D1715133

ANNALS OF THE NEW YORK ACADEMY OF SCIENCES

Volume 645

EDITORIAL STAFF

Executive Editor
BILL BOLAND

Managing Editor
JUSTINE CULLINAN

Associate Editor
JOYCE HITCHCOCK

The New York Academy of Sciences
2 East 63rd Street
New York, New York 10021

TOWARDS A TRANSNATIONAL PERSPECTIVE ON MIGRATION

Race, Class, Ethnicity, and Nationalism Reconsidered

ANNALS OF THE NEW YORK ACADEMY OF SCIENCES
Volume 645

TOWARDS A TRANSNATIONAL PERSPECTIVE ON MIGRATION
Race, Class, Ethnicity, and Nationalism Reconsidered

Edited by Nina Glick Schiller, Linda Basch, and Cristina Blanc-Szanton

The New York Academy of Sciences
New York, New York
1992

Library of Congress Cataloging-in-Publication Data

Towards a transnational perspective on migration: race, class, ethnicity, and nationalism reconsidered / edited by Nina Glick Schiller, Linda Basch, and Cristina Blanc-Szanton.
    p. cm. – (Annals of the New York Academy of Sciences, ISSN 0077-8923 ; v. 645)
    Includes bibliographical references and index.
    ISBN 0-89766-703-4. – ISBN 0-89766-704-2 (pbk.)
    1. Emigration and immigration – Social aspects – Congresses.
2. International economic relations – Congresses. 3. Internationalism – Congresses. I. Schiller, Nina Glick. II. Basch, Linda G. (Linda Green), 1938- . III. Blanc-Szanton, Cristina. IV. Series.
Q11.N5 vol. 645
[JN6225]
500 s – dc20
[304.8]   92-10551
                                             CIP

CCP
Printed in the United States of America
ISBN 0-89766-703-4 (cloth)
ISBN 0-89766-704-2 (paper)
ISSN 0077-8923

ANNALS OF THE NEW YORK ACADEMY OF SCIENCES

Volume 645
July 6, 1992

TOWARDS A TRANSNATIONAL PERSPECTIVE ON MIGRATION
Race, Class, Ethnicity, and Nationalism Reconsidered[a]

Editors and Workshop Organizers
NINA GLICK SCHILLER, LINDA BASCH, and CRISTINA BLANC-SZANTON

CONTENTS

[a] This volume is the proceedings of a workshop with the same title held on May 3–4, 1990
at the New York Academy of Sciences and co-sponsored by the Research Institute for the Study
of Man and the Wenner-Gren Foundation for Anthropological Research.

Preface

LAMBROS COMITAS

Departments of Anthropology and Education
Teachers College, Columbia University
New York, New York 10027
and
Research Institute for the Study of Man
162 East 78th Street
New York, New York 10021

If people never left their place of birth, never sought refuge nor scrambled for opportunity in other lands, what a different world we would live in and what a different history we would celebrate! However, mass migration, more often the theme for political diatribe or melancholy ballad than for scientific inquiry, is an indisputable phenomenon of profound significance that permeates the fabric of contemporary society. It gives me great pleasure, therefore, to introduce this publication drawn from the proceedings of a conference on transnationalism held in May of 1990 which expanded our understanding of current patterns of migrant behavior and traced, as well, the multi-faceted impact of these mass movements on both sending and receiving societies. Transnationalism, as a conceptual framework, was examined in detail at this meeting along with its implications, both theoretical and policy, on currently accepted wisdom about race, class, ethnicity, and nationalism.

Significant advances in scientific theory do not spring *de novo* from the minds of individual scholars. In fact, social science has long flirted with questions about the movement of people and the transfer, even the clash, of cultures. The first part of this century saw a burgeoning of historical and sociological studies of new immigrants to America and the fitful start of more abstract anthropological explorations of cultural diffusion and cultures in contact, the latter with particular reference to the frayed relationship between indigenous people and European settlers in the New World. From these early, field-defining probes, concepts or terms such as melting-pot, integration, assimilation, syncretism, reinterpretation, pluralism, diffusion, cultural exchange, and acculturation came into technical and popular usage. These, in turn, stimulated debate, reaction, and reformulation in the context of competing theoretical camps.

One such reformulation, that of the eminent Cuban sociologist and committed functionalist Fernando Ortiz, may be considered progenitor of the transnationalism paradigm elaborated in this volume. Taking umbrage at what

he perceived as the scientific rigidities and inadequacies of the concept of acculturation, Ortiz in 1940 sought to replace it by another neologism, that of
transculturation. This term and concept, he claimed,

> better expresses the different phases of the process of transition from one
> culture to another because this does not consist merely in acquiring an-
> other culture, which is what the English word *acculturation* really implies,
> but the process also necessarily involves the loss or uprooting of a previous
> culture, which could be defined as a deculturation. In addition it carries
> the idea of the consequent creation of new cultural phenomena, which
> could be called neoculturation. In the end, as the school of Malinowski's
> followers maintains, the result of every union of cultures is similar to that
> of the reproductive process between individuals: the offspring always has
> something of both parents but is always different from each of them.

Ortiz's immediate goal was to construct a more efficient conceptual tool for
exploring the transmutation of a Cuban culture battered over time by waves
of culturally differing settlers. Ortiz's antipathy to the concept of acculturation and his replacement of it by transculturation presaged a number of recent
advances in migration theory, including transnationalism. In later years, more
highly focused conceptual tools for the study of migration have been forged,
various types of migration – permanent, temporary, circulatory, and sojourn –
have been identified, and appropriate units of analysis such as social field and
remittance society have been operationalized.

Major scientific advances never develop in a vacuum; nor are they merely
conditioned reflexes of past achievement. They do, in fact, mirror the concerns of the day, the issues and questions of public moment. After World War
II, release from war-time bondage, the specter of economic crisis, the development of inexpensive transportation and almost instantaneous communication led to a veritable world-wide explosion of migratory activity. It was monitored in part by the field-based research of sociologists and anthropologists.
In the past few years, this worldwide search for a better life has almost expo-
nentially increased as one political barrier after another has been removed – as
the many Berlin Walls come tumbling down. In these new, politically fluid
environments, the concept of transnationalism and the quotidian reality of
transnationalism are joined.

The organizers of the conference and editors of this volume, Drs. Nina
Glick Schiller, Linda Basch, and Cristina Blanc-Szanton are to be heartily com-
mended for the enormous organizational effort and scholarly contribution
that have led to this most valuable publication.

Towards a Definition
of Transnationalism
Introductory Remarks and Research Questions

NINA GLICK SCHILLER, LINDA BASCH,
AND CRISTINA BLANC-SZANTON

In the course of the past few years, anthropologists have increasingly noted that immigrants live their lives across borders and maintain their ties to home, even when their countries of origin and settlement are geographically distant. To describe this new way of life, some social scientists have begun to use the term "transnational." However, this term is being used loosely and without specificity. Much conceptual work needs to be done to move from the perception that "something new is happening here" to the development of a new conceptual framework within which to discuss contemporary international migration.

As part of an effort to conceptualize and analyze transnational migration in May of 1990 we brought together a group of researchers who had found in their own field work evidence of a new pattern of migration and who had each been trying to grapple with the implications of what they were seeing all around them. The decision to have a workshop was a result of an odyssey that we had embarked upon several years before. When comparing our observations of the social relations of immigrants to the United States from three different areas–the eastern Caribbean, Haiti, and the Philippines–we found that migrants from each population were forging and sustaining multi-stranded social relations that linked their societies of origin and settlement. We called this immigrant experience "transnationalism" to emphasize the emergence of a social process in which migrants establish social fields that cross geographic, cultural, and political borders. Immigrants are understood to be transmigrants when they develop and maintain multiple relations–familial, economic, social, organizational, religious, and political–that span borders. We came to understand that the multiplicity of migrants' involvements in both the home and host societies is a central element of transnationalism. Transmigrants take actions, make decisions, and feel concerns within a field of social relations that links together their country of origin and their country or countries of settlement.

Having identified and defined transnationalism, we sought to locate this process historically and theoretically. Was transnationalism actually a new im-

ix

migration experience or was it rather that previous conceptualizations of immigrants and migration had precluded us from perceiving the manner in which immigrants, as they settle in a new society, extend their social fields to include their home societies? A research agenda developed: 1) to examine the manner in which transnational migration is shaped by and contributes to the encompassing global capitalist system; 2) to examine the analytical categories with which social scientists have approached the study of migration; and 3) to analyze the manner in which transmigrants – caught between the experience of transnationalism and the dominant discourse on migration – construct their racial, ethnic, class, national, and gender identities. We hypothesized that transnational migration differs significantly from previous migration experience and is becoming increasingly a global phenomenon as populations in capital-dependent countries are everywhere forced to migrate to centers of capital in order to live. However, the manner in which transmigrants conceptualize their experiences, including their collective identities, is very much shaped by both the political and economic context of the country of origin and the countries of settlement of the transmigrants.

In order to pursue this research agenda we formulated an initial conceptual framework (Glick Schiller, Basch, and Blanc-Szanton, this volume), continued our own comparative studies (Basch, Glick Schiller, and Blanc-Szanton, n.d.), and organized a workshop with others who were embarked on similar explorations. Although the perspective of the workshop was global, to keep the scope of analysis manageable we confined our focus to migration to the United States. The workshop was jointly sponsored by the Anthropology Section of the New York Academy of Sciences, the Research Institute for the Study of Man, and the Wenner-Gren Foundation for Anthropological Research. It advanced our research agenda in many ways by providing invaluable documentation of the transnational migrant experience and by honing and shaping the nature of the theoretical inquiry. The papers and discussion presented in this volume are the fruits of that process.

The papers prepared for this workshop can be grouped around three themes, which we have used in the organizational structure of this book. In Part I, the Introduction, we propose a transnational perspective on migration. We argue for a global perspective, linking the emergence of transnationalism to recent changes in the world economy, especially the extensive penetration of capital into the third world. We suggest that the transnational lives of contemporary migrants call into question the bounded conceptualizations of race, class, ethnicity, and nationalism which pervade both social science and popular thinking. The papers in Part II proceed by discussing the ways in which the identity of the new transnational subject is currently being constructed. Transformations of class practices and racial categories and the restructuring of women's and men's lives in the deployment of cultural capital are all detailed. In Part III, the relationship between transnational populations and nation states is examined, and the challenge posed to nationalism by the existence of these transnational populations is described.

The discussion at the workshop was far-ranging, touching both on the specifics of the papers and on the global perspective in which the presenters placed their data. Although we have located the discussion papers at the end of the book, they serve not so much as a summary but as a springboard for further thought. The papers and discussion in this book represent some of the first steps in what is proving to be a fruitful journey.

» «

The workshop participants were also provided with a series of questions that we felt need to be addressed. We include these in the hope that they may contribute to the development of a research agenda to accompany this new transnational perspective on migration.

A. Analytical Methodology

1. Analytically, what tools do we as social scientists have available to develop a better understanding of transnational processes and to formulate a conceptual framework that allows us to see these processes more clearly and chart changes as we move into the 21st century?

2. What concepts and terms should we use to describe the identities, personhoods, social fields, subjects, cultural citizenships, and psychic stresses that are emerging from the practice of transnational migrants?

B. The Global Perspective

1. What is the relationship between transnationalism and global capitalism— both in terms of the current historical moment and how this moment is being experienced within the particularities of both third world sending countries and the receiving countries?

2. How does the emergence of transnationalism relate to neocolonialism?

C. The Historical Perspective

1. Comparing past and present migrations, to what extent is this transnationalism a new phenomenon?

2. What continuities exist between past and present practices of immigrants, who have maintained home ties and yet settled in new geographical locations?

3. How does what we are observing now differ from the experiences of earlier migrant populations?

4. Were earlier migrants able to sustain active involvement in the two or more geographical and national settings—in terms of kinship, friendship networks, organizational alliances, political activities?

5. How did the maintenance of home ties in earlier generations affect the construction of national, racial, and ethnic identities?

6. How does the emergence of this new transnational subject reflect the major recent technological leaps in the areas of communications and media that put the world in much more immediate interaction technologically as well as facilitate transnational processes?

D. Transnational Social Fields

1. What are the implications of current day transnationalism for kinship relations, family organization, and the form and content of social networks?

2. To what extent are family networks now multi-class in composition and are multiple class locations reproduced within the familial networks?

3. Do transnational networks develop new economic activities or drain capital from immigrant enterprises?

4. How do transmigrants develop organizations that span national borders and how do these organizations deploy resources and leadership positions?

5. Under what conditions do transnational media develop and how do such media serve to develop the transnational social field?

E. Class Background, Class Mobility, and the Emergence of Class Globally

1. What classes and strata (skilled workers, unskilled workers, small business people, professionals, capitalists) are currently becoming transmigrants?

2. Why are different strata moving?

3. What do the similarities and differences in the flows and agendas of different classes and strata suggest for defining this new transnationalism?

4. Where do transmigrants end up in the stratification and class structure of each different country to which they have moved?

5. How do migrants gain access to resources, education, and capital, and how does this access assist in the reproduction of classes and affect the class position of individual migrants?

6. To what degree is the immigrant's class position in the home society transferable to the host society?

7. To what extent can class position attained in the host society be transferrable back home?

8. How are we to understand class formation, position, and consciousness as transmigrants participate in both home and host societies?

9. What kinds of leadership roles do transmigrant political and economic elites assume within their immigrant populations, their host societies at large, and in their home societies?

10. What are the implications of transnationalism for global capitalism and concepts of class?

11. Is transnationalism contributing to the emergence of new class and racial structures that cut across national boundaries?

F. Identity, Hegemony, and Resistance

1. How and to what degree are hegemonic constructions in home and host societies affected by the presence of transnational populations and their practices?

2. What types of racial and ethnic constructions emerge when transmigrants participate simultaneously in two or more polities and are exposed to two or more hegemonic systems with differing constructions of identity?

3. What role do the governments of the home and host societies play in developing and/or shaping the identities of the transmigrant populations?

4. How do dominant strata and political and economic elites use culture to further their own agendas, grounded in the political economy of each location in the transmigrant field?

5. How do transmigrants confront, resist and accommodate to the different racial, social, and political structures of the several societies in which they take part?

6. When transmigrants participate in several different racial systems simultaneously how are their sense of social position, their concepts of race, and their emergence as political actors affected?

7. Capital and labor are global yet the world is still very much divided into nation states, and internal and external oppositions are expressed in nationalist terms. To what extent does transnationalism perpetuate nationalist identifications or will it lead to more encompassing forms of identification?

8. How aware are transmigrants of their particular locations within a global labor force when they adopt strategies of migration or when they utilize one aspect of identity or another derived from the different hegemonic contexts that they have experienced?

9. To what extent and in which ways are consciousness of class, race, and national identities being transferred, reinterpreted, resisted and transformed as a result of transnationalism?

10. To what extent is a new transnational subject being formed who transcends the hegemonic context and its disciplining practices in each nation?

11. Are we all faced with the emergence of new transnational subjectivities that are shaping us in ways we are only barely starting to comprehend?

G. The Future

1. Is transnationalism a phenomenon of the first generation only or is it transmitted across generations? If it is transmitted, how is this and to what extent?

2. What are the harmful effects of these processes on individuals, institutions, and whole societies?

3. By defining, raising awareness, and naming these new transnational phenomena are we contributing to the development of transnationalism as a new form of hegemonic construction?

4. To what extent does transnationalism produce conscious resistance to global capitalism, and to what degree might this resistance go beyond limited challenges and contribute to calls for a reconsideration of the whole global capitalist system and its premises?

REFERENCES CITED

Basch, Linda, Nina Glick Schiller, and Cristina Blanc-Szanton
    n.d.   *Rethinking migration, ethnicity, race and nationalism in transnational perspective.* New York: Gordon-Breach. Forthcoming.
Glick Schiller, Nina, Linda Basch, and Cristina Blanc-Szanton
    1992   Transnationalism: A new analytic framework for understanding migration. In *Towards a transnational perspective on migration: Race, class, ethnicity, and nationalism reconsidered*, edited by Nina Glick Schiller, Linda Basch, and Cristina Blanc-Szanton. *Annals of the New York Academy of Sciences* 645:1–24. This volume.

Acknowledgments

The conference upon which this book is based and the book itself were made possible through the support of numerous people whom we wish to thank. We especially acknowledge the contributions of Dr. Constance Sutton who, as the chair of the Anthropology Section of the New York Academy of Sciences, encouraged us to hold this conference, and who, as a teacher and friend, inspired the theoretical framework that informed it; Dr. Sydel Silverman, President of the Wenner-Gren Foundation, who provided advice, support, and co-sponsorship and has been a continuing source of encouragement; Dr. Lambros Comitas, Director of the Research Institute for the Study of Man, who was a source of support for this project from its first conceptualization to completion; and June Anderson, Executive Assistant of the Research Institute for the Study of Man, whose wisdom and assistance made the conference as productive as it was. We also acknowledge the assistance and guidance of the New York Academy of Sciences, the organization that hosted the conference, and its staff: Mathew Katz, Manager of Meeting Services, and Bill Boland, Executive Editor of the *Annals*. We especially recognize the invaluable contribution of Joyce Hitchcock, Associate Editor of the *Annals*, whose skills and patience made this book possible.

» «

We would like to gratefully acknowledge the role of our families, who through their continuing support for our project have contributed to its completion.

Naomi	Sam	Peter
Rachel	Ethan	Julia
	Arielle	
	Abigail	

NINA GLICK SCHILLER
LINDA BASCH
CRISTINA BLANC-SZANTON

Transnationalism: A New Analytic Framework for Understanding Migration

NINA GLICK SCHILLER

Department of Anthropology
University of New Hampshire
Durham, New Hampshire 03824

LINDA BASCH

School of Arts and Sciences
Manhattan College Parkway
Bronx, New York 10471

CRISTINA BLANC-SZANTON

Southern Asian Institute
International Affairs
Columbia University
New York, New York 10027

Our earlier conceptions of immigrant and migrant no longer suffice. The word immigrant evokes images of permanent rupture, of the uprooted, the abandonment of old patterns and the painful learning of a new language and culture. Now, a new kind of migrating population is emerging, composed of those whose networks, activities and patterns of life encompass both their host and home societies. Their lives cut across national boundaries and bring two societies into a single social field.

In this book we argue that a new conceptualization is needed in order to come to terms with the experience and consciousness of this new migrant population. We call this new conceptualization, "transnationalism," and describe the new type of migrants as transmigrants. We have defined transnationalism as the processes by which immigrants build social fields that link together their country of origin and their country of settlement. Immigrants who build such social fields are designated "transmigrants." Transmigrants develop and maintain multiple relations—familial, economic, social, organizational, religious, and political that span borders. Transmigrants take actions, make decisions, and feel concerns, and develop identities within social net-

1

works that connect them to two or more societies simultaneously (Basch, Glick Schiller and Blanc-Szanton n.d.).[1]

The following vignettes based on our observations of migrants from Haiti, the eastern Caribbean, and the Philippines now living in New York allow a glimpse of the complexities and intricacies of transmigrant experience and identity that, we believe, calls for a new analytical framework.

The ten men sat around a living room on Long Island. The occasion was a meeting of their regional association. Each member of the association had pledged to send $10.00 a month to support an older person living in their home town in Haiti. They came from different class backgrounds in Haiti, although all were fairly successful in New York. But one of the members, a successful doctor, expressed dissatisfaction–although he has a lucrative practice, a comfortable life style in New York and a household in his hometown which he visits every year "no matter what." As he stated it, "I'm making money and I am not happy. Life has no meaning."

His speech about his emotional state was a preamble to his making an ambitious proposal to his hometown association. He called on his fellow members to join him in the building of a sports complex for the youth in their hometown. He indicated that he already had bought the land which he would donate and he would also donate $4,000–5,000 for the building and called on others to assist in the construction. He had given no thought to maintaining the building or staffing it.

The doctor was not alone in his aspirations to make a mark back home in a way that maintains or asserts status both in Haiti and among his personal networks in New York. There were more than 20 Haitian hometown associations in New York in 1988. Their memberships were composed of people who have lived in New York for many years. Many of them undertook large scale projects back "home," projects which often are grand rather than practical. For example, an ambulance was sent to a town with no gasoline supply and no hospital.

These associations differ dramatically in the activities and audience from hometown associations of earlier immigrants whose main, if not only thrust of activity was to help the newcomers face social welfare issues in the new land. Russian Jewish immigrants in the beginning of the 20th century, for example,

---

[1] The term "transnational" has long been used to describe corporations that have major financial operations in more than one country and a significant organizational presence in several countries simultaneously. The growth of transnational corporations has been accompanied by the relocation of populations. It therefore seems appropriate to use the term "transnational" as a description for both the sectors of migrating populations who maintain a simultaneous presence in two or more societies and for the relations these migrants establish. In 1986 the American Academy of Political and Social Science employed the term as the theme of a conference publication entitled *From foreign workers to settlers?–Transnational migration and the emergence of a new minority*. The conference papers dwelt more on the effect on public policy of this type of migration, but did so without developing the concept of transnational migration.

founded "landsman" associations to provide their members with burial funds and assist the poor and orphaned in the United States. In contrast, the members of Haitian hometown associations, much as the participants in similar Filipino and Grenadian and Vincentian associations, are part of a social system whose networks are based in two or more nation states and who maintain activities, identities and statuses in several social locations.

Approximately 200 well-dressed Grenadian immigrants, mostly from urban areas in Grenada and presently employed in white collar jobs in New York, gathered in a Grenadian-owned catering hall in Brooklyn to hear the Grenadian Minister of Agriculture and Development. The Minister shared with Grenada's "constituency in New York," his plans for agricultural development in Grenada and encouraged them to become part of this effort.

By being addressed and acting as Grenadian nationals, these immigrants were resisting incorporation into the bottom of the racial order in the United States that categorizes them as "black," much as Haitians do when they construct hometown associations or meet as members of the Haitian diaspora to discuss the situation in Haiti.

By having their views elicited by a government minister from home, the Grenadians were exercising a status as Grenadian leaders, a social status generally unavailable to them in the racially stratified environment of New York. Their perceptions of themselves as Grenadian "leaders" were further activated by the minister's suggestion that these migrants have the power to convince their relatives at home that agricultural work, generally demeaned as a productive activity, is worthwhile and important.

But the Minister was also addressing the migrants as Grenadian ethnics in New York when he asked them to try to assist in introducing Grenadian agricultural goods to the United States market by using their connections in New York within the fledgling Caribbean American Chamber of Commerce to which many of them belonged. And of particular significance, the organizers of this meeting, who had each been in the United States a minimum of ten years, were as involved in the local politics of New York City as in Grenada. In fact, they were able to transfer—and build on—the political capital they gained in New York to Grenada, and vice versa. Grenada's ambassador to the United Nations has been a leader in the New York Caribbean community for 20 years. And so often did these political actors travel between Grenada and New York, that it became difficult for the anthropologist to recall where she had last seen them.

Well-established Filipino migrants are also periodically visited by representatives of the Philippines government urging transnational activities including strong encouragement to reinvest their American earnings into Philippine agriculture. The role of the Philippines state in contributing to the construction of transnational migrant fields extends even further.

At a desk, an employee was helping a customer close her box and complete the listing of items it contains. We were in the offices of a company in New Jersey (the only company where boxes can be delivered directly to the warehouse rather than being picked up for delivery). A regular flow of such boxes leaves every day from seven to eight major Filipino shipping companies. Anything can be sent back door-to-door and with limited taxes—appliances, electronic equipment and the like—as long as it fits the weight and size prescriptions defining a *Balikbayan* box.

President Marcos had created the term *balikbayan* (literally homecomers) during a major national speech encouraging immigrants to visit their home country once a year during the holidays. He developed economic and legal means to facilitate their return and allowed each of them to bring yearly two *Balikbayan* boxes duty-free. Mrs. Aquino restated her concern for the numerous silent "heroes and heroines of the Philippines." She then enabled them to purchase gifts of up to $1,000 duty-free upon entering the Philippines. Contracting for overseas labor and the system of sending remittances, so very important now for the country's economy, has been similarly institutionalized. The existence of transnational migration is thus officially sanctioned and highly regulated by the Philippine state.

We thus see how the transnational social field is in part composed of family ties sustained through economic disbursements and gifts. At the same time this field is sustained by a system of legalized exchanges, structured and officially sanctioned by the Philippine state.

As these examples show, transnational migrants arrive in their new country of residence with certain practices and concepts constructed at home. They belong to certain more or less politicized populations and hold particular class affiliations. They then engage in complex activities across national borders that create, shape and potentially transform their identities in ways that we will begin to explore in this paper and in these conference proceedings. This is not to say that this phenomenon has not been observed by others. However, an adequate framework for understanding this phenomenon or its implications has yet to be constructed. Building on our own research with transmigrants from Haiti, the English-speaking Caribbean, and the Philippines[2] as well as the earlier observations of others, we seek in this paper to develop such a framework. This framework we argue allows an examination of how transmigrants use their social relationships and their varying and multiple identities generated from their simultaneous positioning in several social locations both to accommodate to and to resist the difficult circumstances and the dominant ideologies they encounter in their transnational

[2] A fuller development of the themes in this article can be found in our book, *Rethinking migration, ethnicity, race, and nationalism in transnational perspective* (Basch, Glick Schiller, and Blanc-Szanton, forthcoming). See also Glick Schiller and Fouron (1990) and Basch *et al.* (forthcoming).

fields. We start our analysis by identifying and developing six premises that situate transnationalism in time, space, world systems and sociological theory.

The six premises central to our conceptualization of transnationalism are the following: 1) bounded social science concepts such as tribe, ethnic group, nation, society, or culture can limit the ability of researchers to first perceive, and then analyze, the phenomenon of transnationalism; 2) the development of the transnational migrant experience is inextricably linked to the changing conditions of global capitalism, and must be analyzed within that world context; 3) transnationalism is grounded in the daily lives, activities, and social relationships of migrants; 4) transnational migrants, although predominantly workers, live a complex existence that forces them to confront, draw upon, and rework different identity constructs–national, ethnic and racial; 5) the fluid and complex existence of transnational migrants compels us to reconceptualize the categories of nationalism, ethnicity, and race, theoretical work that can contribute to reformulating our understanding of culture, class, and society; and 6) transmigrants deal with and confront a number of hegemonic contexts, both global and national.[3] These hegemonic contexts have an impact on the transmigrant's consciousness, but at the same time transmigrants reshape these contexts by their interactions and resistance.

SOCIAL SCIENCE UNBOUND

For the past several decades descriptions of migrant behavior that could be characterized as transnational have been present in the migration literature, but these descriptions have not yielded a new approach to the study of migration. Students of migration did not develop a conceptual framework to encompass the global phenomena of immigrant social, political, and economic relationships that spanned several societies.

There was a certain recognition that the constant back and forth flow of people could not be captured by the categories of "permanent migrants," "return migrants," "temporary migrants," or "sojourners." In fact, Richardson, whose own work documents Caribbean "migration as livelihood" states that "students of the movements of Pacific islanders have found human mobility there so routine that they now employ the term circulation rather than migration" (1983:176). Chaney astutely noted that there were now people who had their "feet in two societies" (1979:209). Noting that many Garifuna "today have become United States citizens, yet they think of themselves as members of two (or more) societies," Gonzalez described migrants from Belize as forming "'part societies' within several countries" (1988:10).

---

[3] The concept of hegemony, long embedded in Marxism but developed by Gramsci (1971), facilitates the discussion of the relationship between power and ideology.

In part, the recognition by social scientists that many migrants persist in their relationship to their home society, not in contradiction to but in conjunction with their settlement in the host society, did not develop beyond the descriptive level because migrant experiences in different areas of the world tended to be analyzed as discrete and separate phenomena rather than as part of a global phenomenon. For example, students of Caribbean migration noted the tendency of generations of migrants from the Caribbean to spend long periods away from home, yet support their families and often family landholdings or small enterprises with the money they sent home. They identified Caribbean nations as "remittance societies" and viewed this as a Caribbean phenomenon (Wood and McCoy 1985; Rubenstein 1983). Yet remittances are now part of the economies of nations in disparate parts of the world.

In all the social sciences, analyses of immigrant populations, their patterns of social relations and systems of meaning have continued to be enmeshed within theories that approached each society as a discrete and bounded entity with its own separate economy, culture, and historical trajectory. That the study of immigrant populations should have been built upon such a bounded view of society and culture is not surprising considering that all social sciences had for decades been dominated by such static models.

Anthropologists, for example, were long constrained by the closed models of "structural functionalism" (Radcliffe Brown 1952) that endowed populations, variously designated as "tribes," "peoples," "ethnic groups," or simply "cultures," with given, "natural," and group-specific properties. Each population was studied as a bounded unit, living in one place, bearing a unique and readily identifiable culture.[4] Sociology, meanwhile, had fastened on Parsons' emphasis on "social system" and the development of systems theory, and political scientists created models of "traditional" versus "modern" societies (Parsons 1951). In the comparative study of "social systems," all fields of scholarship projected an ethnographic present in which the stasis of tradition was broken apart only by 19th and 20th century European or American "contact," resulting in migration, urbanization, and acculturation. Anthropologists may have expressed uneasiness about the consequences of the very same processes that produced the political scientists' quintessential goal of modernization, but until the 1970s all disciplines remained constrained by their bounded categories of social analysis.

For the past two decades, such views have been subject to powerful critiques generated by several different analytical paradigms. But these critiques have yet to lead to new approaches to the study of immigrant populations. In anthropology, efforts to break free from bounded thinking have gone in

---

[4] While the concept of uniform patterns of culture (Benedict 1959) has been thoroughly critiqued by numerous anthropologists it persists in the profession and is a basic building block of most introductory texts.

two directions. Some analysts "deconstruct" culture, recognizing the artifice of the bounded unit of analysis by replacing conceptions of a single uniform "pattern" with multiple visions of individual, gendered and particularized experiences. By and large, as Marcus has noted, "ethnographers of an interpretive bent–more interested in problems of cultural meaning than in social action–have not generally represented the ways in which closely observed cultural worlds are embedded in larger, more impersonal systems" (Marcus 1986:166). The emphasis is on the formulation of the ethnographic text as a product of the interaction between the individual ethnographer and the "informant" (Rosaldo 1989). For those writers who, in their discussion of "text construction," acknowledge a global context the question becomes "once the line between the local worlds of subjects and the global world of systems becomes radically blurred, . . . (h)ow, . . . is the representational space of the realist ethnography to be textually bounded and contained in the compelling recognition of the larger systems contexts of any ethnographic subjects?" (Marcus 1986:171).

Others, such as Wolf (1982; 1988) and Worsley (1984), building on a Marxist-influenced anthropology which decades earlier had expressed disquietude about the reification of the concept of "tribe,"[5] have called for a global level of analysis. Sectors of sociology and political science share this global vision and look to the "world capitalist system" as a unit of analysis. Wallerstein, a sociologist, developed a "world systems theory" in which different geographic regions of the world performed different and unequal functions in a global division of labor (Wallerstein 1974; 1982). World systems theory allowed social science to move beyond the examination of the structures of individual economies and to link the penetration of capital into previously non-capitalized sectors of production to the movements of people into the labor market.[6]

However necessary this global perspective, it has proved to be insufficient on several counts.[7] Little has been done by world systems theorists to explain the continuing significance of nation-states within these larger global processes, and world systems theorists have tended to ignore the legal, military, and ideological basis for the continuing existence of nations. In fact, the international flow of capital and distribution of labor takes place in a world that continues to be very much politically divided into nation-states that are un-

---

[5] The authors represented in *Essays on the problem of the tribe* (Helm 1975) and Morton Fried's (1975) insightful work on primordial state formation and the tribe made seminal contributions to the effort to move anthropology beyond the conceptualization of cultures as tightly bounded, and discrete.

[6] Important early work in a global analysis was carried out by André Gunder Frank (1966). Work to link world system theory to migration has been carried out by numerous authors including Bach (1980), Portes and Walton (1981), Pessar (1982) and Sassen (1988).

[7] For efforts to both critique and build upon a world systems framework see Smith (1984), Lozano (1984), Portes and Bach (1985).

equal in their power, and which serve differentially as base areas of international capital. Wallerstein has addressed the constructed nature of nationalism and has recognized the significance of nationalism in the development
of states. Nevertheless, a great deal more needs to be said about the fact that
nation-states, although they exist within the world capitalist system, continue
to control armies and nuclear weapons. Much world system analysis has focused on the economic rather than the political aspects of the system, especially in discussions of migration.[8]

Another shortcoming of world systems theorists who have built upon Wallerstein has been their tendency to view migrants as essentially units of labor.
While the direction has been set by authors such as Portes and Bach (1985)
and Sassen (1988) who acknowledge that a global perspective must include
the social, cultural, and political dimensions of migrant experiences, this work
has yet to be done. Our observations suggest that the transnational context
of migrants' lives develops from the interplay of multiplex phenomena—
historical experience, structural conditions, and the ideologies of their home
and host societies.

In developing the concept of transnationalism we wish to provide those
studying contemporary migrating populations with a framework in which
global economic processes, and the continuing contradictory persistence of
nation-states can be linked to migrants' social relationships, political actions,
loyalties, beliefs, and identities. At this juncture in the social sciences, it is essential that the study of migrating populations combine an emphasis on social
relations, understood to be fluid and dynamic, yet culturally patterned, with
an analysis of the global context. Such an approach is certainly necessary to
elucidate the processes underlying the experience of those sectors of migrating
populations who become transmigrants.

Transnationalism as a Product of World Capitalism

To analyze transnationalism we must begin by recognizing that the world
is currently bound together by a global capitalist system. Such a perspective
allows us to examine the economic forces that structure the flows of international migration and to place the migrants' responses to these forces and
their strategies of survival, cultural practices and identities within the world-
wide historical context of differential power and inequality.

Because of the growing internationalization of capital, by the 1980s the
structure of employment in the United States had undergone transformations
often called "restructuring" or "deindustrialization" (Block 1987:136). Many
stable industrial-sector jobs had been lost through the export of manufac-

---

[8] Zolberg (1983) has emphasized the political and legal structuring of international migration.

turing industries and related jobs abroad, frequently to Third World countries. In many large urban areas in the United States well-paying, unionized, industrial employment was replaced by service sector and clerical employment. Sweat shops and home work proliferated. The newly created employment was characterized by low pay and little or no benefits or security.

At the same time, in the global restructuring of capital, the local economies of the Third World were disrupted by the intrusion of large scale agrobusinesses, the investment of transnational corporations in export processing industries, and tourism (Nash and Fernandez 1983). These economic shifts created a displaced, underemployed, labor force, not easily absorbed by the growing but still relatively small highly capitalized sector of the economy. The economic dislocations in both the Third World and in industrialized nations increased migration, yet made it difficult for the migrants to construct secure cultural, social or economic bases within their new settings. This vulnerability increased the likelihood that migrants would construct a transnational existence.

Understanding this global context has led to new perspectives on migration, perspectives that can contribute to an understanding that current migration is a new and different phenomenon. There is, however, no consensus among analysts on the character of the new migration. There are some who point to the invention of rapid transportation and communication systems, rather than the current state of the world social and economic system, as the reason why modern-day migrants are more likely than their predecessors to maintain ongoing ties to their societies of origin (Wakeman 1988). Others continue to view migrants within a classic "push-pull" model in which migration is seen as a product of separate and unrelated forces in the society of origin and the society of settlement (Lee 1966). Using recent historiography that has revised our picture of 19th century immigrants, one might argue that there has been no major change in migration patterns. Apparently many earlier migrants were, in some sense, transmigrants who remained in communication with their home country and participated in its national movement (Vassady 1982). We believe that current transnationalism does mark a new type of migrant existence and that only by more fully developing a global perspective on the transnational life experience of migrants, will social scientists be able to understand the similarities and differences between past and present migrations.

Transnationalism as Cultural Flow or as Social Relations?

The word transnationalism has recently become popularized in the realm of cultural studies with references made to "transnational phenomena" and "transnational research" (Wakeman 1988:85). However, this usage of transnationalism stands conceptually apart from the entire bodies of literature on migration and on the world system. Instead, those who speak of "transnational phenomena" focus on flows of meanings and material objects in an effort to describe "transnational" culture, and put the discussion of culture in a world-wide framework.

Appadurai and Breckenridge seek to explain the recent development of a "public culture" in India, which they see manifested in public foods, entertainment, goods and services that largely transcend national boundaries. Such a public culture, they argue, is a response to India's cultural interactions and exchanges with other nations (Appadurai and Breckenridge 1988). They highlight the complexities, the back-and-forth transferences, and the contradictions that characterize transnational flows of objects and cultural meanings.

A similar approach to global cultural trends has been taken by Hannerz (1989). Critiquing those who see the diffusion of cultural goods and ideas only from powerful core nations to those on the economic periphery, Hannerz argues against notions of a "global village" or the "homogenization" of culture. Hannerz rightly emphasizes the constant tendency of people to creatively reinterpret, a process he calls "creolization." Focusing largely on movements of cultural items and flows of media images, he also emphasizes "cultural flows." The concurrent movement of peoples, and the activities, networks, relationships, and identities of transnational migrants have yet to be addressed.

In our task of developing a transnational framework that is of use in the analysis of migration, we can build on some ground-breaking work that has directed our attention to systems of social relations that are wider than national borders. In their 1975 description of Barbadian immigrants, Sutton and Makiesky-Barrow spoke of a "transnational sociocultural and political system" (1987).[9] They posited that migration provides "an important channel for the bi-directional flow of ideas such that political events at home (e.g., independence) had an impact on the migrant communities abroad while migrant experiences were relayed in the opposite direction" (1987:114). Portes and Walton suggested that migration could be "conceptualized as a process of network building" (1981:60). Rouse introduced the concept of "transnational migrant circuits" that encompass several societies (1988; 1989).

As the work of these authors and our own research makes clear, to understand current day migrants we must not only map the circulation of goods and ideas, but understand that material goods are embedded in social relations. If someone sends home a barbecue grill to Haiti, the grill does not stand in and of itself as an item of material culture that will change the material culture of Haiti. While it is interesting to talk about the new development of cultural forms around imported items, something else needs to be said. The grill is a statement about social success in the United States and an effort to

---

[9] See also Sutton's more recent discussion of "the emergence of a transnational sociocultural system" (1987).

build and advance social position in Haiti. It will be used in a fashionable round of party-going in which status is defined and redeemed in the context of consumption.

When someone from a small town in Haiti, St. Vincent, or the Philippines who now lives in New York sends home a cassette player, how are we to interpret this flow? The player can be used along with imported cassettes to bring the latest musical forms and themes from around the world into the most remote rural area. But on this same cassette those sitting on a mountainside in Haiti, in a rural village in the Philippines, or on a family veranda in St. Vincent send messages, warnings, information about kith and kin "at home" that influence how people behave and what they think in New York, Los Angeles, and Miami (Richman 1987). Connections are continued, a wider system of social relations is maintained, reinforced, and remains vital and growing.

Whether the transnational activity is sending the barbecue to Haiti, dried fruits and fabric home to Trinidad so these goods can be prepared for a wedding in New York, or using the special tax status of *Balikbayan* boxes to send expensive goods from the United States to families back home in the Philippines, the constant and various flow of such goods and activities have embedded within them relationships between people. These social relations take on meaning within the flow and fabric of daily life, as linkages between different societies are maintained, renewed, and reconstituted in the context of families, of institutions, of economic investments, business, and finance and of political organizations and structures including nation-states.

The Complex Identities of Transnational Migrants

Within their complex web of social relations, transmigrants draw upon and create fluid and multiple identities grounded both in their society of origin and in the host societies. While some migrants identify more with one society than the other, the majority seem to maintain several identities that link them simultaneously to more than one nation. By maintaining many different racial, national, and ethnic identities, transmigrants are able to express their resistance to the global political and economic situations that engulf them, even as they accommodate themselves to living conditions marked by vulnerability and insecurity. These migrants express this resistance in small, everyday ways that usually do not directly challenge or even recognize the basic premises of the systems that surround them and dictate the terms of their existence.

As transmigrants live in several societies simultaneously, their actions and beliefs contribute to the continuing and multiple differentiation of populations. The creolization observed by Hannerz is not only a product of intensified world-wide product distribution systems, but also of this dynamic of migration and differentiation.

In order for us to be able even to perceive, much less analyze, the role played by migration in the continuing differentiation of the world's population, we must add to the study of international migration an examination of the identities and aspirations of transmigrants. This perspective should accompany our understanding that such migrants compose a mobile labor force within a global economic system. This is a labor force that acts and reacts in ways that emphasize, reinforce, or create cultural differentiation and separate identities.

For example, the same individual may attend a meeting of U.S. citizens of the same "ethnic group," be called as a New Yorker to speak to the Mayor of New York about the development of "our city," and the next week go "back home" to Haiti, St. Vincent, or the Philippines and speak as a committed nationalist about the development of "our nation." A migrant may pray in a multi-ethnic congregation that identifies itself as a common community in Christ, attend rallies for racial empowerment that emphasize Black or Asian identities, and dance at a New Year's Eve ball organized for members of the migrant's "own" ethnic community. This same person may swear allegiance to his or her fellow workers at a union meeting in the United States while sending money back home to buy property and become a landlord. Through these seemingly contradictory experiences, transmigrants actively manipulate their identities and thus both accommodate to and resist their subordination within a global capitalist system.

Transnational social fields are in part shaped by the migrants' perceptions that they must keep their options open. In the globalized economy that has developed over the past several decades, there is a sense that no one place is truly secure, although people do have access to many places. One way migrants keep options open is to continuously translate the economic and social position gained in one political setting into political, social and economic capital in another.

Sometimes the transnational field of relations extends to the leadership of nation-states. The Aquinos rallied political support among Filipinos in the United States and brought many of them back to the Philippines in Cory Aquino's first government. Some of these people were sent back to the United States in turn to pressure American politicians with regard to key issues such as economic aid and the United States military bases in the Philippines.

Social scientists are only now beginning to comprehend the significance of these developments and to develop an appropriate analytical framework. What is needed is a reconceptualization of culture and society, work that is only now beginning (Wolf 1982, 1989; Worsely 1984; Rollwagen 1986). As a first step we must rethink our notions of nationalism, ethnicity and race.

RETHINKING CLASS, NATIONALISM, ETHNICITY AND RACE

As we indicated above when we traced the link between transnationalism and world capitalism, transnational migrants are primarily proletarian in their placement within the host labor force if not in their class origins. At the same time each transmigrant population is class differentiated. The Chinese trans-migrant population contains powerful elements of the Hong Kong capitalist class, for example, while the Indian, Caribbean and Filipino populations have important petit bourgeois and professional strata.

The identity of the transmigrant population is contested terrain. Both the capitalist class forces within the dominant society and the leading class forces of the migrating population collude and compete in their interests and out-look with respect to the domination of the migrant workforce. Note those Grenadian leaders who defined the entire transmigrant population in terms that minimized class stratification, yet reinforce their class position by empha-sizing Grenadian transmigrants as both citizens of the Grenadian nation and members of a U.S. Caribbean ethnic group. Thus that sector of the migrant workforce that is proletarian whether in origin or in insertion is both subject/actor in a continuing discourse about not only how they should be-have, but just as importantly about who they are. Their loyalty and sense of self, both individually and collectively, are the subjects of hegemonic construc-tions that emanate both from the place of settlement, such as the United States, and from their home society. Hegemony is at its root a conceptuali-zation about the process by which a relationship is maintained between those who dominate within the state and those who are dominated (Gramsci 1971; Williams 1977; Brow 1988; Comaroff 1991). While ultimately relations of domination are maintained by force, the social order is enforced by the daily practices, habits and common sense through which the dominated live their lives, dream their dreams, and understand their world. By conceptualizing hegemony we are led to see, as Raymond Williams pointed out, that

> (Hegemony) is a lived system of meanings and values—constitutive and constituting—which as they are experienced as practices appear as recipro-cally confirming. . . . It is . . . a culture which also has to be seen as the lived dominance and subordination of particular classes. (Williams 1977:110).

Hegemonic constructions and practices are constantly created, reenacted, and reconstituted. These conceptions and categories are in part internalized by both dominant and dominated alike and create a sense of common loyalty and legitimacy for the dominant classes. In the United States, hegemonic construc-tions speak little of class but much more directly of race, ethnicity, and nation-alism. Simultaneously these constructions serve to discipline a "classless" public into capitalist subjects through practices of consumption, leisure, and work.

The socially constructed nature of our entire repository of terms used to define and bound identity—"nationality," "race," and "ethnicity"—has just recently begun to be scrutinized adequately by social scientists. And the implications of transnationalism for hegemonic constructions of identity have yet to be analyzed.

The different hegemonic contexts to which these transnational migrants relate must be examined. Within both the United States and the home countries the state and the dominant classes attempt to establish and perpetuate control over their populations. They do this by elaborating systems of domination based on hegemonic constructions and practices in a process that is closely related to nation-building. These emergent formulations will speak to and build on the experiences and consciousness of the transnational migrants, directing the migrants' incorporation into the class relations of the nation states in which they are living—both home and host. As we have seen, the activities of the transmigrants within each state and across national boundaries are influenced by, but also influence, all aspects of this hegemonic process in each nation-state.

In the United States these hegemonic constructions, though not uniform, have certain basic themes. The possibility of class identities is not only negated but cross-cut by constructions of race and ethnicity. The racial categories of their new setting, in this case the United States, are imposed on those incoming populations, though this occurs in different ways and with different emphases if they are Caribbeans, Chicanos, or Asians for example. At the same time, demands are placed on those same populations to identify "ethnically." The hegemonic context imposes a discipline on newcomers who develop self-identifications, if not broader collective action, in accordance with categories and related behaviors that are not of their own making. But transnational migrants, with variation linked to their class background and racial positioning, have their own notions about categories of identity and their own conceptions of the rules of the hegemonic game. People live in and create a new social and cultural space which calls for a new awareness of who they are, a new consciousness, and new identities. However, both the actors and analyst still look around them with visions shaped by the political boundaries of nation-states.[10]

Nationalism has been identified as an early 19th century invention (Kedourie 1960; Kamenka 1973), resulting from the rapid replacement of existing absolute monarchies in Europe by units called nation-states and the subsequent establishment of such polities in other parts of the world. While the unifying content of nationalism varied from country to country, it was based

---

[10] For a more complete explanation of these processes see Basch, Glick Schiller and Blanc-Szanton, 1992; n.d.

on an ideology of the commonness of origins, purposes, and goals that allowed those in power to legitimate rule over large and diverse populations. Nationalism gave heterogeneous groups a sense of a shared common interest, and carried a vision of a nation-state as a "people," each nation making up a separate, equal, and natural unit.

Intellectuals provided these new formulations with their own rationality, describing religion, ethnicities, and kinship as archaic, whereas the new nations were seen as moving towards a rational and scientific modernity—part of an unending spiral of forward-looking improvements. Nations were defined as the necessary outcome of commercialism, scientific culture, and industrial progress occurring in Europe. By the 20th century the concept of nation-state embodied a series of ideological constructions including scientific rationality, the economic role of the State, the institutionalization of economic calculations, and modernism.

Only recently have intellectuals begun to approach the study of nationalism more critically, and a number of authors have conceptualized nationalism as a historically specific construction in which the country's leaders and populations play an active role (Anderson 1983; Worsely 1984; Chatterjee 1986; Kapferer 1988; Fox 1990). Some writers link the construction of nationalism to the colonial venture. This work has provided the social sciences with an analysis of nationalism that highlights its construction, through shared symbolism, of an imaginary common interest that may occasionally galvanize rebellion to existing authority or more often allow such authorities to control their national populations most effectively.

Despite the internationalization of capital and the transnationalization of populations, nation-states and nationalism persist and must be the topic of further analysis. For our purposes, it is important to recognize that transnational migrants exist, interact, are given and assert their identities, and seek or exercise legal and social rights within national structures that monopolize power and foster ideologies of identity. At the same time, it is clear that the identity, field of action, ideology, or even legal rights of citizenship of transnational migrants are not confined within the boundaries of any one single polity. The development of transnationalism challenges our current formulations about nationalist projects. We must ask whether transmigrants will continue to participate in nationalist constructions that contribute to the hegemony of the dominant classes in each nation state as they live lives that span national borders (Basch, Glick Schiller and Blanc-Szanton 1992).

As with nationalism, the constructed, manipulated, variable, flexible nature of ethnicity is only now becoming clear. *Ethnicity* first emerged as a key concept in social science in the United States during the late 1960s. Until that time, despite the multitude of indicators that sectors of populations of immigrant descent continued to maintain or even develop separate identifications, often including some ties to their country or region of origin, social science maintained that the appropriate mode of analysis for the study of immigrant populations was "assimilation."

The assimilationist framework that envisioned the melting of the prior national identities of immigrants into a single new American nationality has been shown to be a construction reflecting and contributing both to a myth of social mobility (Omi and Winant 1986) and to the construction of American nationalism. The assimilationist framework and its concomitant popularization as an ideology, with America cast as a "melting pot," promoted a consistent message: a universal promise of mobility and success based on individual motivation and effort in a society in which there were no class barriers.

The assimilationist model had little to say about race. Often African-Americans were seen as a recently arriving immigrant group in the North, even though a section of this population had helped construct and then continued to live in these cities.[11] However, in the 1960s, as demands for civil rights and full assimilation changed to demands for Black Power, the entire nature of ethnicity in America was re-examined by social scientists. The result was the creation of new theoretical models. First, Glazer and Moynihan's (1963) effort to look "beyond the melting pot" took up and popularized pluralist ideology first articulated in the 1920s (Kallen 1956). The enthusiastic reception of the notion of cultural pluralism several years later by media, academics, and white "ethnics" (Greeley 1971; Novack 1974) seems linked to the development of minority demands for empowerment. A structuralist approach which emphasized the role of the larger society in fostering ethnic difference developed soon after as a critique (Alba 1985; Yetman 1985). Neither approach provided insights into racial divisions in the United States, however. Both were products of and contributed to the continuation of paradigms that conceptualize populations as divided into discrete, tightly bounded groups, and explain persisting identities as products of forces contained within separate nation-states.

In the United States, the cultural pluralists focus attention on cultural differentiation which they maintain divides the populace into separate, but equivalent, "ethnic groups," each with its own history, culture, and political interests. Central to the entire paradigm of cultural pluralism is the fact of persisting cultural differentiation traced by some pluralists to primordial sentiments described as virtually a "tribal" instinct (Isaacs 1975).

Pluralists have paid scant attention to differences within the populations labeled as ethnic. Jews and Italians, for example, are categorized as single

---

[11] Classic assimilationist works are those of Wirth (1928) and Park (1950). This framework was extended to African-Americans in the work of Myrdal 1962 (1944) and E. Franklin Frazier (1957). Critiques of this approach have been made by numerous authors. For writers who specifically compare the experiences of immigrants and African-Americans see Stanley Lieberson (1980) and Omi and Winant (1986).

ethnic groups, whereas in both cases they in fact originated from different classes, regions, or countries, arrived with profound internal cultural differences, and in the course of settlement, developed new internal differentiations of class, region, and outlook (di Leonardi 1984; Gorelick 1974). National loyalties that link incoming populations to ancestral homes may be acknowledged by pluralists, but such relations are believed to fade over time.

The structuralists focus more on the economic and social forces within the polity that foster divisions between ethnic populations and thus the persistence of ethnic groups (Alba 1988; Glick 1975). They pay more attention to the constructed and manipulated nature of ethnic boundaries and ethnic differentiation. The term "ethnogenesis" is sometimes used to distinguish a process of cultural differentiation that develops from forces found within the larger society (Gonzalez 1988). In its extreme, all cultural differentiation is seen as not just "invented" but imagined, so that no actual cultural differences separate populations conceived to be culturally distinct. Bentley (1987) has labeled this the "empty vessel" approach to the study of culture to highlight the tendency of structuralist analysis to discount the role of the members of ethnically defined populations to actively employ ongoing cultural repertoires.

The current critique of pluralist and structuralist arguments has called for an analysis of ethnicity that leaves room both for "cultural practice" and human agency. There is an understanding that ethnicity is a product of the dialectic between continuities of cultural behavior and social constructions that are defined or reinforced by a particular nation-state (Blanc-Szanton 1985a,b; Basch 1985). However, a growing tendency in writing on ethnicity to focus on individual choice reduces rather than expands our analytical horizons (Cohen 1978). With the emergence of transnationalism the individual migrant is now embedded in a wider social field that spans two or more nations. A transnational perspective on ethnicity must be developed that includes an examination of culture and agency within this expanded social field.

Race is also a social construction but one with a different history and a different relationship to the growth of the global system. It is useful to recall that until recently race and nation often were used interchangeably, as in the construction "the British race," in order to make clear that race is no more a product of genetics than nationality or ethnicity.[12] Over time, however, in places like the United States, the set character of race was imposed by the insistence that biology rather than culture is to be determinative of differentiation. In other national settings, ethnic divides may be used as race is—in this sense both are social constructions used to order social and economic relations.

---

[12] Park (1950), whose writings contributed to the assimilationist framework, spoke of the "race-relations cycle" and used the terms "nationality" and "race" interchangeably, thereby sidestepping the historic separation in the United States between people of color and white America.

At the same time, the historical construction of race is so firmly entrenched within the structure of global capitalism, and in the structures of inequality of particular societies, that some argue that social organization on the basis of race is best described as a "racial order" (Greenberg 1980), besides which ethnic categories seem ephemeral and fluid.

Eric Wolf has stressed the historical difference between the operation of ethnic and racial categories in the development of capitalism. "Racial designations, such as "Indian" or "Negro" are the outcome of the subjugation of populations in the course of European mercantile expansion" (1982:380). Formulations of cultural difference do not apply to race—as we saw in the 1990 census—when one could only be black, not African-American, West Indian, or Haitian. While ethnic or national terms stress cultural difference, Wolf makes it clear that racial terms disregard "cultural and physical differences within each of the two large categories, denying any constituent group political, economic, or ideological identity of their own."

The analytical mandate here is urgent and complex. Because race permeates all aspects of the transnational migrant's experience, it is important to analyze its several components. First of all, migrant identity and experience are shaped by the position of their country within the global racial order just as they are affected by the social location of their racial group within the nation state. Secondly internal class differentiation exists within the racial group to which transmigrants are assigned. For example, all those designated black in the United States can hardly be said to share the same class position. Moreover, the population designated as black in the United States is culturally differentiated (Basch 1987; Bryce-Laporte 1972, 1980; Foner 1983; Fouron 1983; Charles 1989; Glick Schiller and Fouron 1990). Migrants coming from the Caribbean, for example, confront an African-American population that shares several centuries of historical experience. At the same time the global construction of race provides the basis for affinity and communality.

Yet all of these factors do not encompass the complexity of the racial identity of migrants who are transnationals. An analysis of the conceptions of race of transnational migrants also must examine the constructions of race that persist "back home." Talking about "back home" emphasizes the necessity of examining how the several nation-states within which transmigrants reside influence constructions of identity that draw on race, ethnicity and nationalism and the manner in which transmigrating populations, with their own internal differences, process these constructions within their daily lives.

CONCLUSION

We have emphasized the constructed nature of the identities of nationality, ethnicity, and race, and stressed the necessity of looking beyond the boundaries of existing analytical categories of social science. To conceptualize transnationalism we must bring to the study of migration a global perspective. Only a view of the world as a single social and economic system allows us to comprehend the implications of the similar descriptions of new patterns of migrant experience that have been emerging from different parts of the globe. At the very same time, it is in terms of these bounded identity constructs that migrants frame their individual and collective strategies of adaptation. In forging a framework of analysis capable of comprehending the life experiences of transnational migrants, social scientists cannot merely dismiss categories of identity as artificial and reified constructions that mask more global processes.

A focus on transnationalism as a new field of social relations will allow us to explore transnational fields of action and meaning as operating within and between continuing nation-states and as a reaction to the conditions and terms nation-states impose on their populations. Migrants will be viewed as culturally creative but as actors in an arena that they do not control. Transnational flows of material objects and ideas will be analyzed in relation to their social location and utilization—in relation to the people involved with them. This approach will enable us to observe the migrant experience in process, analyze its origins, monitor changes within it, and see how it affects both country of origin and countries of residence. Such a perspective will serve as a necessary building block for the reformulation of such key social science concepts as society and culture.

ACKNOWLEDGMENTS

This article was co-written, but it is based on research carried out by the individual authors. We gratefully acknowledge the material and intellectual support we have received. We also wish to thank Iching Wu for his assistance and support. Glick Schiller's work was funded first by a doctoral fellowship from the National Institute of Mental Health Doctoral and then by a grant to Josh DeWind and Nina Glick Schiller from the National Institute for Child Health and Human Development (Grant HD 18140-02). This latter research was conducted jointly by a team of researchers which included Marie Lucie Brutus, Carolle Charles, George Fouron, and Luis Antoine Thomas. Basch's early research on the Caribbean was supported by a doctoral dissertation grant from the National Institute of Mental Health. Her subsequent research, conducted together with Rosina Wiltshire, Winston Wiltshire, and Joyce Toney, and with the assistance of Isa Soto, Margaret Souza, and Colin Robinson, was funded by grants from the International Development Research Centre of Ottawa, Canada and the United Nations Institute for Training and Research the United Nations Fund for Population and Activities. Blanc-Szanton's initial research in the Philippines was funded by a grant from a joint Penn State—

Ateneo de Manila University research project. Her subsequent work was carried out while living and working for many years in the Philippines and Thailand and most recently in the process of carrying out a research project for the Ford Foundation in the region. Additional funding was received from Columbia University and the New York Council for the Humanities.

REFERENCES CITED

Alba, Richard, Ed.
    1985   *Ethnicity and race in the U.S.A. Toward the twenty-first century.* New York: Routledge.
American Academy of Political and Social Science
    1986   From foreign workers to settlers?–Transnational migration and the emergence of new minority. *The Annals of the American Academy of Political and Social Science 485 (May):*9–166.
Appadurai, Arjun and Carol Breckenridge
    1988   Why public culture. *Public Culture 1(1):*5–9.
Anderson, Benedict
    1983   *Imagined communities: Reflections on the origins and spread of nationalism.* London: Verso.
Bach, Robert
    1980   On the holism of a world system perspective. In *Processes of the world-system,* edited by Terrace Hopkins and I. Immanuel Wallerstein. Beverly Hills: Sage. Pp. 289–310.
Basch, Linda
    1985   *Workin' for the Yankee dollar: The impact of a transnational petroleum company on Caribbean class and ethnic relations.* Unpublished Ph.D. dissertation, New York University, 1978.
    1987   The politics of Caribbeanization: Vincentians and Grenadians in New York. In *Caribbean life in New York City,* edited by C. Sutton and E. Chaney. New York: Center for Migration Studies. Pp. 160–181.
Basch, Linda, Nina Glick Schiller, and Cristina Blanc-Szanton
    1992   Transnationalism and the construction of the deterritorialized nation: An outline for a theory of post-national practice. Paper delivered at the annual meetings of the American Anthropological Association. Chicago.
    n.d.   *Rethinking migration, ethnicity, race, and nationalism in transnational perspective.* New York: Gordon and Breach. Forthcoming.
Basch, Linda, Rosina Wiltshire-Brodber, Winston Wiltshire, and Joyce Toney
    n.d.   Caribbean regional and international migration: Transnational dimensions. In *Caribbean international migration and labor movements,* edited and published by the International Development Research Centre, Ottawa. Forthcoming.
Benedict, Ruth
    1959 [1934]   *Patterns of culture.* Boston: Houghton Mifflin.
Bentley, G. C.
    1987   Ethnicity and practice. *Comparative studies of society and history 24:*24–55.
Blanc-Szanton, Cristina
    1985a   Thai and Sino-Thai in small town Thailand: Changing patterns of inter-ethnic relations. In *The Chinese in Southeast Asia, Volume II: Identity, culture*

and politics, edited by Peter Gosling and Linda Lim. Singapore: Maruzen Press. Pp. 99–125.

1985b Ethnic identities and aspects of class in contemporary central Thailand. Paper presented at the symposium on Changing Identities of the Southeast Asian Chinese since World War II, Canberra, Australia.

Block, Fred
1987 *Revising state theory: Essays in politics and postindustrialization.* Philadelphia: Temple University Press.

Brow, James
1988 In pursuit of hegemony. *American Ethnologist 15(2)*:311–327.

Bryce-Laporte, Roy, Ed.
1972 Black immigrants: The experience of invisibility and inequality. *Journal of Black Studies 3*:29–56.
1980 *Sourcebook on the new immigrants.* New Brunswick: Transaction Books.

Chaney, Elsa
1979 The world economy and contemporary migration. *International Migration Review 13*:204–212.

Charles, Carolle
1989 *Dialectics of race, class, and ethnicity among Haitian immigrants: A case study of Haitian leaders.* Ph.D. dissertation, SUNY, Binghamton.

Chatterjee, Partha
1986 Nationalist thought and the colonial world: A derivative discourse. London: Zed Books.

Cohen, Ronald
1978 Ethnicity: Problem and focus in anthropology. *Annual Review of Anthropology 7*:379–403.

di Leonardi, Michaela
1984 *The varieties of ethnic experience: Kinship, class, and gender among California Italian-Americans.* Ithaca: Cornell University Press.

Foner, Nancy
1983 Jamaican migrants: Comparative analysis of the New York and London experience. New York Research Program in Inter-American Affairs. *Occasional Paper No. 36.* New York.

Fouron, Georges
1983 The black immigrant dilemma in the United States: The Haitian experience. *Journal of Caribbean Studies 3(3)*:242–65.

Fox, Richard
1990 Nationalist ideologies and the production of national cultures. Washington, DC: American Anthropological Association.

Frank, André Gunder
1966 The development of underdevelopment. *Monthly Review 18*:17–31.
1969 *Capitalism and underdevelopment in Latin America: Historical studies of Chile and Brazil.* New York: Modern Reader Paperbacks.

Frazier, E. Franklin
1957 The Negro in the United States. New York: MacMillan. (revised edition)

Fried, Morton
1975 *The notion of tribe.* Menlo Park, CA: Cummings Publications.

Glazer, Nathan and P. Moynihan
1963 *Beyond the melting pot.* Cambridge, MA: MIT Press.

Glick, Nina
1975 *The formation of a Haitian ethnic group.* Ph.D. dissertation. Colombia University.

Glick Schiller, Nina and George Fouron
   1990   'Everywhere we go we are in danger': Ti manno and the emergence of a
          Haitian transnational identity. *American Ethnologist 17(2)*:329–347.
Gonzalez, Nancie
   1988   Sojourners of the Caribbean: Ethnogenesis and ethnohistory of the Gari-
          funa. Urbana: University of Illinois Press.
Gorelick, Shirley
   1974   *City College and the Jewish poor.* New York: Schocken.
Gramsci, Antonio
   1971   *Prison notebooks: Selections*, translated by Quinton Hoare and Geoffrey Smith.
          New York: International Publishers.
Greeley, Andrew
   1971   The rediscovery of cultural pluralism. *The Antioch Review 31*:343–367.
Greenberg, Stanley
   1980   *Race and state in capitalist development: Comparative perspectives.* New Haven,
          CT: Yale University Press.
Hall, Stuart
   1988   The toad in the garden: Thatcherism among the theorists. In *Marxism and
          the interpretation of culture.* Urbana: University of Illinois Press. Pp. 35–57.
Hannerz, Ulf
   1989   Scenarios for peripheral cultures. Paper presented at the symposium on Cul-
          ture, Globalization and the World System, University of Stockholm, Sweden.
Helm, June
   1975 [1968]   *Essays on the problem of the tribe.* St. Louis: Washington University
          Press.
Isaacs, Harold
   1975   Basic group identity: The idols of the tribe. In *Ethnicity: Theory and experi-
          ence*, edited by Nathan Glazer and Daniel Moynihan. Cambridge, MA: Har-
          vard University Press. Pp. 29–52.
Kallen, Horace
   1956 [1924]   *Cultural pluralism and the American idea: An essay in social philosophy.*
          Philadelphia: University of Philadelphia Press.
Kamenka, Eugene
   1973   Political nationalism: The evolution of the idea. In *Nationalism: The nature
          and evolution of an idea*, edited by E. Kamenka. Canberra: Australia National
          University Press. Pp. 2–20.
Kapferer, Bruce
   1988   *Legends of people, mythos of state: Violence, intolerance, and political culture in Sri
          Lanka and Australia.* Washington, D.C.: Smithsonian Institution Press.
Kedourie, Eli
   1960   *Nationalism.* New York: Praeger.
Lee, Everett
   1966   A theory of migration. *Demography 3*:47–57.
Lozano, Beverly
   1984   The Andalucia-Hawaii-California migration: A study in macrostructure and
          microhistory. *Comparative studies in society and history 26(2)*:305–324.
Lieberson, Stanley
   1980   *A piece of the pie: Blacks and white immigrants since 1880.* Berkeley: University
          of California Press.
Lerner, David
   1958   *The passing of traditional society.* Glencoe, IL: Free Press.

Marcus, George
1986   Contemporary problems of ethnography in the modern world system. In *Writing culture*, edited by James Clifford and George Marcus. Berkeley: University of California Press. Pp. 165–193.
Myrdal, Gunnar
1962 [1944]   *An American dilemma: The Negro problem and modern democracy.* New York: Harper and Row.
Nash, June and Maria Patricia Fernandez
1983   *Women, men and the international division of labor.* Albany: State University of New York Press.
Novack, Michael
1974   The Seventies: Decade of the ethnics. In *Race and ethnicity in modern America*, edited by R. Meister. Lexington, KY: D.C. Heath.
Omi, Michael and Howard Winant
1986   *Racial formation in the United States.* New York: Routledge and Kegan Paul.
Park, Robert
1950   *Race and culture.* New York: Free Press.
Parsons, Talcott
1951   *The social system.* Glencoe, IL: Free Press of Glencoe.
Pessar, Patricia
1982   The role of household in international migration and the case of U.S. bound migration from the Dominican Republic. *International Migration Review* 16(2):341–364.
Portes, Alejandro and Robert Bach
1985   *Latin journey: Cuban and Mexican immigrants in the United States.* Berkeley: University of California Press.
Portes, Alejandro and John Walton
1981   *Labor, class, and the international system.* New York: Academic Press.
Radcliffe Brown, A. R.
1952   *Structure and function in primitive society.* London: Cohen.
Richman, Karen
1987   They will remember me in the house: The song-pwen of Haitian cassette-discourse. Paper delivered at the meetings of the American Anthropological Association, Chicago, IL.
Rollwagen, Jack
1986   Reconsidering basic assumptions: A call for a reassessment of the general concept of culture in anthropology. *Urban Anthropology* 15:97–133.
Rosaldo, Renaldo
1989   *Culture and truth: The remaking of social analysis.* Boston: Beacon.
Rouse, Roger
1988   *Mexican migration and the social space of postmodernism.* Center for U.S. Mexican Studies. University of California, San Diego.
1989   *Mexican migration to the United States: Family relations in the development of a transnational migrant circuit.* Ph.D. dissertation, Stanford University, Stanford, CA.
Rubenstein, Hymie
1983   Remittances and rural underdevelopment in the English speaking Caribbean. *Human Organization* 42(4):306.
Sassen, Saskia
1988   *The mobility of labor and capital: A study in international investment and labor flow.* New York: Cambridge University Press.

Smith, Carol
    1984   Local history in global context: Social and economic transitions in western
            Guatemala. *Comparative Study of Society and History 26(2)*:193–227.
Sutton, Constance
    1987   The Caribbeanization of New York City and the emergence of a trans-
            national socio-cultural system. In *Caribbean life in New York City: Socio-
            cultural dimensions*, edited by Constance Sutton and Elsa Chaney. New York:
            Center for Migration Studies. Pp. 25–29.
Sutton, Constance and Susan Makiesky-Barrow
    1987 [1975]   Migration and West Indian racial and ethnic consciousness. In *Carib-
            bean life in New York City: Sociocultural dimensions*, edited by Constance
            Sutton and Elsa Chaney. New York: Center for Migration Studies. Pp. 92–116.
Vassady, Bella
    1982   'The homeland cause' as a stimulant to ethnic unity: The Hungarian Ameri-
            can response to Karolyi's 1914 tour. *Journal of American Ethnic History 2(1)*:
            39–64.
Wakeman, Frederic, Jr.
    1988   Transnational and comparative research. *Items 42(4)*:85–88.
Wallerstein, Immanuel
    1974   *The modern world system.* New York: Academic Press.
    1982   The rise and future demise of the world capitalist system: Concepts for com-
            parative analysis. In *Introduction to the sociology of 'developing societies'*, edited
            by Hamza Alavi and Teodor Shanin. New York: Monthly Review Press.
            Pp. 29–53.
Williams, Raymond
    1977   *Marxism and literature.* Oxford: Oxford University Press.
Wirth, Louis
    1928   *The ghetto.* Chicago: University of Chicago Press.
Wolf, Eric
    1982   *Europe and the people without history.* Berkeley: University of California Press.
    1988   Inventing society. *American Ethnologist 15*:752.
Wood, Charles and Terrance McCoy
    1985   Migration, remittances and development: A study of Caribbean cane cutters
            in Florida. *International Migration Review 19(9)*:251–277.
Worsely, Peter
    1984   *The three worlds.* Chicago: University of Chicago Press.
Yetman, Norman
    1985   Introduction: Definitions and perspectives. In *Majority and minority, the dy-
            namics of race and ethnicity in American life*, edited by Norman Yetman.
            Boston: Allyn and Bacon. Pp. 1–20.
Zolberg, Aristide
    1983   International migrations in political perspective. In *Global trends in migra-
            tion*, edited by Mary Kritz, Charles Keely, and Silvano Tomasi. New York:
            Center for Migration Studies. Pp. 3–27.

Making Sense of Settlement:
Class Transformation, Cultural
Struggle, and Transnationalism
among Mexican Migrants
in the United States

ROGER ROUSE

Department of Anthropology
1054 LSA Building
University of Michigan
Ann Arbor, Michigan 48109

Mexicans have been migrating to the United States in significant numbers for more than a hundred years. From the outset, the great majority of this migration has been temporary and circular. Contrary to popular opinion, people have generally come for periods ranging from a few months to a couple of years and then returned home (Cockcroft 1982; Cornelius 1979). Since the late 1960s, however, there has been a marked growth in settlement. While temporary migration continues to predominate, it has become increasingly common for people to stay for extended periods and to establish new homes north of the border (Chavez 1988; Cornelius, in press).

How should we understand the experiences of these recent settlers? What kinds of influence have they faced, and how have they responded? More importantly, how should we theorize and conceptualize their relationship to the contexts in which they have lived? For more than forty years, the ethnographically based literature on Mexican migration has been dominated by two closely related tendencies.[1] First, migration in general has been analyzed

---

[1] There is surprisingly little ethnographically based literature that deals directly with Mexican migration to the United States and even less that draws on fieldwork conducted north of the border. Until the 1980s, much of the work empirically most relevant to an understanding of Mexican settlement was found in studies of Chicano neighborhoods that contained at least some settlers and much of the work conceptually and theoretically most relevant was found in studies of migration within Mexico. My introductory remarks refer to all three kinds of literature. It is important to point out that I am concerned to identify general tendencies and trends in these related areas over a period of almost half a century. I cannot do justice to the subtlety of particular studies or to evolving differences and debates. For an overview of work on Mexican migration to the United States prior to the 1980s, see Kemper (1979); for reviews of anthropological work on Chicanos see Romano-V. (1968, 1970), Rosaldo (1985), and Vaca (1970a,b); and for a review of general anthropological work on migration, informed by a detailed knowledge of the Mexican literature, see Kearney (1986).

mainly in *bipolar* terms (Uzzell 1976) as a move between essentially autonomous communities and, within this framework, settlement has been treated
as a process in which people steadily shift their focus of attention and the locus
of their principal social ties from one community to another.[2] Second, the
attitudes and practices of those involved have been understood primarily from
a *neofunctionalist* perspective as more or less effective forms of adaptation to
a new environment.[3]

There have, of course, been important changes in the literature dealing
with Mexican migration and settlement. Most notably, it has been common
since the late 1960s to challenge earlier studies in which people's problems
were attributed primarily to the difficulties they experienced in modifying
their existing values and beliefs (*cf.* Romano-V. 1968, 1970; Vaca 1970a,b).
Environments once deemed homogeneous and beneficent have been reconstituted as differentiated, exploitative, and oppressive; people once treated as
passive and bound by custom have been reconceptualized as active and creative agents; and responses once considered maladaptive have been reinterpreted as rational reactions to structurally conditioned problems. No longer
seen as victims of their own cultural inertia, settlers have increasingly been
lauded for developing effective forms of coping under difficult conditions.[4]

Yet the literature remains problematical in several respects. In the first
place, the growing emphasis on creative adaptation has been accompanied by
a marked retreat from culture. Responding to the fact that culturally oriented
analyses often seemed to "blame the victims," scholars have come to understand migrants' experiences increasingly in behavioral terms as manifest responses to particular configurations of opportunity and constraint. We thus
know very little that is analytically significant about the ways in which recent
settlers have made sense of their lives. At the same time, the emphasis on a
bipolar framework has obscured the ways in which many settlers during the

---

[2] This approach is most clearly manifest in studies that compare sociocultural forms in the
destination community with those manifest in the community, or general area, from which the
settlers came. For examples from work on migration within Mexico, see Butterworth (1962),
Kemper (1977), and Lewis (1952). For examples from work on Mexican settlers and Chicano
neighborhoods in the United States, see Achor (1978), Horowitz (1983), Humphrey (1944),
Madsen (1964), Rubel (1966), and Thurston (1974).

[3] For a general review written from this perspective, see Graves and Graves (1974). A particu-
larly clear statement of its significance in the study of a Chicano neighborhood can be found in
Achor (1978: 166–176). For examples of its use in the study of migration within Mexico, see
Butterworth (1962), Hendricks and Murphy (1981), Kemper (1977), Lomnitz (1976, 1977), and
Ugalde (1974). Examples of its use in the study of Mexicans migrating to and living in the United
States can be found in Alvarez (1987), Alvirez and Bean (1976), Baca and Bryan (1983), Carlos
(1975), Humphrey (1944), and Rubel (1966).

[4] See, for example, Alvarez (1987), Alvirez and Bean (1976), Carlos (1975), Hendricks and
Murphy (1981), Kemper (1977), Lomnitz (1977), and Ugalde (1974). During the last decade,
this approach has moved in a more Malinowskian direction with a growing emphasis on treating
migration itself as an "adaptive household strategy." Examples in the Mexican context include
Dinerman (1978) and Wood (1981); for a critical response, see Rouse (1989b).

last two decades have managed to maintain active involvements with the people and places they have left behind and, in so doing, have often helped create new kinds of communities that span the international border. And finally, the emphasis on adaptation has made it difficult to conceptualize and identify the contradictions and potential conflicts that are entailed in the class-related dimensions of settlement.

In this article, I shall outline an approach that addresses all three problems. Giving particular emphasis to the ways in which recent settlers have evaluated and interpreted their lives, I shall argue that we should view their understandings from a theoretical perspective attentive to the cultural struggles associated with class transformation and that we should view these struggles within a conceptual framework sensitive to the emergence of transnational forms of organization. That is, while emphasizing the importance of approaching settlement from a transnational perspective, I shall argue that it is equally important to approach transnationalism from a perspective attentive to the interplay of culture, class, and power.

To give these general claims a particular point of reference, I shall draw on my knowledge of a single case, the migration that has taken place since the early 1940s between the *municipio* (or "county") of Aguililla in the west-central region of Mexico and Redwood City, an urban jurisdiction in northern California. More narrowly, I shall focus on the experiences of *men* who spent extended periods in Redwood City between the late 1960s, when an Aguil-illan community began to emerge there on a significant scale, and the mid-1980s, when I concluded my research. More narrowly still, I shall develop my argument through an account that concentrates on just two men, brothers whom I shall refer to as "Carlos" and "Antonio."[5] While the evidence that informs my analysis comes from work with a large and varied group of settlers, I hope in this way to show how the cultural politics of class transformation and the workings of transnationalism have been played out concretely in the details of people's daily lives.

Before proceeding, I should emphasize two points about this analysis. First, its basic elements are by no means novel. In theoretical terms, it owes a great deal to E.P. Thompson's magisterial study of the making of the English working class (Thompson 1966) and to the varied treatments of the relationship between culture, power, and practice in the work of Raymond Williams

[5] My understanding of Aguilillan migration is based largely on twenty-seven months of fieldwork carried out between October 1982 and December 1984. During this period, I spent almost equal amounts of time in Aguililla and Redwood City. To minimize the threatening nature of my research, I did not carry out a formal survey but relied instead on participant observation and the collection of oral histories. It is important to appreciate the historical specificity of this research. Since its completion, the context in which Aguilillans operate has been significantly altered by passage of the Immigration Reform and Control Act of 1986 and by dramatic changes in the politics and economics of the *municipio* (Ramírez 1988; Reding 1990). It is to encourage a sense of historical specificity that I refer to the experiences of Aguilillans in the past tense.

(1977), Michel Foucault (1979, 1983), Pierre Bourdieu (1977) and Michel de
Certeau (1984). Moreover, in stressing the significance of transnational arrangements, it parallels important developments made recently both within
the literature on Mexican migration and beyond.[6] My aim is simply to bring
these elements together in a manner that illustrates their capacity for mutual
illumination.

The second point to stress is that, in concentrating on Aguilillan men, I
do not mean to deny the importance of women's contributions to the process
of settlement. Nor do I mean to suggest, more generally, that men forged
their attitudes and practices in isolation. The two sexes influenced one another in numerous ways and their lives were inextricably linked. At the same
time, however, the cultural and political contexts in which they operated
meant that their experiences were significantly different. My focus on the lives
of men reflects both a recognition of these differences and a more general concern to approach the experience of settlement in a manner that is properly
attentive to the specificities of gender.

Having made these points, I shall begin by providing some preliminary
information on the history of Aguilillan migration to the United States and
on the particular trajectories that Carlos and Antonio described.

~ I ~

The *municipio* of Aguililla is located in the southwest corner of the state
of Michoacán in a mountainous region known locally as the Costa Sierra.[7]
Sandwiched between the Tepalcatepec Valley to the north and the Pacific
Ocean to the south, this region was for many years a marginal and isolated
zone remote from major centers of power and wealth in the interior of the
country. In the early 1940s, the *municipio* was dominated by a way of life organized around small-scale ranching and peasant farming, one in which
people strove locally to create and maintain their own independent, family-
run operations. At that point, however, Aguilillans began migrating in significant numbers to the United States and, over the next four decades, the
municipio came increasingly to serve as a nursery and nursing home for people
working in wage-earning jobs north of the border.

---

[6] The concept of multilocational communities was first developed in the Mexican context
during the 1970s in studies dealing with internal migration. A seminal analysis by Roberts (1974)
on migration in Peru and Guatemala, itself apparently influenced by earlier work in Africa, was
followed by articles on Mexico from Lomnitz (1976) and Uzzell (1976). More recently, the concept has been elaborated in studies of migration to the United States by Baca and Bryan (1983),
Kearney (1986), Kearney and Nagengast (1989), Massey *et al.* (1987), and Mines (1981). My own
contributions appear in Rouse (1989a, 1991). Parallel developments regarding other migrations
are summarized by Glick Schiller, Basch and Blanc-Szanton (this volume).

[7] A fuller version of this account can be found in Rouse (1989a).

For the first two decades, the great majority of the migration was temporary and circular. The most common pattern was one in which men left their families in the *municipio* to work seasonally in agricultural jobs in the rural southwest. The numbers migrating in any one year were relatively low and, in aggregate terms, the impact of migrants' earnings was limited. From the mid-1960s onwards, however, the level of migration rose significantly and the *municipio's* economy became increasingly dependent on the influx of dollars. Moreover, the patterns of movement changed. A growing proportion of Aguilillans headed for urban destinations, where it was easier to find employment on a year-round basis. Women and children began to migrate in greater numbers. And, reflecting broader trends, it became steadily more common for people to settle north of the border.

As settlement increased, Aguilillans rapidly established a series of satellite communities in the United States. From the late 1960s, by far the largest of these was in Redwood City, an urban jurisdiction on the northern edge of California's famous "Silicon Valley."[8] In the early 1980s, when there were roughly 26,000 people living in the *municipio*, there may have been as many as 7,000 Aguilillans (including their U.S.-born children) in the Redwood City area. As a function of the growing restrictions on legal entry to the United States, many were undocumented. Despite this difficulty, however, people found jobs throughout the valley, almost invariably working in the region's burgeoning secondary labor market. Although some were employed in light assembly, the great majority worked in the service sector. Men found jobs as gardeners, landscapers, janitors, and dishwashers, while women who earned wages generally did so as hotel cleaners, child-minders, and domestic servants.

Beginning in the early 1940s, then, the population of the *municipio* experienced a dramatic and accelerating dispersion. But more was involved than a simple change in spatial distribution. At the same time, and in some respects more crucially, Aguilillans underwent a major shift in the ways in which they made a living. In general terms, they moved from an emphasis on various forms of petty production to a growing dependence on wage-labor; more specifically, they came increasingly to rely not only on working for wages but on selling their labor power as a carefully calibrated and readily alienable commodity within the context of contractual relations. That is, put simply, they underwent a process of "proletarianization."[9] Some experienced this shift without leaving the *municipio*, but for most people it was an integral part of their first trip to the United States.

[8] Redwood City is located in San Mateo county, on the western side of the San Francisco Bay, roughly half way between San Francisco and San Jose. Many analysts locate "Silicon Valley" entirely within Santa Clara county, to the south, but high technology firms have in fact been a significant force in southeast San Mateo county as well.

[9] It is important to point out, however, that very few Aguilillans experienced the move into blue collar factory work that is normally suggested by the use of this term.

These broad processes are clearly illustrated in the lives of Carlos and Antonio. Between the early 1940s and the early 1960s, their parents, Enrique and María, devoted themselves to building up a farming operation in a small *rancho* (or "hamlet") called La Pitaya. From this operation, they hoped to meet the immediate needs of their rapidly growing family. More ambitiously, they also hoped to provide each of their ten children with capital endowments large enough to let them stay in the area and continue making a living as petty producers. By the early 1960s, however, it was apparent that the farm would not yield enough resources to endow everyone, and so Enrique and María began encouraging their younger children to develop an alternative basis of support by continuing their education. Yet the income from the farm was soon unable to meet even the family's most immediate needs and so the older children turned to migration, hoping that the money they earned in the United States would enable them to both help their parents and finance the formation of their own operations.

So it was that Carlos, as the oldest son, left for the United States in 1966 and found his way to Redwood City, where he obtained work first as a dishwasher and later as an assistant cook. Antonio, the middle son, remained behind in school and, a few years later, managed—quite remarkably given his parents' poverty and lack of formal education—to gain admission to the state university where he began studying to be a doctor. In 1971, however, after two years in college, he dropped out and a year later migrated northwards to join his brother. Despite his advanced education, he ended up working first as a dishwasher and later as a janitor. Like his older brother, he entered the United States without papers.

Although Carlos and Antonio initially planned to stay only briefly, they became increasingly embroiled in life in the United States. Carlos married a Chicana, started having children with her and, through his marriage, obtained legal status. Antonio married a woman from Aguililla whom he had met in Redwood City, also started having children, and, in 1979, sought to legalize his status on the grounds that he had been in the country continuously for seven years without getting into trouble with the law or becoming a public charge. Significantly, in the early 1980s, both men purchased houses in the Redwood City area. By late 1984, when my fieldwork ended, they had clearly become long-term settlers. Carlos, by then 38, had been in Redwood City eighteen years, and Antonio, 34, had been there twelve. More importantly, they had spent the great majority of their adult lives rehearsing the daily routines of proletarian labor.

~ II ~

How should we understand their relationship to the context in which they lived? As I have already indicated, the dominant tendency over the last two decades has been to construe it in terms of adaptive responses to a new environment, one deemed to present people with a particular configuration of opportunities and constraints. But this tendency is problematical in several respects. It represents adult migrants as pre-formed subjects, it treats the settings in which they operate as too external—as a kind of maze or labyrinth laid out inertly before them; and it obscures both the cultural dimensions of contextual influence and the politics of daily life.

As an alternative, I would argue that we should view the experiences of Carlos and Antonio within an agonistic frame as active engagements with class-related forms of discipline. That is, having set their lives in the context of proletarianization, we should appreciate that this involves not only politico-economic developments that undermine people's attachments to subsistence farming and throw them into wage-labor but also cultural pressures that work to make their daily habits and routines more consistent with the interests of capital. Moreover, we should recognize that, while these pressures are directed partly at people's behavior, they are also, and more profoundly, directed at their values and beliefs so that eventually they will regulate themselves (Thompson 1966). Put another way—one that enables a selective appropriation of poststructuralist insights—we should treat proletarianization as an integral part of broader processes involving the disciplinary production of class-specific subjects (cf. Althusser 1972; Foucault 1979, 1983).

Such processes place a heavy emphasis on producing workers who, in contracting to sell their labor power as a commodity, are able to deliver it in a steady and dependable manner. They must turn up at the workplace regularly and punctually, be sober and rested so that the labor they provide is uniform and predictable, and use the time for which they are paid exclusively for work. But the production of "good" proletarians requires more than this. It has always involved the development of "good" citizens, people who devote their time outside work to individual and familial activities rather than to forms of collective interaction that might encourage concerted challenges to the status quo. And, increasingly since the 1920s, it has also involved the production of "good" consumers, people who not only spend freely but do so within approved circuits of capitalist exchange. To some extent, of course, these demands have been directed at everyone within the reach of consumer capitalism but, as I shall illustrate below, there are many ways in which both the demands themselves and the manner of their enforcement have varied along lines of class. Most notably, the habits and dispositions required of proletarian subjects have differed markedly from those considered appropriate for people in professional and managerial positions.

As Carlos and Antonio entered within the compass of such disciplinary mechanisms, they encountered challenges to many aspects of the way of life they had known in La Pitaya. It is impossible to cover all of these aspects here or to explore the differences between the pressures exerted in the United States and the similar but much less rigorous influences emerging in the *municipio*.

I shall therefore focus on the workings of proletarian discipline in Redwood City and confine myself to just two areas of challenge: first, definitions of personal fulfillment and the ways in which it should be manifested, and second, ideas about the organization of space and the ways in which it should be used. Moreover, as I indicated earlier, I shall consider these issues specifically in relation to adult men.

The way of life that Carlos and Antonio knew as members of a farming family in La Pitaya defined fulfillment primarily in terms of the capacity to create and maintain independent, family-run operations, ideally based in land. In a setting that lacked overarching mechanisms of arbitration and protection and a cultural context that off-set an emphasis on family unity with a strong commitment to personal independence, such operations were constantly vulnerable to the unwanted intrusion of outsiders and to desertion from within. Correspondingly, the conduct of everyday life was organized to a large degree around attempts to maintain effective boundaries and regulate their crossing. Under these circumstances, both the family's house and the bodies of its members served as ready analogues of the collective property and, as such, were meant to exhibit and project a strong immunity to transgression. Houses were meant to present an austere and forbidding face to the outside world and, even on the inside, were meant to be unassuming in appearance. Bodies, particularly the bodies of the family's women, were meant to move demurely and to present an insistent modesty. Clothes were designed to cover the whole body and make-up was rarely used.

The standards and practices that Carlos and Antonio found pressed upon them in Redwood City were quite different. Fulfillment was associated with the capacity to earn well and to spend appropriately and, within this framework, people's houses and their bodies were treated as primary vehicles for the conspicuous expression of claims to success. Houses were meant to invite people's inspection and to serve as an effective medium for the display of prestigious consumer goods. And bodies, particularly female bodies, were meant to draw attention to an active participation in the costly world of fashion. For young Mexican women in the early 1980s, this meant wearing high-heeled shoes, plunging necklines, skin-tight jeans, and heavy make-up.

Regarding the organization of space, the way of life that Carlos and Antonio knew in La Pitaya gave primary emphasis to a familiar opposition between the domestic and the public.[10] A bounded domestic realm, considered ordered, cooperative, and safe, was contrasted with an encompassing and unbounded public realm deemed chaotic, conflict-ridden, and dangerous.

---

[10] My analysis of spatial factors has been stimulated by the work of Yanagisako (1984) and by lectures given at Stanford University in 1980–81 by Jane Collier and the late Michelle Rosaldo. For a review of convergent attempts to explore the politics of space, see Soja (1989). A fuller account of the spatial dimensions of Aguilillan experience can be found in Rouse (in press).

This opposition was, of course, both gendered and asymmetric, the domestic domain being associated with women and young children while the more highly valorized public domain was associated with adult men. In this context, women and young children were meant to stay within the domestic arena, either literally in their own homes or in places that were similarly bounded and protected such as the church and the houses of relatives and friends. Men, by contrast, were meant to move as freely as possible within the public realm and between the public and the domestic, furthering the interests of their family operations not only by working in the fields but also by meeting with other men so that they could reproduce vital social ties and shape the continuous negotiation of personal and familial reputations. In the process, as the heads of families, they were meant to regulate movement of all kinds across the boundaries of their property, mediate relationships between family members and the wider world, and ensure the maintenance of internal hierarchies that ascriptively privileged not just men over women but parents over children and old over young.

Once again, the standards and practices that Carlos and Antonio found pressed upon them in Redwood City were quite different. Space was organized in terms of a fundamental opposition between two equally bounded domains, home and the workplace (or its formal equivalent, the school), and these were distinguished not so much by their relative danger as by the idea that the workplace was the proper locus of socially valued labor, namely labor rewarded by a wage. Men's privileged access to the workplace and their privileged identity as primary wage-earners gave them greater authority than women, but the spatial implications of their authority were again quite different. Because women and children were construed as potential laborers, they too were meant to move outside the home. Women, as a crucial reserve, were meant to be given qualified access to the workplace and children, as workers in the making, were meant to move freely to and from school. Correspondingly, men were meant to let the state, as both a source of education and a regulator of domestic practices, have relatively unmediated access to the members of their families.

In this framework, then, proper movement for everyone involved a disciplined but "free" alternation between home and the workplace. Correspondingly, considerable stress was placed on avoiding a third realm made up of places such as street corners, bars, brothels, and gambling clubs, a realm commonly referred to as "the street." While attacks on the use of this realm were generally phrased in terms of immorality and personal danger, it is important to note that it was also an area in which people threatened to undermine their qualities as sober and rested workers, to meet in ways that might allow the development of collective challenges to the status quo, and to spend their money outside the approved circuits of capitalist exchange. If people did spend time neither at home nor at work, they were meant to do so primarily in malls, theme parks, and cinema complexes. These pleasure palaces of corporate capitalism, together constituting a fourth domain in the logic of spatial discipline, were often represented as privileged sites for large-scale gathering and collective interaction, equivalent in many ways to public settings in Aguililla. Yet they were in fact privately owned and carefully regulated arenas designed almost exclusively for individual and familial forms of use.

To some degree, of course, these arrangements and ideas were pressed on everyone in the Redwood City area. Yet, as Antonio knew from his advanced education and unfinished training as a doctor, this pressure also varied along lines of class and gender. Men subject to proletarian discipline were pressed to accept the constant scrutiny of supervisors, to see their labor power as a commodity measured in carefully calibrated units of time, and to distinguish sharply between the workplace as the site in which they delivered their labor power and the home as a locus of leisure and relaxation.[11] In contrast, professional and managerial workers, whether salaried or self-employed, were encouraged to operate independently, to think of their labor power as something delivered according to the demands of the task, and to accept a much more fluid relationship between the workplace and the home.

~ III ~

The influences that Carlos and Antonio encountered in Redwood City were not just politico-economic; they were also cultural. And the cultural context in which they operated was neither uniform nor neutral; it was differentiated along lines of class and served as a crucial medium of discipline. How did such discipline work?

In part, of course, proletarian discipline worked *discursively* through techniques aimed directly at the ways in which people evaluated and construed the world around them. Most notably, a multitude of messages in the mass media emphasized the fulfillment to be gained through appropriate consumption while attacking everything associated with the street. And although such messages were initially delivered almost exclusively in English, the introduction of a Spanish-language television channel and the steady growth of Spanish-language radio stations meant that, as the 1970s progressed, they were increasingly disseminated in Aguilillan's native tongue. Above all, however, proletarian discipline worked *non-discursively* through techniques directed primarily at the ways in which people acted.[12] And, in this regard, the

[11] The recent growth of industrial homework, performed almost exclusively by women, both illustrates and extends the ways in which the distinction between home and the workplace has been pressed differently on women and men.

[12] This distinction between the discursive and the non-discursive follows Bourdieu (1977: 87–90).

most important sources of influence were the police and the INS (the Immigration and Naturalization Service, commonly referred to by Mexican migrants as "*la migra*").

The impact of these agencies was particularly significant regarding Aguilillans' use of space. Officers from the INS frequently approached people on the street and also patrolled many of the bars, dance halls, and recreational areas where Aguilillan men assembled.[13] Those who were found to be undocumented were simply taken across the border to northern Mexico and, as a result, many were able to return within a few days. But the unpleasantness of temporary imprisonment, the costs involved in getting back to Redwood City, and the possible loss of valued and familiar jobs meant that many people without papers were cautious about attracting unnecessary attention. The local police also stopped Aguilillans on the street, especially those who were driving old and damaged cars or who were walking late at night in the wealthy neighborhoods surrounding Redwood City (something that their jobs as restaurant workers and office cleaners often obliged them to do). And they kept a close eye on many of the bars that migrant men frequented and on gatherings for illegal activities such as cock-fights and gambling. Even migrants who were doing nothing wrong found this kind of attention troubling. There was uncertainty about how the law would be applied and, for those without papers, the added fear that the police might hold them for collection by the INS. Influenced by the dangers that these two agencies posed, many Aguilillans moved as quickly and inconspicuously as they could between home and work and avoided any kind of large-scale gathering in public.

Yet the influences exerted by the INS and the police were not confined to constraints on people's use of space. In an indirect way, they also played an important part in encouraging Aguilillans to be good consumers. Given the fact that officers from both agencies paid most attention to people who looked out of place, there was a strong incentive for new arrivals to replace their cheap, Mexican clothes with a more expensive U.S. wardrobe and for settlers in general to find themselves good-looking cars and to move from barrack-like apartment buildings and multi-family homes into owner-occupied, single-family dwellings. At the same time, to the extent that Aguilillans were obliged by the activities of the two agencies to spend their leisure hours at home, they were given added reason to acquire sources of entertainment such as stereo systems, radios and televisions. Indeed, Aguilillans' susceptibility to the media was first dependent on the effective operation of forces that sought to turn them away from public, interpersonal forms of activity towards domestic settings.

Carlos and Antonio knew such disciplinary influences well. Both had been

---

[13] For a summary account of INS practices prior to passage of the Immigration Reform and Control Act of 1986, see West and Moore (1989:3–5).

arrested and expelled by the INS and both had been challenged frequently
by the police, especially during their early years in Redwood City. Moreover,
the ways in which they talked suggested that the two agencies had played a
significant part in changing their behavior. When I asked Carlos what he did
for entertainment when he was first in Redwood City, he told me:

> I didn't do anything . . . I couldn't even go to the movies . . . My cousin said
> the *migra* was there . . . I used to stay in the house all day long . . . In the
> end I got a radio . . . There was a bar called "The Vietnam." I passed it every
> night but I never went in because they had fights there all the time and so the
> police would come . . . The police got very suspicious if you were on the streets
> after ten at night. They used to stop me on my way to the bus and ask me
> for my papers . . . A friend started driving me home in his car, but he didn't
> have a license and we got stopped one time, so after that I started going home
> by taxi.

Antonio's observations were very similar:

> The police ask for your papers if you don't have other identification and they
> take you off if you don't have them. They pick up people in the bars especially.
> When I was a bachelor, there were dances at St. Anthony's [the local Catholic
> church] but I didn't go because people said that the *migra* used to come . . .
> Coming back from work, I was always scared because the *migra* used to stop
> you all the time . . . so it was better to go home by car . . . Carlos used to
> take me or I'd get a taxi . . . In the end I learned to drive and got a car of my own.

The police and the INS, then, affected settlers such as Carlos and Antonio
not only as enforcers of law and order but also, and in some ways more power-
fully, as agents of class-related discipline, encouraging them to become "good"
proletarian subjects who would appear at work both sober and rested and who
would use their earnings to further individual and familial interests through
the rivalrous medium of conspicuous consumption.

It is important to point out, however, that the interventions of these agencies were not the only forms of non-discursive influence that Aguilillans faced.
Behind them lay a series of ostensibly more neutral and benign processes that
shaped the very terrain on which they were obliged to move and that influenced both the nature and efficacy of more immediate controls. Policies concerning zoning and the construction of low-income housing, for example,
served to open up significant gaps for many Aguilillans between the places in
which they could afford to live and the places in which they worked (Bernstein
et al. 1977). And these gaps, in conjunction with the limited availability of
public transportation, played a crucial role in increasing people's vulnerability
to the attentions of the police and the INS as they moved to and from their
work. Concomitantly, modernist forms of urban planning, apparently influenced by Le Corbusier's injunction to "kill the street," markedly reduced the
availability of large, genuinely public spaces in which Aguilillans could con-

gregate and, in so doing, channelled them to places such as bars and street corners that were much more readily monitored and controlled.

Operating in tandem, in fact, these different kinds of influence did not just shape the ways in which Aguilillans behaved. Through a complex process of habituation, they also worked indirectly to shape people's values and beliefs. By inscribing crucial oppositions in the area's landscape and by carefully regulating how this landscape was used, they worked to habituate people to desired patterns of action and, in so doing, encouraged them unconsciously to internalize the principles that guided this double structuring.[14]

Moreover, while in some respects this process affected everyone in the Redwood City area equally, its impact was also class-specific. The gap between home and work was generally much greater and more extreme for proletarian workers than for members of the professional-managerial elite, and the spatial practices of working people were much more carefully regulated than those of the upper middle classes. In the case of migrants like Carlos and Antonio, whose skin-color, lack of papers, and night-time work in wealthy neighborhoods made them especially vulnerable, the differences in regulatory attention were considerable. As Antonio once told me, "It's difficult, you know. You always have this fear that anyone you meet could be *la migra*."

~ IV ~

In the process of becoming long-term settlers, then, Carlos and Antonio came within the compass of disciplinary forces that insistently worked to change their whole way of life so that they would better serve the interests of capital. How did they respond?

When I began my discussions with the two men, they gave numerous indications that, after so many years of laboring for wages in the United States, they had not only adjusted their behavior to meet the requirements pressed upon them but had come to internalize the values and beliefs that these pressures worked to inculcate. Their compliance was indicated partly by the ways in which they talked about fulfillment. Both men emphasized their relative success as wage-earners and took considerable pride in the fact that they had been able to use their earnings effectively to benefit their families. Regarding their own conjugal families, they drew attention to the homes they had bought in Redwood City, to the work they had done to improve the outward appearance of these homes, and to the prestigious items such as televisions and stereos with which they had filled them. And, regarding their natal family

---

[14] This argument builds on Bourdieu's account of "bodily hexis" and "the hysterisis effect" (1977:72ff.) but extends the workings of these non-discursive processes beyond childhood and beyond the confines of the house.

back in Mexico, they described with equal pride how their material success and continued provision of remittances had been reflected, and made apparent to the wider community, in their family's move from La Pitaya into the *municipio*'s one large town (also named Aguililla), in the large house that their parents had acquired there, in the consumer goods that adorned the house, and in the fashionable clothes that their youngest sister was able to wear while out in public.

Their internalization of these values and beliefs was also indicated by the way they talked about their work habits and their use of space. Both men spoke proudly of being good workers, people who were well-liked by their bosses for turning up on time and providing their labor in a steady and dependable manner. And they frequently drew attention to their careful avoidance of the diversions of the street. Echoing a refrain I heard numerous times during the course of my research, they both told me that they were the kind of people who went "from home to work and straight back home again."

As our conversations continued, however, I heard increasing evidence of a different response. To borrow—and rework—an image used by Robert Bellah and his colleagues in *Habits of the Heart*, Carlos and Antonio supplemented the "first language" I have described with a "second language" that articulated a markedly different set of attitudes and standards (Bellah *et al.* 1985).[15] This second language was expressed most clearly in a series of criticisms that the two men directed at the kinds of lives they and their children were obliged to live in the United States.

Carlos and Antonio were particularly critical of the ways in which the rhythms and routines of proletarian labor impinged on their sense of independence. They complained quite often about having to labor subject to the dictates of the clock and the scrutiny of supervisors; they talked wistfully of the opportunities they had enjoyed in the *municipio* to "*andar libre en los cerros*," ("to move around freely in the mountains"); and they mentioned on several occasions their desire eventually to run their own operations rather than continue working for others. From their point of view, daily movement between home and the bounded, supervised realm of the workplace was a feminized kind of activity that threatened their self-worth as men.

They also criticized the forces that challenged their authority within the home. They disliked the fact that women and, above all, children were able to leave the house at will, and they were particularly critical of the ways in which the state could intervene between male heads of household and the women and children under their control. Both of them repeated stories, widely circulated among Aguilillans in Redwood City, which suggested that

[15] Bellah *et al.* use the term "languages" to refer to "modes of moral discourse that include distinct vocabularies and characteristic patterns of moral reasoning" (1985:334).

the spanking of a child or an argument between spouses could trigger the immediate intervention of the police. As Antonio told me on one occasion:

> I love the children a lot and feel ashamed when I hit them. But occasionally it's necessary. It's important to have a little fear, in this case of God. Without it, people are more uncontrolled . . . I don't like the government poking its finger into family life over something like spanking a child. There's too much of an attempt to tell us how to live.

On another occasion, he complained:

> Here the kids have lost their respect for their parents . . . They can do whatever they like. If you try to stop them, they run away. If you try to spank them, they call the police. I'd like everyone to be here quietly in the house until they marry. But it's impossible to control the children . . . At eighteen or so they want to leave and go off on their own.

The fears that Carlos and Antonio felt concerning influence over their children were also expressed in a series of criticisms directed at the nature of U.S. schooling. In part, they worried that the knowledge their children might acquire in school would upset domestic hierarchies by giving them too much knowledge too soon and by enabling them to act more effectively than their parents as mediators between the family and the wider world. More generally, they expressed doubts about whether U.S. schools were capable of providing the moral guidance they considered necessary. The teachers, they felt, were rarely strict enough and, as a result, proper hierarchies were undermined, leaving children exposed to the dangerous influence of their peers. In a phrase I heard repeatedly from Aguilillan parents, the two men claimed that children educated in such circumstances were especially vulnerable to "*drogadicción y prostitución*" ("drug addiction and prostitution"). Thus Carlos told me once, "I don't like the way that kids are raised in this country . . . They learn too much here about some things . . . And they easily go onto drugs and all that stuff." Antonio's observations were similar:

> The biggest problem with education here is the drugs . . . The children begin to pay more attention to people of their own age than to their parents . . . There is no control. In the United States, things are very liberal . . . freedom becomes hedonism . . . I'd prefer to bring up the children in the house and teach them my own ideas of right and wrong. In school, here they learn different ways . . . They say that young people are lost when they take drugs.

What is striking about these comments, I think, is not the revelation that Carlos and Antonio were dissatisfied with aspects of life in Redwood City. This is scarcely surprising among first generation settlers, or anyone else for that matter. Rather, it is the fact that the imagery they used was tied so closely to the normative and cognitive frames they had acquired in La Pitaya and, in particular, to the problems of boundary control that were associated with running a family operation. The criticisms that the brothers directed at threats to their domestic authority were articulated largely in terms of the dangerous permeability of domestic boundaries: women and children could leave without permission and agents of the state could intervene without regard to the mediations of the male head. And the concerns that they expressed about their children were crystallized in a pair of images emphasizing the equally dangerous permeability of bodies. Among Aguilillans, drugs were held to bring chaos to the ordered logic of the body and prostitution was thought to turn a woman *loca* ("crazy"), to rob her of the vital guidance provided by a regulating mind.

~ V ~

Thus, while Carlos' and Antonio's first language implied that they had changed their values and beliefs, their second suggested that they had, instead, retained their old ways of evaluating and interpreting the world, even after becoming long-term settlers in the United States. How should we construe the relationship between these languages? Which of them more accurately articulated their responses to the pressures that they faced?

There are many analysts who would treat the second language as relatively unimportant. As part of the wide-ranging reaction to studies that construed settlers as victims of cultural inertia, it has become common since the late 1960s for scholars to argue that people's references to their values and beliefs often contain the linguistic remnants of convictions they no longer hold and that, if their attitudes and standards are to be considered at all, they should be inferred primarily from what they do (or, more accurately if more complexly, from what they tell us about what they do).[16]

In the case of Carlos and Antonio, this trivializing of their second language seems encouraged by the fact that, in their daily routines, they rarely acted out the values and beliefs that it expressed. Yet I am inclined to treat this language more seriously, to see it as articulating attitudes and standards that continued to concern them. In principle, it is dangerous to imagine that people are free to express their desires and commitments fully in their actions, especially if they occupy subordinate positions (see Griswold del Castillo 1984). In practice, Carlos and Antonio expressed their criticisms with an intensity that suggested a continued investment in the principles on which they were based; and, rather than inertly holding on to established dispositions, they actively strove to maintain them, even in the face of concerted pressures to

---

[16] See, for example, Baca Zinn (1979), Romano-V. (1970), and Vaca (1970b). A similar argument is made by Lamphere (1987) regarding Portuguese immigrants in New England.

change. One way they did so was by regularly articulating the reservations I have described. Another was by telling stories at family gatherings and in other contexts about the years they had spent in the hamlet. Through affectionate descriptions of the time they had spent there and through admiring references to the ways in which their parents had behaved, they simultaneously preserved clear images of a different kind of life and reinforced their commitment to the values and beliefs that it expressed.

Given that these values and beliefs ran counter to the ones that proletarian discipline worked to inculcate, it seems reasonable to characterize Carlos and Antonio's second language as a language of resistance and, at the same time, to emphasize with this example that people challenge dominant systems not only in manifest acts but also by working hard to sustain compelling images of alternative possibilities. Indeed, it is tempting simply to invert the reading I have described and to privilege this second language while trivializing the first. There is certainly encouragement to do so from the burgeoning literature on everyday forms of popular resistance. In its more extreme versions, this literature suggests that people in subordinate positions continuously challenge the various forms of domination that they face and that apparent signs of compliance should be treated simply as forms of disguise used to mask the insistent pursuit of different goals (de Certeau 1984; Scott 1985). In the case of Carlos and Antonio, however, this alternative reading seems equally difficult to justify. As I suggested earlier, the two men gave every indication of having internalized many of the values and beliefs associated with being good proletarian workers, not only acting in the manner demanded of them but evaluating and interpreting much of their experience from the perspective that proletarian discipline worked to inculcate.

At the risk of seeming to offer a bland compromise, I would argue that we should take both languages seriously. From this perspective, Carlos and Antonio had neither abandoned the perspective they had learned in La Pitaya nor resolutely retained it to the exclusion of the new one pressed on them in Redwood City. Instead, they had broadened their cultural repertoire to include both. Yet this did not result in some ordered kind of synthesis. The two perspectives were in many ways quite contradictory and, although the implications of these contradictions could often be obscured, the basic tensions were always present, always capable of manifesting themselves in confusion and conflict. What the two men had developed was a cultural bifocality, a capacity to see the world alternately through quite different kinds of lenses.

~ VI ~

Carlos and Antonio were not alone. Many Aguilillan settlers in Redwood City developed a similar bifocality. How should we make sense of this contradictory vision? It is not enough, I believe, to challenge the neofunctionalist emphasis on adaptation. It is also necessary, as a final step, to reconsider the bipolarism that has so often been used to frame analyses of settlement.[17]

In its simplest form, the bipolar model assumes that migration takes place between territorially discriminable communities that retain their essential autonomy even as they grow more closely linked. More complexly and somewhat less explicitly, it also assumes that, in the long run, people are unable to remain involved in communities from a distance. Settlement is therefore seen as a process in which people inevitably reorient to their new locale, steadily transferring their home base, contextual focus, and locus of social activity from one place to another. Class transformation, when it is addressed, is deemed to involve a similarly clear and unambiguous shift. And the difference of degree between settlers and sojourners, based on length of stay, is also treated as a difference of kind, based on focus of orientation. Sojourners, it is suggested, remain oriented to the community they have left and therefore stay in the United States only briefly, while settlers, by reorienting to their new locale, tend increasingly towards permanent relocation. Thus the logic of bipolarism conduces readily to a binary framework that extends the basic distinction between mutually exclusive communities ("sending" and "receiving") into similar kinds of opposition between sojourners and settlers, migrants and immigrants, and the temporary and the permanent, while encouraging analysts to treat these oppositions as if they were identical.[18]

From this perspective, the bifocality I have described has been understood in three ways: as a combination of old dispositions too deeply inculcated to be shed and new ones adopted in reaction to the fresh environment; as a transitional state for people in the early stages of settlement; and as a product of contradictory forces intrinsic to life in the United States. Yet the assumptions central to the bipolar model and the readings it produces are too limiting. In particular, they are unable to deal with the ramifications of major changes in the workings of international capitalism, notably the reorganization of production on a transnational basis and capital's growing reliance since the late 1960s on strategies of flexible accumulation (Harvey 1989; Sassen 1988). Through the dialectical interplay between these broad material developments and the culturally mediated agency of the migrants themselves, new arrangements have emerged during the last two decades that the bipolar framework

[17] For a fuller version of the argument that follows, see Rouse (1991).

[18] See, for example, Chavez (1988) and Cornelius (in press). This binarism is particularly common in analyses which argue that governments and capital gradually lose control of systems of temporary labor recruitment and that this loss of control is most clearly marked by steady shifts from sojourning to settlement and from settlement to permanent relocation (e.g., Piore 1979). It is manifest even in analyses which emphasize the development of translocational ties. See, for example, Dinerman (1982), Mines (1981), Reichert and Massey (1982), and Mines and Massey (1985). An early critique of such binarism can be found in Uzzell (1976).

is unable to contain. An understanding of these arrangements and their gene-sis is crucial in the Aguilillan case.

From the beginnings of U.S.-bound migration in the early 1940s, people from the *municipio* were subject to contradictory influences. Mexican policies diverting capital from small-scale farming into industry and commercial agri-culture, mounting U.S. demand for foreign labor, and marked differences be-tween wage rates in the two countries encouraged many Aguilillans to migrate northwards. And, from the mid-1960s onwards, the growing need for workers in urban services and light assembly prompted increasing numbers to settle. But other factors discouraged settlers from feeling that they were making a simple, unidirectional shift.

Against the background of U.S. capital's general interest in minimizing its contributions to the reproduction costs of labor (Burawoy 1976; Meillassoux 1981), the selective but increasingly intense use of INS pressure and the growing restrictions on access to governmental sources of support made set-tlers uncomfortable about staying, especially when chronic illness, injury and aging or a downturn in the local economy reduced their attractiveness to em-ployers. Meanwhile, the increasing bifurcation of the U.S. job market (Sassen-Koob 1982), steadily eroding the middle rungs between low-paid, non-unionized work and professional-managerial employment, made it difficult for settlers to see chances of upward mobility for themselves and, perhaps more significantly, for their children.

At the same time, most settlers remained committed to the goal of run-ning their own operations and, while they saw little opportunity for realizing this ambition in the United States, a variety of factors encouraged them to feel that it was still a possibility back in Mexico, especially in the *municipio*. Given the area's remoteness and the lack of large tracts of readily irrigated land, agribusiness had not made the kinds of intervention that in other parts of Mexico had often led to the effective expropriation of local holdings; occa-sional government aid designed to prevent the complete collapse of subsis-tence agriculture had provided a limited buttress to local farming; and dollar remittances had managed to sustain many peasant operations that might other-wise have failed while stimulating new possibilities for petty entrepreneurship in areas such as construction, transportation and commerce.[19]

Quite a few settlers in Redwood City did in fact go back, even after lengthy stays in the United States. Some returned when they felt they had saved enough to fund an operation of their own; some when their children began to enter elementary school or when their eldest daughter reached puberty; and some when they retired. Many, exercising less choice in the matter, went

---

[19] An emphasis on the contradictory forces affecting Third World migrants is found most commonly in analyses guided by "articulation theory" (Kearney 1986). See, for example, Burawoy (1976), Cockcroft (1982), Kearney (1986), Kearney and Nagengast (1989), and Meillassoux (1981).

back when they were expelled by the INS, when they could no longer deal with the pressure or when injury or chronic illness made it difficult to find work. By no means everyone returned for good. But people did go back. For Aguilillans, long-term settlement did not lead inexorably to permanent relocation.[20]

In these circumstances, many settlers remained oriented to the *municipio* even as they developed new involvements in the Redwood City area (Baca and Bryan 1983). People who had owned property before leaving generally held on to it, and those who were able to accumulate savings while abroad often used them to acquire houses and land back home. Many continued to contribute to enterprises in the *municipio* that were run by their parents and siblings, and those who had left operations in the hands of others often tried to preserve general control over their administration. In addition, many settlers maintained social ties with people who were based in the area, not only members of their immediate family but more distant relatives, friends and allies as well. The impetus to sustain these ties came in large part from the people left behind, for relatives and friends based in the United States could serve as vital sources of remittances and as key providers of support to those who followed in their footsteps. But many settlers also valued these relationships. Some relied on family and friends to look after the people and property they had left behind and most knew that, if they did return, they would be able to do so much more effectively if a solid network of support were already in place. Finally, given these varied attachments, most settlers worked hard to keep abreast of what was happening in the area, monitoring both general developments and particular events.

In the early years of Aguilillan migration, settlers found it difficult to sustain these involvements at a distance. But, from the late 1960s onwards, the obstacles were steadily diminished, especially for those in the Redwood City area. The emergence of a large and concentrated community that still attracted many short-term migrants enabled settlers to interact with people who were based in the *municipio* without having to return there. Growing access to affordable air travel and improvements to the transport system in Mexico dramatically reduced the time involved in moving back and forth, thus making it much easier for settlers both to visit briefly without surrendering homes and jobs in the United States and to reserve their trips for moments of urgent need. The construction of a secondary school in the town allowed parents to send their children back to the *municipio* for at least part of their education. And, most crucially, the growing availability of telephones in the area not only made it much easier for settlers to maintain ties and keep abreast of developments while they were away but also allowed them to participate

---

[20] For examples of similar situations, see Baca and Bryan (1983), Fernández (1988), Massey *et al.* (1987), and Stuart and Kearney (1981).

immediately in family celebrations and discussions about major decisions. Instead of leaving one community and reorienting to another, then, many settlers developed transnational involvements that encompassed both. While they lived in Redwood City, they were also living deep in western Mexico.

In this context, focus of orientation did not serve clearly to distinguish settlers from sojourners. Many Aguilillans long resident in Redwood City tried to maintain involvements in the *municipio*. At the same time, many short-term migrants tried to develop involvements in Redwood City. Indeed, by the early 1980s, forms of orientation and patterns of movement varied immensely; they were rarely correlated in a simple way; and, more generally, the complexities of Aguilillan migration pressed well beyond the limits of familiar oppositions. Perhaps most notably, the basic distinction between the polar communities no longer held. Through constant movement back and forth, the energetic efforts to reproduce involvements across space, and the accompanying circulation of money, goods and services, the *municipio*, Redwood City and the other settlements in the United States had been woven together so tightly that, in an important sense, they had come to form a single community spanning the various locales, an arrangement I have referred to elsewhere as a "transnational migrant circuit."[21] It was the circuit as a whole that constituted the main arena in which Aguilillans developed and maintained social ties and the primary setting in which they orchestrated their lives. Moreover, while its continued existence depended on the efforts of those who actively reproduced their transnational connections, its workings exerted an effect on everyone who lived within its compass.

It is important to point out, however, that the circuit was not a homogeneous space. While life in Redwood City was dominated for Aguilillans by the rhythms and routines of proletarian labor, life in the *municipio* continued to be organized around petty production and its attendant cultural logic. Abstractly, this implied a certain coherence, the allocation of distinct but complementary activities to different sites within a single, integrated system. But experientially, for those immediately involved, it was an arrangement riven with contradictions. In mixing two quite different ways of making a living, Aguilillans found themselves obliged to balance two quite different ways of life.

It is in this context, I believe, that we should understand the bifocality developed by Carlos, Antonio and so many of their peers. Despite the tenor of my preliminary description, they were not undergoing a simple, unilinear shift from one country to another or from petty production to proletarian labor. Instead, they were becoming members of a transnational semiproletariat, caught chronically astride borders and class positions. All of the settlers in Redwood City inhabited a neighborhood dominated by this process; most

---

[21] See Rouse (1989a, 1991). *Cf.* Baca and Bryan (1983), Kearney (1986), Kearney and Nagengast (1989), Massey *et al.* (1987), and Mines (1981).

envisaged futures for themselves and for their children that might involve re-turning to petty production in Mexico and that, more generally, would require the capacity to move effectively between these different worlds; and many par-ticipated actively in the *municipio* and in operations that were based there even as they worked for wages in the United States. Carlos and Antonio were not as fully involved as some. They did not own property in the *municipio* and they visited only occasionally. But they continued to contribute to the family opera-tion headed by their parents and they thought quite often and in detail about going back. Their bifocalism stemmed not from transitional adjustments to a new locale, but from a chronic, contradictory transnationalism.

~ VII ~

In this article, I have outlined a way of understanding the experiences of recent Mexican settlers that counters several trends long dominant (though not ubiquitous) in the literature. In particular, while stressing the need to re-store a cultural dimension to the study of settlers' lives, I have challenged both the frequent use of bipolar models and the widespread emphasis on adapta-tion. Through an analysis focusing on migration from a single locale and, more narrowly, on the lives of just two men, I have tried to illustrate the merits of a perspective attentive to both class transformation and transnation-alism. To conclude, I shall rearticulate the main points of my argument in a series of general suggestions relevant to the analysis of any given case.

First, we should insistently relate migration and settlement to the repro-duction and transformation of class relations. This does not mean that settlers invariably undergo a process of proletarianization or, indeed, that they go through any kind of class transformation at all. It simply means that it is im-portant to identify their class trajectories and, in particular, to be attentive to the difficulties that arise when people not only move between countries that are markedly different but also experience a major change in the ways in which they make a living.

Second, we should recognize that the reproduction and transformation of class relations is not simply an economic matter. It is also a cultural and political process in which people are subject to a wide array of disciplinary pres-sures working to shape their subjectivities in class-specific ways. For many people within the United States, these pressures simply reinforce existing ten-dencies and dispositions. For those settlers accustomed to making a living in ways quite different from the ones that they adopt in the United States, how-ever, class-related discipline can represent a thoroughgoing challenge to their whole way of life.

Third, given the politically charged nature of the pressures that most set-tlers face, we should construe their responses not in the anodyne language of adaptation, coping, and fit but within an agonistic framework marked by terms such as compliance, accommodation, and resistance. We should not assume that discipline is automatically successful, but we should also avoid assuming that members of subordinate groups invariably resist. It is important to note, however, that, in dealing with class-related forms of discipline, settlers can often draw more directly than citizens on practical knowledge of an alternative way of life. Correspondingly, it is necessary to distinguish between the criticisms that settlers level at the United States as a country and the resentments that they express about the way of life associated with a particular way of making a living.

Fourth, we should analyze the nature of settlers' experiences from a perspective attentive to the emergence of transnational arrangements. These arrangements should be understood at a variety of levels. We should examine the local ramifications of the ways in which international capitalism has been reorganized on a transnational basis. We should consider whether, in a given case, the process of settlement has been accompanied by the emergence of a transnational circuit. And we should explore the extent to which individual settlers have developed and maintained transnational involvements. Neither circuits nor these kinds of involvement are inevitable features of migration under transnational conditions: there is, in fact, significant variation. But, to make sense of this variation, we must first possess a conceptual framework that allows us to identify it.

Finally, coming full circle, we should insistently relate transnational arrangements to the cultural politics of class relations. This is particularly important for those cases in which the multiple engagements that transnationalism involves link worlds associated with quite different ways of making a living. Under these conditions, the images of an alternative way of life which settlers draw upon in responding to class-related discipline affect them not simply with the cloying power of a formative past but as vital aspects of their existing lives and crucial guides to future possibilities.

ACKNOWLEDGMENTS

This article is based on research that was funded in large part by the Inter-American Foundation. I began writing it while a visiting research fellow at the Center for U.S.–Mexican Studies at the University of California, San Diego in 1987–88 and completed it while a visiting scholar at the Center for Comparative Research in History, Society and Culture at the University of California, Davis in 1990–91. I am grateful to all three institutions for their support. Between the article's inception and its surrender, I presented various versions of the argument to Departments of Anthropology at Princeton, Michigan, Portland State, Emory, Boston, and SUNY Albany, and to the participants in the conference from which this collection derives. I would like to thank the many people in these settings who provided me with helpful questions and comments. I am also grateful to Eugenia Georges, Pierrette Hondagneu-Sotelo, and Sherry Ortner for careful readings of the text at various stages in its development. Finally, I would like to thank Nina Glick Schiller, Linda Basch, and Cristina Blanc-Szanton for their immense efforts as organizers of the initial conference and as editors of the present volume.

REFERENCES CITED

Achor, Shirley
1978 *Mexican Americans in a Dallas barrio.* Tucson: University of Arizona Press.
Althusser, Louis
1972 Ideology and ideological state apparatuses (Notes Towards an Investigation). In *Lenin and philosophy and other essays*, translated by Ben Brewster. New York: Monthly Review Press. Pp. 127–186.
Alvarez, Robert R., Jr.
1987 *Familia: Migration and adaptation in Baja and Alta California, 1800–1975.* Berkeley: University of California Press.
Alvirez, David and Frank D. Bean
1976 The Mexican American family. In *Ethnic families in America: Patterns and variations*, edited by Charles H. Mindel and Robert W. Habenstein. New York: Elsevier. Pp. 271–292.
Baca, Reynaldo and Dexter Bryan
1983 The "assimilation" of unauthorized Mexican workers: Another social science fiction. *Hispanic Journal of Behavioral Sciences 5(1)*:1–20.
Baca Zinn, Maxine
1979 Chicano family research: Conceptual distortions and alternative directions. *Journal of Ethnic Studies 7(3)*:59–71.
Bellah, Robert N., Richard Madsen, William M. Sullivan, Ann Swidler, and Steven M. Tipton
1985 *Habits of the heart: Individualism and commitment in American life.* Berkeley: University of California Press.
Bernstein, Alan, Bob de Grasse, Rachael Grossman, Chris Paine, and Lenny Siegel
1977 *Silicon Valley: Paradise or paradox? The impact of high technology industry on Santa Clara Valley.* Mountain View, CA: Pacific Studies Center.
Bourdieu, Pierre
1977 *Outline of a theory of practice*, translated by Richard Nice. Cambridge: Cambridge University Press.
Burawoy, Michael
1976 The functions and reproduction of migrant labor: Comparative material from South Africa and the United States. *American Journal of Sociology 81(5)*: 1050–1087.
Butterworth, Douglas S.
1962 A study of the urbanization process among Mixtec migrants from Tilaltongo in Mexico. *América Indígena 22*:257–274.
Carlos, Manuel L.
1975 Traditional and modern forms of compadrazgo among Mexicans and

Mexican-Americans: A survey of continuities and changes. *Atti del XL Congresso Internazionale Degli Americanisti, Roma-Genova*, 1972 (Vol. 3). Genoa: Tilgher. Pp. 469–483.

Chavez, Leo R.
1988   Settlers and sojourners: The case of Mexicans in the United States. *Human Organization 47(2)*:95–107.

Cockcroft, James D.
1982   *Mexico: Class formation, capital accumulation, and the state.* New York: Monthly Review Press.

Cornelius, Wayne A.
1979   *Mexican and Caribbean migration to the United States: The state of current knowledge and recommendations for future research.* La Jolla, CA: Program in United States-Mexican Studies.

in press From sojourners to settlers: The changing profile of Mexican migration to the United States. In *U.S. Mexican relations: Labor market interdependence*, edited by Jorge Bustamante, Raul Hinojosa and Clark Reynolds. Stanford, CA: Stanford University Press.

de Certeau, Michel
1984   *The practice of everyday life*, translated by Steven F. Rendell. Berkeley: University of California Press.

Dinerman, Ina R.
1978   Patterns of adaptation among households of U.S.-bound migrants from Michoacán, Mexico. *International Migration Review 12(4)*:485–501.
1982   *Migrants and stay-at-homes: A comparative study of rural migration from Michoacán, Mexico.* La Jolla, CA: Center for U.S.-Mexican Studies.

Fernández, Celestino
1988   Migración hacía los Estados Unidos: Caso Santa Inés, Michoacán. In *Migración en el occidente de México*, edited by Gustavo López Castro and Sergio Pardo Galván. Zamora, Michoacán: El Colegio de Michoacán. Pp. 113–124.

Foucault, Michel
1979   *Discipline and punish: The birth of the prison*, translated by Alan Sheridan. New York: Vintage Books.
1983   *The history of sexuality. Volume I: An introduction*, translated by Robert Hurley. New York: Vintage Books.

Graves, Nancy B. and Theodore D. Graves
1974   Adaptive strategies in urban migration. *Annual Review of Anthropology 3*: 117–151.

Griswold del Castillo, Richard
1984   *La familia: Chicano families in the urban Southwest, 1848 to the present.* Notre Dame, IN: University of Notre Dame Press.

Harvey, David
1989   *The condition of postmodernity: An enquiry into the origins of cultural change.* Oxford: Basil Blackwell.

Hendricks, Janet and Arthur D. Murphy
1981   From poverty to poverty: The adaptations of young migrant households in Oaxaca, Mexico. *Urban Anthropology 10(1)*:53–70.

Horowitz, Ruth
1983   *Honor and the American dream: Culture and identity in a Chicano community.* New Brunswick, NJ: Rutgers University Press.

Humphrey, Norman D.
1944   The changing structure of the Detroit Mexican family: An index of acculturation. *American Sociological Review 9(6)*:622–626.

Kearney, Michael
  1986   From the invisible hand to visible feet: Anthropological studies of migration
          and development. *Annual Review of Anthropology* 15:331–361.
Kearney, Michael and Carole Nagengast
  1989   Anthropological perspectives on transnational communities in rural Cali-
          fornia. *Working Paper 3, Working Group on Farm Labor and Rural Poverty.*
          Davis, CA: California Institute for Rural Studies.
Kemper, Robert V.
  1977   *Migration and adaptation: Tzintzuntzan peasants in Mexico City.* Beverly Hills,
          CA: Sage Publications.
  1979   Frontiers in migration: From culturalism to historical structuralism in the
          study of Mexico-U.S. Migration. In *Migration across frontiers: Mexico and the
          United States*, edited by Fernando Cámara and Robert V. Kemper. Albany:
          State University of New York.
Lamphere, Louise
  1987   *From working daughters to working mothers: Immigrant women in a New England
          industrial community.* Ithaca, NY: Cornell University Press.
Lewis, Oscar
  1952   Urbanization without breakdown. *Scientific Monthly* 75:31–41.
Lomnitz, Larissa A.
  1976   An ecological model for migration studies. *Rice University Studies 62(3)*:
          131–146.
  1977   Networks and marginality: Life in a Mexican shantytown, translated by
          Cinna Lomnitz. New York: Academic Press.
Madsen, William
  1964   *The Mexican Americans of South Texas.* New York: Holt, Rinehart & Winston.
Massey, Douglas S., Rafael Alarcón, Jorge Durand, and Humberto González
  1987   *Return to Aztlán: The social process of international migration from western
          Mexico.* Berkeley: University of California Press.
Meillassoux, Claude
  1981   *Maidens, meal and money: Capitalism and the domestic community.* Cambridge:
          Cambridge University Press.
Mines, Richard
  1981   *Developing a community tradition of migration: A field study in rural Zacatecas,
          Mexico, and in California settlement areas.* La Jolla, CA: Program in United
          States–Mexican Studies.
Mines, Richard and Douglas S. Massey
  1985   Patterns of migration to the United States from two Mexican communities.
          Latin American Research Review 20(2):104–123.
Piore, Michael
  1979   *Birds of passage: Migrant labor and industrial societies.* Cambridge: Cambridge
          University Press.
Ramírez, Ignacio
  1988   Aguililla: Todo un pueblo dedicado al cultivo de amapola y mariguana.
          Proceso 599:10–13.
Reding, Andrew
  1990   Drugs, politics and reform in Mexico. *Z Magazine 3(12)*:88–93.
Reichert, Joshua S. and Douglas S. Massey
  1982   Guestworker programs: Evidence from Europe and the United States and
          some implications for U.S. Policy. *Population Research and Policy Review 1*:
          1–17.

Roberts, Bryan
  1974   The interrelationships of city and provinces in Peru and Guatemala. *Latin American Urban Research* 4:207–235.
Romano-V., Octavio I.
  1968   The anthropology and sociology of the Mexican-Americans: The distortion of Mexican-American history. A review essay. *El Grito* 2:13–26.
  1970   Social science, objectivity and the Chicanos. *El Grito* 4:4–16.
Rosaldo, Renato J.
  1985   Chicano studies, 1970–1984. *Annual Review of Anthropology 14:* 405–427.
Rouse, Roger
  1989a   *Mexican migration to the United States: Family relations in the development of a transnational migrant circuit.* Ph.D. dissertation, Department of Anthropology, Stanford University.
  1989b   Migration and the politics of family life: Divergent projects and rhetorical strategies in a Mexican transnational migrant community. Ms. Department of Anthropology, University of Michigan, Ann Arbor.
  1991   Mexican migration and the social space of postmodernism. *Diaspora 1(1):* 8–23.
  in press Men in space: Class relations and the politics of urban form among Mexican migrants in the United States. In *Culture, power, place: Explorations in critical anthropology,* edited by Roger Rouse, James Ferguson and Akhil Gupta. Boulder, CO: Westview Press.
Rubel, Arthur J.
  1966   *Across the tracks: Mexican-Americans in a Texas city.* Austin: University of Texas Press.
Sassen, Saskia
  1988   *Mobility of capital and labor: A study in international investment and labor flow.* Cambridge: Cambridge University Press.
Sassen-Koob, Saskia
  1982   Recomposition and peripheralization at the core. *Contemporary Marxism 5:* 88–100.
Scott, James C.
  1985   *Weapons of the weak: Everyday forms of peasant resistance.* New Haven, CT: Yale University Press.
Soja, Edward W.
  1989   *Postmodern geographies: The reassertion of space in critical social theory.* London: Verso.
Stuart, James and Michael Kearney
  1981   *Causes and effects of agricultural labor migration from the Mixteca of Oaxaca to California.* La Jolla, CA: Program in United States-Mexican Studies.
Thompson, Edward P.
  1966   *The making of the English working class.* New York: Random House.
Thurston, Richard G.
  1974   *Urbanization and sociocultural change in a Mexican-American enclave.* San Francisco: R & E Associates.
Ugalde, Antonio with Leslie Olson, David Schers, and Miguel Von Hoegen
  1974   *The urbanization process of a poor Mexican neighborhood.* Austin: Institute of Latin American Studies, University of Texas.
Uzzell, Douglas
  1976   Ethnography of migration: Breaking out of the bi-polar myth. *Rice University Studies* 62:45–54.

Vaca, Nick C.
  1970a The Mexican-American in the social sciences, 1912–1970. Part I: 1912–1935.
         El Grito 3:3–24.
  1970b The Mexican-American in the social sciences, 1912–1970. Part II: 1936–
         1970. *El Grito* 4:17–51.
West, Martin and Erin Moore
  1989   Undocumented workers in the United States and South Africa: A compara-
         tive study of changing social control. *Human Organization* 48(1):1–10.
Williams, Raymond
  1977   *Marxism and literature.* Oxford: Oxford University Press.
Wood, Charles H.
  1981   Structural changes and household strategies: A conceptual framework for
         the study of rural migration. *Human Organization* 40(4):338–344.
Yanagisako, Sylvia J.
  1984   Explicating residence: A cultural analysis of changing households among
         Japanese-Americans. In *Households: Comparative and historical studies of the do-
         mestic group*, edited by Robert McC. Netting, Richard R. Wilk and Eric J.
         Arnould. Berkeley: University of California Press. Pp. 330–352.

Investing or Going Home?
A Transnational Strategy
among Indian Immigrants
in the United States[a]

JOHANNA LESSINGER

Southern Asian Institute
Columbia University
New York, New York 10027

INTRODUCTION

As we come to understand the transnational strategies of immigrant populations, it is clear that such strategies resonate through the cultural, economic and political realms of both home and host countries. This paper examines a particular transnational economic strategy which developed among immigrants from India from the early 1980s to 1991, when laws pertaining to all foreign investment in India were liberalized. Some recent Indian immigrants now settled in the United States, Europe, Southeast Asia, and the Middle East are returning as capitalist investors to the land of their birth. They are attracted by the potential for profit in India's cheap, skilled labor force and its growing middle-class consumer market.

These investors are emerging as a new transnational business class which is attempting to carve out a role for itself, both in India and globally. The presence of these expatriate investors has already had political repercussions in India and has fed an ongoing debate there about national identity and about the role of the state in development. Since common culture was the basis for immigrant investors' privileged economic relationship with India as well as for their unique role within the society, there also developed a wide-ranging cultural debate in India and in Indian immigrant communities around the world

---

[a] The research for this paper was begun in 1985 under a Rockefeller grant on immigration which involved interviews with a large number of New York area Indian business people and community leaders. Since then the work has continued part-time both in New York and in India. Two major Indian immigrant newspapers in the area, *News India* and *India Abroad* (the latter with close ties with the Indian government) have proved invaluable. Eva Friedlander, Delmos Jones, Betty Levin, Nina Glick Schiller, Shekhar Ramakrishnan, George Rosen, Frances Rothstein and Ida Susser have patiently commented on earlier versions of this paper. Their critiques have been extremely helpful.

about national identity and the definition of "Indian-ness." Although a sudden opening of India to foreign investment in the summer of 1991–a response to economic and political crisis–may eventually undermine the competitive advantage of expatriate Indian investors, the cultural debate will continue.

This form of investment by departed immigrants is very recent in India; it has been made possible by the last decade's restructuring of the global economy, by Indian government efforts to adjust to that restructuring through recourse to foreign investment, and by pressure from indigenous Indian capital for greater contact with world markets. In the last eight years India has abandoned its "inward-oriented" development policies (Sen 1991) in favor of a search for foreign investment. As former socialist societies have abandoned their planned economies, India has been under increasing pressure from international capital to jettison its own protectionist economic policies. Significant numbers of first-generation Indian immigrants, primarily residents of the United States and Britain, and to a lesser degree of Europe, Southeast Asia and the Middle East, have become investors in India's newly opened economy. These expatriates, known as Non-Resident Indians or, more popularly, NRIs, invest their savings–accumulated overseas from professional salaries, business enterprises and profitable domestic investments–in Indian industrial ventures and Indian banks. In the process, immigrant investors themselves are altering their class relationships. They have seized a unique historical moment in order to move from the ranks of the professional and entrepreneurial bourgeoisies of their adopted countries into the ranks of transnational capitalists. As NRI investors become aware of their distinct interests, they are beginning to organize internationally to pursue them.

Initially a response to urgings and incentives offered by the Indian government in the early 1980s as part of its own push for industrial modernization, this form of investment from within the Indian immigrant community quickly took on a life of its own. As the investors organized to further their economic and political interests, they have exerted mounting pressure on the Indian government to facilitate still more investment, provide more incentives, and to grant investors an overt political role. Within India, however, there is growing unease about immigrant entrepreneurs as polluters, union-breakers, and recipients of vast amounts of state subsidy. Their bids for political representation are rejected as yet another effort at outside domination of India.

The phenomenon of immigrant investment has other implications as well. The process touches on India's changing path of economic development, and is closely involved in the polarization of class relations within India, a country where extreme social stratification is already a source of political instability. The overseas investment process has also played a role in the development of class stratification within the Indian immigrant community here in the United States.

One of the most important steps paving the way for Indian immigrant investors was the decision of the Indian government in the late 1970s to make foreign investment an active priority, the centerpiece of a new industrialization drive (Jain 1987:1–8). The economic ascendancy of various Southeast Asian countries like Taiwan or South Korea, which already outstrip India in productivity, access to foreign investments and foreign markets, and standard of living, gave real urgency to India's efforts to do likewise. As I have argued elsewhere, the turn toward greater foreign investment and the abandonment of 25 years of Indian "self-reliance" was the culmination of years of internal ideological struggle within the Indian elite (Lessinger 1991). By the time Rajiv Gandhi was elected in 1985, the modernizers were in the ascendancy, rallying under Rajiv's slogan, "Forward to the Twenty-first Century." In July 1991 the newly elected Congress Party government of P.V. Narasimha Rao made one of its first acts the relaxation of foreign investment regulations. For the first time since the mid-1970s, foreign firms will be able to hold a controlling 51% interest in companies in India. Real estate, the stock market and even certain "strategic" industries will no longer be off-limits to foreign investors. These changes may eventually undermine the privileges, and the competitive advantages over foreign competitors, NRIs have enjoyed so far.

The proponents of a self-contained and highly regulated economy, whose stance was forged in India's long anti-colonial struggle, are not wholly defeated, however. Against this backdrop, discussions about NRI investment become, automatically, part of a nationalist discourse about Indian economic autonomy.

As India made cautious overtures toward foreign capital in the early 1980s, however, planners and economists advocating economic "liberalization," were chagrined that no eager flood of foreign investors materialized, clamoring to invest money in Indian industry as they did in Taiwan, South Korea, Singapore, or Hong Kong (Reserve Bank of India 1989, 1985). In this situation, the NRIs seemed appealing as a kind of "third force," combining the advantages of foreign capital with a native's tolerance of Indian society. India's expatriate immigrant population–an estimated 10 million people worldwide, with perhaps 650,000 of them living in the United States–seemed to offer a reservoir of capital, skills and entrepreneurial zeal which might be of great benefit to India. The government singled out NRIs in North America and Europe precisely because of the ways these immigrants in particular are situated within Western economies and institutions. The employment histories of Indian immigrants in the United States have given them money to spare, technical and management expertise, and important networks within scientific, industrial and financial institutions. In contrast, many within Britain's large Indian immigrant population are lifelong entrepreneurs skilled in running small industrial firms, as Nowikowski (1984) and Tambs-Lynch (1980) note. These skills also foster NRI investment in India.

As part of its outreach to NRIs, the government offered to treat these investors as a special, favored subcategory of foreign investor, exempt from some – but not all – of the tight restrictions which applied until the summer of 1991 to non-Indian investment from abroad. The new allocation of privileges was designed to spur investments – in sought-after Western currencies – from individual immigrants or from groups of immigrants. Yet this influx of NRI capital, technology, skills, and perhaps personnel was to be carefully regulated and controlled by the Indian state in accordance with its own nationalist agenda.

NRIs – defined in the text of a Citibank advertisement soliciting NRI deposits as "Indian nationals and foreign passport holders of Indian origin. They include even wives of Indian citizens and those whose parent/s or grandparent/s was/were resident in undivided India" (*India Abroad*, March 1, 1991b:15) – were given wide-ranging government assistance in setting up new industries, in becoming partners in existing firms, in investing savings in Indian banks. NRI industrial investors got help from state and federal governments in planning and siting an industry, in acquiring raw materials, in borrowing start-up money and in finding the necessary Indian co-investors (since NRIs who planned to repatriate profits could not be the sole shareholders in a venture.) In some cases state governments themselves became partners in NRI ventures. Tax concessions were offered along with special rights to import equipment, move currency in and out of the country and to repatriate profits. Much assistance available to NRI investors was not available to local Indian capitalists. Some of it was not available to non-NRI foreign investors either. It is this competitive edge which the new regulations may have eliminated.

The impetus for NRI investment does not come entirely from the Indian government, of course. In larger terms it coincides with the push for the internationalization of capital and labor which emanates from the very Western capitalist centers where NRIs are now concentrated. The preponderance of investments from North American and British NRIs suggests that these immigrant investors are propelled by capitalist strategies current in their adopted countries. India's sudden about-face in terms of foreign investment policy suggests that India is under many of the same pressures as recently unravelled socialist economies. Attempts to insulate local economies from wider capitalist forces have failed.

From the viewpoint of the Indian government NRIs, particularly those in the United States, are attractive as investors because of their unique class position; they are especially well-positioned to become investors and active participants in the kind of high-tech, export-oriented industrialization which India must pursue if it is to compete with Singapore or South Korea. The clear recognition of the social and economic ramifications of the immigrants' class position has obviously shaped the Indian government's decision to pursue NRI investment actively. What is sought is not just the money which NRIs might put into fledgling industries in India, but also NRI technical and managerial expertise garnered abroad, and NRI social networks within the scientific, business and financial worlds of the West. At the same time, Indian government planners clearly see NRI investment, with its cultural nationalist overtones, as more manageable, less disruptive and threatening than investment from wholly foreign investors and firms.

In cultural terms, the process has intensified the kind of debates common among all immigrants and the societies that send them: debates about post-migration identity and cultural change. Both Indians and Indian immigrants in the United States are involved in endless discussion about what it means to be Indian as India itself changes, what constitutes Indian-ness, and whether one can remain truly Indian outside of India. There is an ongoing attempt on the part of those groups involved in NRI investment to break with a narrow, nationalist definition of "Indian" and to recast that identity in new, global terms. Meanwhile people in India tend to see NRIs as no longer fully Indian, and to blame them for the social and spiritual dislocations inherent in the modernization process itself. In some ways NRIs have come to stand for a whole category of India's urbanized, superficially Westernized "new rich" who have flourished with modernization.

THE SCOPE OF NRI INVESTMENTS

Figures about the actual scope of NRI investment in India are hard to come by and often contradictory. However, India's former Union Minister of Finance, speaking to a business seminar in the summer of 1989, announced that 957 NRI project proposals had been sanctioned between late 1983 and the end of 1988 (*The Hindu*, July 13, 1989:9). The total value of their investment from 1984–88 was some $240 million, poured into fields such as metallurgy, electronic and electrical equipment, paper making, engineering, chemicals, textiles, telecommunications and hospitals (*India Today*, July 31, 1989:92 and Gopalakrishnan 1989a:16). Over the same 4-year period 43% of the total value of NRI investment came from investors in Britain, 31.2% from Canada and the United States, 6.7% from the rest of Europe, 10.3% from the Middle East and 6% from Southeast Asia (*India Today*, July 31, 1989:93). Similarly there are no figures on the kinds of industries NRIs choose to invest in. The case material collected from interviews and newspaper articles suggests that many NRI ventures are of the light industry variety, but NRI-funded heavy industries do exist, including a steel plant partially owned by a British NRI (*India Today*, July 31, 1989:91–92).

The degree to which NRI direct investment ventures are successful is not something the government is prepared to talk about, and no reliable figures seem to exist. Since many of these ventures are very new, it is also too early to generalize about overall success or failure trends. Yet officials in the heavily industrialized state of Maharashtra, where a great deal of NRI investment has been poured into the area surrounding Bombay, suggested to journalists for the Indian weekly *India Today* that about a third of the NRI ventures in their state do well, about a third manage to stay afloat, and that about a third fail. (July 31, 1989:90–92). The same journalists quote government officials to the effect that not all NRI investors are well-prepared for their tasks, and that those with prior business experience do best.

The other major form of NRI investment–far larger in monetary terms than direct investment–is in savings deposits and bonds issued by the State Bank of India. The State Bank offered NRIs interest rates significantly higher than those available in U.S. banks; NRI investors also got exemption from certain taxes (*India Abroad*, November 10, 1989:19). These deposits, which help maintain India's ever-precarious foreign currency reserves, are currently worth $10–$12 billion (*News India*, March 9, 1990a:22) and help to finance India's necessary imports from abroad, including the import of industrial machinery and raw materials. Again, these savings schemes were framed to give NRIs privileges unavailable either to other foreign investors or to Indian citizens resident in India.

Plaintive remarks from Indian government officials suggest that although NRI investments in bonds and savings accounts are booming, direct industrial investments have not yet proved as numerous or as profitable as planners initially hoped (Root 1989:17). Nevertheless the subject of NRI investment in India is avidly discussed in both the Indian and the Indian immigrant press, as well as at most Indian official and social gatherings in New York. Among some Indian immigrants there was, until the Gulf war and the subsequent economic slump in India, an atmosphere of goldrush fever around the whole discussion. In India the issue also excites considerable passion. Thus the phenomenon of NRI investment has assumed a place within India's discourse on modernization which is more central than the actual numbers of investments might indicate.

The NRI attitude towards investing in India is that it is still cumbersome and uncertain. They complain at every opportunity that the Indian government should simultaneously do more to facilitate the process and to relax its regulation of a highly planned economy. For instance NRIs frequently claim they would make far more direct investments if there were fewer bureaucratic impediments to their activities. At meetings in which NRI investors gather to talk with Indian government officials, the would-be investors often imply that Indian modernization can proceed only with their aid. There is, in fact, enormous political pressure being placed on the Indian government by NRI interests for a wide variety of economic and political concessions to facilitate investment. In this regard NRIs echo the demands of other capitalist states anxious to penetrate the Indian market.

Meanwhile the indigenous Indian business elite, while welcoming the new government emphasis on deregulation and industrial growth, is hostile and resentful toward NRIs, charging that the government is giving a powerful set of competitors unfair advantages. Yet some Indian businessmen are beginning to turn to NRI capital to fund their ventures or to buy their holdings, as advertisements in the immigrant press make clear. Among India's non-business population, public opinion about NRIs wavers between envy for their presumed wealth and achievements and pity, even contempt, for their presumed loss of essential Indian-ness. There is also a growing edge of anger as some of the social consequences of NRI investment become clearer. The Indian government may, in its search for "safe" foreign investment from NRIs, actually have opened a Pandora's box.

THE INDIAN MIGRATION TO THE UNITED STATES

The post-1965 immigration of Asian Indians to the United States has been a selective one, characterized by the arrival of large numbers of highly educated, urban, middle-class people. It is also a migration spurred by the forces of modernization within India itself. Unlike many other U.S. immigrant groups, Asian Indians have been able to maintain their bourgeois status after arrival here, via the professional jobs they have obtained. If the "traditional" immigrant road to success in the United States is a slow, painful climb into the professions via education in the second generation, many Indian immigrants have been able to capitalize on their knowledge of English, advanced education, skills and/or comparative wealth to insert themselves into U.S. professions at a time when this country has perceived itself as having a shortage of both skilled professionals and of investment capital (Lessinger 1986; Helweg and Helweg 1990).

Thus Indian students come to the United States to specialize in science, technical fields, medicine, business or management, and then arrange to stay on permanently; professionals trained in scientific, technological or medical fields immigrate under professional preference quotas; large-scale entrepreneurs are able to immigrate by virtue of the capital they have available to invest here. Interim figures compiled by U.S. Census Bureau employees and reported in the Indian immigrant press reinforce this picture, suggesting that 62% of the Indians migrating to the United States in 1987 described themselves as executives or professionals in India and showing that 76% of the foreign-born Indian population here in 1986 was college educated (Dutt 1989:12, reporting on figures compiled by Amara Bachu and Michael Hoefer).

Illsoo Kim, in his study of Korean immigrants to New York City, notes some of the ways in which the Korean urban middle class as a whole has been primed to migrate to the United States, long before individuals actually decided to leave, by the penetration of U.S. capital and U.S. cultural influences there (1981). In fact a similar pattern is observable in India as well. There a Western-style, technically oriented system of higher education has played a major part, as have the numerous foreign firms in India which hire Indian professionals. Moreover the immigrant network itself is now a prime source of inspiration for young people planning to leave; quantities of information about the educational and employment strategies for migration now circulate within the middle-class kinship circles of every large Indian city. Virtually every family at a certain social level has at least one member living abroad in Europe, North America or the Middle East; the younger generation, faced with a shortage of good jobs at home, is aching to follow and is willing to pursue any path to get the treasured visa to a Western or Middle Eastern country.

Needless to say this "brain drain" has been of considerable concern to the Indian government for some time, but few effective measures have been found to stem it.[1] The graduates of India's premier science, technology and medical schools are flocking West after receiving a publicly funded education in India (see Ejnavarzala 1986), yet India still lacks enough doctors and claims that it needs scientific and managerial talent. Meanwhile India's own lagging industrial growth has made jobs scarce and working conditions poor for highly trained graduates. Many universities, scientific laboratories, clinics and hospitals lack essential equipment. Certain research institutions are acquiring unsavory reputations as petty fiefdoms where jealous, incompetent older scientists deny opportunities to younger people. Jobs in large "modern" firms or in multinationals are fiercely sought-after, not only for their better pay but because the job experience is highly valued abroad and company transfers overseas facilitate permanent migration. Yet even the most able graduates need patronage and influence to secure any employment. It is no wonder that so many Indian professionals, having made the move to the United States, talk about the sense of freedom, autonomy and accomplishment they find in working here (Lessinger 1986, Helweg and Helweg 1990). In addition, of course, immigrants can also attain a level of material comfort which is becoming increasingly elusive for many segments of India's urban middle class.

In 1988 almost 43% of Indian immigrants in the United States held managerial or professional positions, and another 36% held technical, sales and administrative support jobs. (Ray 1989:15 reporting figures compiled by Amara Bachu). In 1988 almost 46% of the adult foreign-born Indian immi-

---

[1] The NRI investment policy was obviously not designed primarily to reverse the brain drain, but planners and government officials clearly hope it will, and mention the fact in private.

grants in the United States earned $25,000 a year or more, 30% of them earning $35,000 or more annually (Dutt 1989:12, reporting on figures compiled by Bachu). These relatively high individual incomes, combined with a two-earner family structure common among Indian professionals in the United States and a culturally conditioned frugality, mean that many Indian immigrants have considerable savings available for investment. NRIs were, in fact, the answer to a planner's prayer.

At the same time, NRIs seemed attractive investors in the eyes of Indian government experts precisely because the immigrants retain tremendous cultural identification with India and an ongoing involvement with Indian society which allows them to operate within it more like natives than like foreigners. The ambivalence, even guilt, NRIs feel about having left India make them receptive to Indian government pleas for investment. These pleas combine moral and emotional appeals to nostalgia and to (India's) national interest with appeals to NRIs' frank interest in making money. In government advertising NRIs are reminded of how much they can do for themselves while bringing jobs, prosperity and modernity to the struggling, beloved country they once called home (see for instance Basu 1989:17). Private advertisements soliciting NRI investment sound a similar call. "If your heart misses a beat for India . . ." begins a full-page advertisement in the New York-based *News India* of October 19, 1990 which solicits NRI doctors to invest in, and eventually return to practice in, an elaborate new medical center being constructed by the Apollo Hospitals Corporation and the Sterling Group in Ahmedabad (*News India*, October 19, 1990b:15).

Immigrant guilt and ambivalence is on weekly view in the United States in the Indian immigrant press, a tremendously important forum for debate and soul-searching within the community. Articles, letters and opinion columns express, with startling frankness, the agonies of assimilation, divided cultural loyalties and the question of "what does it mean to be Indian?" Writers compare the luxury of life in the United States with India's extreme poverty, India's interpersonal warmth and American coldness, the dangers of American dating versus arranged marriages. They reflect on the care of their aged parents and the kind of old age they themselves face in an alien land hostile to the elderly. They debate the virtues of staying, of going home, or of trying to create some kind of bicultural, bicontinental existence for themselves.

The majority of Indians in the United States maintain close links with friends and relatives at home. Modern technology makes it possible for this generation of immigrants to maintain a kind of intimate contact with the social system they left behind which was impossible for earlier generations. It is the wealthiest and most successful Indian immigrants who are able to maintain the closest links with India—despite their greater Westernization—while the less successful tend to cut all ties. At one extreme is the rich young woman who calls her mother in Delhi every day and the wealthy businessman who flies home on mixed business and pleasure trips three or four times a year. At the other extreme is the modest couple (he has a civil service job, she runs a newsstand) who migrated in 1971 and have returned only once, to marry their daughter to a doctor within their narrow village marriage circle. They swear they will never go back. A more usual pattern is for families to make weekly or biweekly phone calls, and to take their children to visit every year or two years, in combination with a regular exchange of letters, photos and videos chronicling life crisis events. Much of the visiting and the constant contact is described in terms of love for family (itself a hallmark of Indian-ness) but also explicitly in terms of maintaining one's own, and one's childrens', cultural identity.

Ties within the kin network, as well as Indian-based political alliances, are maintained through exchanges of gifts and a strenuous round of visits when people go home. Sometimes local political ambitions are nourished through the sponsorship of extravagant rituals in India. An acquaintance who is considering running for political office in India returned one summer to spend two months organizing an elaborate three-day wedding for a younger brother's child. The man and his American wife took on all the heavy administrative and financial responsibilities traditional to the oldest brother, in a wedding to which 1000 guests were reportedly invited.

The overall impression, therefore, is of an immigrant population in the United States of which a sector is still closely tied to daily life "at home" and maintains a stake in Indian society. For some NRIs, of course, investment in India is just a convenient way to make a profit off a country offering cheap labor, expanding industrial opportunities and booming consumer markets. For many others, however, NRI investment is a more complex process. It offers a welcome profit alongside a way to help those who stayed behind, a way to remain connected to India, an excuse to visit more often, or even a pathway to permanent return—perhaps with higher status. For a smaller number it may facilitate a truly bicultural life lived in both social arenas.

NRI INVESTMENT AND SOCIAL STRATIFICATION

One of the questions which arises around NRI investment is the extent to which it affects socio-economic status, both for the immigrants themselves and for their families in India. Immigrants everywhere have always tried to send remittances back to relatives "at home," and that money was often invested in land or small enterprises which helped raise family status. In many cases the immigrant was paving the way for an eventual return, perhaps on retirement. Certainly NRI investment is closely connected with similar immigrant concerns, but its scope and its power to affect the class standing of those who stay and those who go is very much greater.

Because Indian immigrant family ties remain strong, obligations to the extended family continue to operate across continents and to assist those who do not migrate. The large numbers of NRI savings accounts in India clearly have a role in funding the care of aging parents, the education of younger relatives and the immigrants' own possible retirements to India. Playing on the retirement angle, the State Bank of India (SBI) has recently launched an advertising campaign to attract investments of retirement funds by United States-based immigrants. An SBI offering of special NRI bonds (at 15.94% annual yield) hits all bases with an ad which urges "You can own your dream house in India," "Secure your old age retirement," and "Provide income for your family in India" (*India Abroad*, January 25, 1991a:7). The transfer of Western currencies into India by which to accomplish such ends used to be extremely cumbersome, often impossible. The establishment of interest-bearing NRI savings accounts and bonds which permit money to be withdrawn either in rupees or in Western currency helps to solve this dilemma and has obviously attracted a great deal of money which would otherwise have bypassed official channels. Much of this money seems to be destined for maintenance and improvements in family living standards and family status.

NRI direct investment also assists family members by providing employment and enhanced status for India-based relatives. In a country where highly educated middle-class people often have great difficulty finding work, a NRI manufacturing concern can provide suitable employment for brothers, uncles and nephews, while solving the day-to-day management problems for an NRI investor who does not choose to return to India permanently. One NRI investor remarked that such on-the-spot help from trusted family members was the only way he could manage his Indian business long-distance. At present one of the NRI demands to the Indian government is that tax laws be changed so that NRIs can spend longer periods in India without becoming subject to India's heavy income taxes. For now, however, many investors rely on the traditional managerial functions of the joint or extended family, which has the important effect of leaving the NRI free to pursue a salaried job or run a business in another country. It will be interesting to see, as the NRI investment phenomenon continues, how many of these entrepreneurs eventually resettle in India, just as it will be interesting to see where they reinvest their profits from their initial ventures.

On the other hand, launching an NRI venture is for some immigrants also the chance to return to India permanently with a job of fitting status. Ideally the investment project also allows the immigrant to use his/her technical or managerial skills to their full extent. Immigrants educated in the United States and particularly immigrants who have worked abroad for some years have a difficult time finding work if they return to India. At one time the "foreign returned" were sought after by the most modern Indian industries. Now that is not always true. Local graduates, also highly qualified and probably cheaper, hold all the lifetime jobs in Indian firms. Even Indian companies which are hiring suspect the returned immigrant of having big ideas, big salary demands, and an abrasive, driving, Western style of work. For a NRI a firm of one's own is a highly satisfactory way of returning to India with a prestigious job and an income high enough to sustain some of the comforts of suburban American life: spacious living quarters, air conditioning, a car, good medical care. These are still luxuries for most middle-class Indians.

An enterprise of one's own also solves another common NRI dilemma: inability to climb higher on the professional ladder. A large number of professional Indians moved to the West partly because of frustration over their inability to use their qualifications fully in Indian institutions. On coming to the United States, many Indian immigrants do well in their professions, yet report a growing frustration in middle or late middle age. They find that they cannot rise any further in the companies that employ them. While some resolve the dilemma by forming companies of their own in the United States, (Lessinger 1986) some have extended that strategy to India, where an initial investment will go further because of the greater buying power of U.S. dollars in India. For instance a number of Indian immigrant doctors have returned to India to set up hospitals, clinics, and specialized institutes in which to practice (*India Today*, July 31, 1989:93) Most cite as part of their motivation a desire to excel in their professions. If one makes money off the insatiable demand for modern medical care in India, so much the better.

Finally, of course, the penetration of NRI ventures into the Indian economy will undoubtedly speed the outmigration of the next generation by intensifying trends already visible. The great hope of the Indian government is that industrial growth created by NRI projects will generate industrial and technical jobs for Indian graduates. It will certainly do that, but may also intensify the pressures toward emigration. As some of the cases described later in this paper indicate, the employment of young Indians in NRI enterprises, their training in high-tech procedures, and their exposure to foreign management techniques all prepare them to migrate. The overseas connections of their employers simply facilitate the process.

For many Indian immigrants, the structure of NRI investment offers them a chance to become entrepreneurs on a scale which might be difficult for people of their economic standing to achieve in the West. Because Western currencies will buy a great deal in India, relatively small investments (in Western terms) may be enough to set up a modest industry, particularly if expensive imported machinery is kept to a minimum. More important, government-brokered loans and the sale of stock in India often supply a large percentage of the initial capital, which means that one does not need to have enormous sums to begin. Although no systematic figures are available, scraps of information from individual cases suggest that many NRI investors do not contribute the bulk of the initial funding capital. An entrepreneur who had been living in Kuwait set up a 10-employee die-casting unit in Delhi with about $250,000 of his own savings augmented by loans from friends and a $350,000 loan from the Delhi Finance Corporation. Another entrepreneur, until recently based in Nairobi, set up a camera assembly plant in Bangalore for about $600,000, of which more than half probably came from local bank loans. What is reportedly one of the largest NRI projects, a small steel plant in Maharashtra put up by NRIs in Britain, involved a promoter's contribution of $16.25 million in a total investment of $143.75 million (*India Today*, July 31, 1989:91–92). Again, the balance has come from local loans and the issue of stocks.

Because this form of investment is still new, it is hard to assess its overall social impact. It is not even clear how much long-term profit this group of entrepreneurs can actually extract from small industries set up in India. Some of those with get-rich-quick dreams are clearly going to be disappointed. Some undoubtedly lack the business and managerial experience to keep their firms afloat. One can surmise, however, that those who succeed will form a class of new industrialists–people who under ordinary circumstances would have remained professionals or small businessmen in Western or Middle Eastern societies, dabbling in stocks and bonds on the side. Many have leaped on the NRI bandwagon because they see, very clearly, that this is a unique opening for them, a chance to transform their class standing and their ability to make money.

It is important to remember, however, that not all NRIs do use their investments and their economic involvement with India as a basis for returning permanently. Many clearly prefer to invest while remaining largely rooted in their adopted societies, perhaps continuing to hold professional jobs or to operate businesses there. For this group, overseas investments are primarily a lucrative source of profits and a wellspring of prestige to bolster their standing within the immigrant community or their impact on the host society. The Indian immigrant communities in Britain and the United States already contain a range of individuals, from millionaires to members of the hardscrabble working class (Lessinger 1990). The wealthiest are people who own manufacturing concerns, speculate in real estate or the stock market, or own chains of hotels and restaurants. If NRI investments prove as profitable as they are popularly supposed to be, immigrant communities in both countries will include a significant group of transnational capitalists as well.

One of the aspects of internal differentiation within the immigrant community is the degree of contact individuals have with India. In general the richer and more successful maintain stronger and more extensive ties with India than do the poor and the unsuccessful. Thus the transnational investment strategy, which has placed a whole new emphasis on the question of Indian cultural identity, may eventually contribute to increased cultural differentiation within the immigrant community. The NRI investors may be in the best position to maintain and cultivate their Indian-ness. Whether they will still want to do so remains an open question.

As the process of NRI investment continues, contributing to growing internal social stratification of both India and overseas Indian immigrant communities, it remains to be seen where profits are reinvested. Will they be redirected to the immigrants' adopted countries or remain in India? If NRIs do become a major force within overseas immigrant communities, will they remain encapsulated within their respective ethnic communities or will they merge imperceptibly with larger national or international capitalist classes? What will happen to the sentimental attachment to India and Indian-ness which gave them their initial competitive edge? On the other hand, those NRIs who return more or less permanently to India to focus their future economic activities there will contribute to the growth of a business and professional elite in India which is wealthier and more closely linked to the West than its Indian counterparts.

HOW NRIs INVEST

In this situation, NRIs, simultaneously members of both Western and Indian social systems, share the desirable attributes of foreign investors: access to capital in the form of Western "hard" currencies; access to foreign technology and management techniques; access to foreign markets. Yet their cultural attributes mark them as not foreign but Indian; they are perceived as more controllable, more attuned to Indian aspirations, and less threatening to Indian national interests. It is no accident that Indian government officials made many of their overtures to NRIs in strongly cultural and nationalist contexts, often using events like literary or regional association meetings to frame their pleas for investment in the homeland. It is clear that many in the government saw NRI investment as something beyond a simple development strategy. In part they envisioned it as a mechanism to reverse the brain drain and to make India a world power by wooing the most ambitious of her far-flung sons and daughters home again.

In official terms the Indian government incentives offered NRIs prior to 1991 for direct investment in Indian industry were similar to those offered other foreigners. Thus NRIs could invest (and ultimately repatriate in the form of profits or dividends) 40% of the value of the capital invested in any one venture. The rest of the capital had to come from Indians resident in India. The NRI investor's equity could rise to 74% in the case of priority industries or of industries which undertake to export 60–75% of their output and to 100% for those industries which exported 100% of their output. In addition NRIs, unlike Indian industrialists, were permitted to import certain capital goods, components and raw materials as well as to buy at controlled prices some raw materials destined for exports (Jain 1987). A variety of taxes were waived or postponed.

NRI investors seemed to be most greatly favored in the area of services the government offered investors. In an effort both to guide investment into priority areas and to streamline a complex bureaucratic process, consular offices abroad, the Trade Development Authority in India and the India Investment Center in the United States have all been involved in offering NRI investors advice, acting as advocates in steering licensing applications through committees, helping to assemble groups of Indian co-investors. The provision of loans seems to have been a particularly fruitful area of assistance. In 1987 the State Bank of India began to use its reserves, created by the growing number of NRI deposits, to provide project loans for NRI industries. The state bank also helped NRI industrialists to raise further capital on the Indian stock market (*India Abroad*, November 10, 1989:19). The governments of individual Indian states often provided further loans and investment packages as regions of the country competed to attract NRI investors.

The Indian government went to considerable length to attract and accommodate NRI investors precisely because they were likely to be individual entrepreneurs, or at most consortia of individual investors, new to the process of large-scale overseas investment. This novice quality, rendering NRI ventures initially dependent on the government, has been part of their charm, from the government viewpoint. These were not large, established multinationals whose corporate bases elsewhere in the world gave them economic and political leverage in India. The kinds of wrangling which marked Burmah Shell's ultimate departure from India in 1976 and the nationalization of its assets (Patwardhan 1986) were unlikely to be repeated with the far smaller NRI firms. NRI investors were also more likely, on cultural and ideological grounds, to be sympathetic to government goals of technology transfer and of Indianizing the managerial workforce. NRIs are, by and large, people who lament India's technological and managerial backwardness and left because the country did not offer them enough scope. The chance to improve the situation has posed a challenge for them.

At the same time, NRIs, unlike foreign concerns, were far less intimidated by an Indian entrepreneurial milieu which is simultaneously highly competitive and intensely personalistic. Coming from urban bourgeois backgrounds where familiarity with Indian business culture is widespread, NRIs had a competitive advantage over foreign rivals to offset their relative inexperience and their lower levels of capitalization. NRIs knew the right people and the right approaches to maneuver through the bureaucratic maze, to deal with competitors, to judge the market. The importance of the "insider" role was made explicit by the fact that a great many NRI investors chose to locate businesses in their native regions, where they knew the language and retained influential local contacts.

Because the process of NRI-based industrial development is still new and changing, it is impossible to tell whether NRI investors have really acted any more "altruistically," or in accord with Indian national interests, than foreign capitalists. It is entirely possible that the faith Indian government planners appear to have had in the essentially Indian loyalties of NRI investors will be wholly misplaced. Despite the cultural nationalist rhetoric employed by most immigrant investors and would-be investors, capitalist logic, which treats all labor and all investment opportunities as interchangeable and profit as the major consideration, is likely to prevail in the long run.

The 1991 changes in investment policy may eventually alter NRI investment patterns by removing their competitive advantages. Indian planners clearly hope that the provisions—less stringent licensing regulations, permission for foreign investors (including NRIs) to own 51% of their concerns, and the new accessibility of the stock and real estate markets—will spur foreign investment and make India creditworthy in the eyes of the World Bank and the International Monetary Fund. If multinationals, in particular, do return to India, NRIs' cultural advantages over their competitors may disappear in the face of multinationals' economies of scale. On the other hand, some Indian planners seem to think that the new regulations will prove appealing primarily to large-scale NRI investors.

Several brief profiles of NRI ventures suggest how such investment ventures are put together, and the extent of Indian government assistance. Some are drawn from fieldwork interviews. Others are compiled from accounts in the immigrant press, which lovingly documents success stories. Ads for NRI investment schemes are also a fruitful source of information. The first case represents a business at the small end of the scale. The example illustrates the continuity between NRI strategies and the strategies of a traditional business class which has had transnational social ties for a generation or more, and has used its Indian-based networks to develop import businesses abroad long before NRI investment became possible.

> Mr. B. runs a business importing Indian foodstuffs to New York and distributing them to Indian retail shops around the U.S. He makes use of Indian family ties in Africa to buy lentils and in Indian rice-growing areas to buy basmati rice. Some years ago Mr. B. decided there was a market in the U.S. for a particular kind of Gujarati hot pickle. As Mr. B. describes the situation, this is a kind of pickle once produced only in homes. In the U.S. nobody has time to make pickles, but customers still yearn for the familiar taste, he claims.
>
> Mr. B. provided the capital which allowed a former pickle supplier to expand his tiny factory outside Bombay. In return for the capital and a share of the profits, Mr. B. buys all the factory's output. The factory involves little fancy technology, although standards of cleanliness must be maintained if the pickles are to meet import standards for the U.S. Mr. B. does, however, take advantage of the regulations which permit him to repatriate 100% of his profits, since

this is a 100% export business. A cousin in Bombay handles the shipping of the pickles and keeps a general eye on the concern.

The next two cases involve NRI investors whose prior scientific and industrial experience and choice of high-tech manufacturing make them more typical of NRI investors from the United States. Both firms involve technology transfer. Both involve the production of capacitors, for which South Korea, Taiwan and Japan are currently the major suppliers. Both firms give employment to the major investor's relatives. Both cases show the major involvement of the Indian state in financing the project.

A.S. is a research scientist with a Ph.D. from an American university and her story was presented in an issue of *India Abroad*. She was employed in the labs of a well-known scientific firm in New Jersey. It took her several years of working with Indian officials to put together a project in her home state of Andhra Pradesh. Capital for the $5.35 million project came partly through the State Bank of India. The company, located in a village outside a rapidly growing town, has produced ceramic chip capacitors since late 1988. This is a "40% project," meaning that 40% of its capital value can be repatriated in the form of profits. A.S. has not herself returned permanently to India to manage the project, but relies on close relatives in the area to do so. She herself visits the firm several times a year (Root 1989:17).

» «

K.L. is an American-trained engineer who came to the U.S. initially for graduate work. When interviewed in the offices of the India Investment Center, he explained that he now owns and operates a medium-sized factory making electrolytic capacitors in New Jersey. In his home state of Bihar he and his family run two factories making ceramic capacitors used in electronic goods. The product is sold entirely in India.

One plant is owned by his family and other stockholders. The second is a joint venture with the Bihar state government, which provided 70% of the financing and helped to organize a group of Indian investors. That factory, which is semi-automated, uses imported Japanese machinery and hires 65 people. Most of the employees are local high school graduates whom the factory trains on the job. Several of the young men have moved on to other jobs in multinationals, and two eventually came to the U.S. for further training. Both factories are involved in trying to develop Indian sources of raw materials for the capacitors, since imported raw materials are a heavy expense. K.L. sees Japan, Taiwan and Korea as his major competitors in the ceramic capacitor field.

Daily operations of both factories are supervised by K.L.'s older brother, a doctor, and by his father, a retired civil servant.

The next case, taken from another of the inspirational stories appearing periodically in *India Abroad*, offers even clearer evidence of Indian governmental involvement in financing. As in K.L.'s case, the foreign training these entrepreneurs plan to offer Indian employees will undoubtedly help some to emigrate abroad.

A group of seven NRIs with business, engineering and medical backgrounds incorporated in 1985, and then spent several years looking for a suitable venture to take to India. In 1989 they decided on the production of plastic resin eyeglass lenses, since their research showed that the high cost of labor in the U.S. and Europe meant that production there was falling or being phased out although demand continued to rise. They decided that they could beat competition from Hong Kong, Singapore and South Korea, since Indian labor costs are still lower.

In 1990 they finalized a technical collaboration agreement with an Italian company which has developed a new lens-manufacturing technology, and with an established American lens manufacturer. Two of the original seven have returned to India to supervise factory set-up in an industrial area of Andhra Pradesh. The plant, which is envisioned as a 100% export-oriented unit, will get a tax holiday for five of its first eight years of operation.

The project will cost an estimated $11 million, of which the seven investors and their backers will put up $1.9 million. Some $2.1 million will be raised through stocks sold in India, and $7 million is being loaned by four Indian banks at concessional interest rates. Production is expected to begin in 1991 after local Indian college and high school graduates have been trained in Italy in the new manufacturing techniques (Sikri 1990:21).

The progress of vast schemes to open hospital/medical research/medical training centers can be followed through huge full-paged advertisements in *India Abroad* and *News India*. All of these are clearly attempts to draw investments from NRI doctors, a wealthy group who may not wish to invest in manufacturing concerns. The ads are particularly interesting because they imply that NRIs will wish to return to India, permanently or periodically, to work. Some also remind NRIs that without such centers, elderly parents will be without modern medical care. The ads are notable for the idealism and emotionalism of their language. The planned Apollo Sterling Hospital in Ahmedabad, for instance, addresses prospective investor/employees thus: "USA. The El Dorado of Medical science. Land of opportunities. You're well settled in your profession here; yet India is home and home is where heart is. And you— longing to come home, only if there was, in India, an opportunity apropos to your expertise and seniority and in state-of-the-art environment you're used to." (*News India*, October 19, 1990b:15).

The International Medical Science City outside Hyderabad will, when completed, offer: the most advanced medical research facilities; training for Indian and foreign doctors; free medical care for 40% of its patients, subsidized by charges to the other 60%; a gleaming, well-equipped new hospital; 200 house plots available for sale to those who donate $10,000; a "core group of 100 physicians" drawn from among the trainees; a visiting faculty drawn from among those who contribute $10,000 a year or more; free medical care for the families of those who contribute $10,000 or more. All donations are tax deductible since the enterprise is designated a charity.

At present there are 90 "patrons and benefactors" from 22 U.S. states who are said to have donated more than $500,000 and to have pledged three quarters of a million dollars to begin the facility (*India Abroad*, January 26, 1990:21–22).

» «

The Kalinga Hospital and Research Center, planned for Bhubaneswar, is envisioned as a "264-bed Ultra-modern Super-specialty Hospital of International Standard." It is implied that those who buy equity (minimum 200 shares at $50 each) may be affiliated with the hospital for their own practices. Others may wish simply to invest, to donate time or equipment. Again the originators of the scheme seem to be U.S.-based, although there are undoubtedly also Indians with a financial interest in the project (*India Abroad*, March 1, 1991c:27).

CULTURE AND IDENTITY

As the above makes clear, the rhetoric and the sentiments of Indian nationalism and cultural identity are central to the discourse about NRI investment. Both the Indian government and NRIs themselves use appeals to would-be investors' love of their "motherland." The officials of particular Indian states, competing among themselves for NRI investment, use appeals to intra-Indian regional and linguistic chauvinism in efforts to woo native sons and daughters to invest in their home regions. As noted earlier, immigrant cultural events which symbolize both Indian-ness and regional/linguistic identity within India are favored venues for what are essentially sales pitches for NRI investment. The events lend themselves to elevated and emotional language which temporarily obscures the profit motif. The impediment to such a cultural approach is the universal assumption among both Indians and Indian immigrants that emigration inexorably involves loss of culture, a lessening of one's essential Indian-ness. Central to the whole question, therefore, is the contradiction inherent in NRI identity as simultaneous "insiders" and "outsiders."

The most sophisticated NRI investors are responding to this contradiction as part of their own efforts to develop a class cohesion permitting concerted political action. Part of their effort involves construction of a global, pan-Indian identity. This identity, far from universally recognized yet, nevertheless attempts to accommodate the facts of transnational identity. At the core of this discourse is, of course, Indian society's profound xenophobia and intense conviction of superiority.

Historically, Indians have rejected foreign ways and foreign people as profoundly corrupting, even polluting, as they endured centuries of foreign domination. In the 19th century, Indians who went abroad were obliged to undergo elaborate purification rituals when they returned. Today the problem is identified not as loss of ritual purity but as loss of culture. Immigrants, by leaving the motherland and immersing themselves in an alien cultural context, have lost their Indian-ness. Overseas Indians are thought to have lost their language, their manners, their morals, their religion, their sense of community, and their connectedness to India. In pursuit of foreign wealth they have adopted the soul-less, anomic, and licentious ways of the alien. Immigrants several generations away from India, such as Indo-Caribbeans, Indo-Fijians or the long-term Sikh population in California, are simply rejected (both in India and by first-generation Indian immigrants in the United States) as "not real Indians." The yearnings of many groups within the Indian diaspora to retrieve an Indian heritage are derided. First generation immigrants occupy an intermediate position in the eyes of those remaining "at home." Their cultural loss can sometimes still be remedied by return to the motherland.

In their internal discourse, overseas Indians often agree with aspects of this loss-of-culture critique and the essentialist view that a person can only hold one, unmixed cultural identity. However, the phenomenon of NRI investment, whose legal framework has spotlighted a mixed insider/outsider identity and whose practice has helped reinforce dual cultural allegiances, has created resistance to the dominant ideology. NRIs are beginning to assert that they are, indeed, still Indian and to insist that it is possible to hold dual identities: Indo-American, Indo-French, Indo-Fijian. First- and second-generation immigrants in the United States indignantly deny that they are any less Indian than they were. They stress their retention of food habits and family solidarity, their creation of musical, literary and regional associations, the continued construction of temples, *gudwaras* and mosques abroad in the face of Christian bigotry. Immigrants feel India should be proud that they carry the flame of Indian high culture to foreign shores. Furthermore NRI investors feel India should be grateful for the effort and money they pour into its modernization.

This never wholly convinces Indians who did not migrate. Immigrants visiting relatives for the holidays are scrutinized, their barbarous foreign demeanor and ideas noted. During marriage negotiations prospective bridegrooms sniff that the immigrant girls are "too bold, too American" to make good wives. Immigrants are fully aware of the covert criticism. The international arrivals lounges in Indian airports are full of women nervously adjusting saris they have not worn for several years, teenagers being admonished to throw away their chewing gum, to stop slouching, and to touch Grandmother's feet when she arrives. Whenever NRI enterprises languish, the local competition not only gloats but blames the failure on NRI inability to understand local conditions and local sensibilities. NRIs make the mistake, it is said, of operating as if they are still in the West; the implication is, "They cannot understand us because they are no longer Indian."

It is no surprise, therefore, that NRIs are beginning to assert their essential

Indian-ness in an organized way, often in conjunction with efforts to organize NRIs internationally as an effective political force. A recent event provides an interesting example of such an effort, framed largely in terms of the continuity of Indian culture throughout the world. The First Global Convention of People of Indian Origin[2] was held in New York City in the late summer of 1989. A year of planning had taken United States-based Indian immigrants on organizing visits to Indian immigrant communities in Europe and the Caribbean and brought representatives of the immigrant communities in the Middle East and the Philippines to New York for planning discussions. Many of the organizers were NRIs with political ambitions or economic interests in India. Much of the funding was raised from United States-based entrepreneurs – both NRI investors and potential investors. There was also major financial support from two major firms in India and from the State Bank of India (which is heavily involved in promoting NRI bonds and savings accounts.) The event was sponsored by the Federation of Indian-American Associations, a national umbrella group of Indian immigrant associations in the United States.

The actual event was complex and multi-layered. Attendees came from the immigrant communities of the United States, Canada, Europe, the Caribbean, Fiji, Sri Lanka, South Africa, Southeast Asia, and the Middle East. High-ranking representatives of the Indian government spoke – indeed their participation was essential both in authenticating the event as an item of Indian cultural identity, in offering a channel for NRI contact with the Indian government, and in forming an audience for the event's assertion of a global Indian identity.

A great many different issues were discussed among the several hundred people who attended each day: discrimination against Indian ethnic minorities in various countries and India's moral obligation to protect minority populations of Indian origin in countries like Fiji, Guyana, and South Africa; the importance of political participation in one's adopted country; the transcultural dilemmas of Indian immigrant youth; the power of Indian spirituality, and, in various forms, the eternal question "What is an Indian?" There were music and dance performances and a day devoted to intense discussions of NRI investment which brought together in sometimes heated discussions inves-

---

[2] Conference organizers were undecided about how to label the conference, and the group of Indian immigrants to whom the conference was directed. Early plans called for the term "Indian diaspora," a title used by a primarily Indo-Caribbean group for a 1988 conference. Apparently, however, it was feared that the term had been appropriated by Jews and carried overtones of victimization. For many months the working title referred to "Overseas Indians." At the last minute the phrase "People of Indian Origin" was substituted, apparently to include foreign-born Indians like those from the Caribbean who did not want to erode their claim to citizenship in the countries of their birth. This group felt unable to label itself "overseas Indian," unlike the United States-based, first-generation conference organizers who have fewer qualms about asserting a dual identity.

tors, potential investors and representatives of various government departments in New Delhi.

One of the underlying themes elaborated by the event was the existence of a single Indian identity among immigrants separated from India by thousands of miles, and in some cases by several generations. Perhaps this shone through most vividly in the evening cultural performances in which established artists from India appeared alongside largely amateur groups from Canada, the Caribbean, and the United States. The works they performed were drawn from a common repertoire of music, dance, dance-drama and religious ritual. The clear message, articulated by many conference participants in subsequent days, was the tangible existence of a single, unifying Indian identity, persisting over time and space, which ties the overseas Indian community together, and links it firmly with India. Furthermore, the clear message of the entire event was that this common heritage gives the overseas Indian community moral claims to Indian-ness, and thus on India itself. For NRIs this moral claim bolsters their demand for freer access to the Indian economy.

Obviously this question of Indian immigrant identity can have two resolutions. One is that posed by many immigrants – an insistence that it is possible to be Indian even abroad, amid some kind of pan-Indian identity which the transnational migrants can inhabit. The other resolution, and one which the Indian government clearly favors, is to bring the immigrants, their talent, and their money, home for reintegration into India. Certainly some immigrants do eventually return permanently to India, but a larger number clearly want to remain part of two cultures.

THE POLITICAL BACKLASH IN INDIA

Although the Indian government clearly feels that it is doing a vast amount for NRIs, these investors, like capitalists everywhere, want more – more bureaucratic efficiency, quicker licensing procedures, more politeness among officials, speedier answers to queries, quicker access to money in savings accounts, and a clearcut political role inside India. Simultaneously they call for "deregulation" of economic processes. In recounting their grievances, NRIs are quick to cite, and to exaggerate, the amount of money they, as a group, have invested in India and the importance of the technical assistance they extend, or might extend. Sometimes one hears the ghost of the Raj speaking behind the NRI – why aren't the bloody natives *grateful?* In recounting their horror stories – a motif of any meeting between NRI investors and Indian government officials – the NRIs sound much like any frustrated, high-pressure Westerner fuming about Asiatic red tape and bureaucratic sloth. Indian government officials note, in return, that NRI investment is still new, and that its total value has not yet made much impact on India's economy.

Most NRI complaints have to do with delays potentially fatal to people trying to get small industries up and running so they can pay off loans. Direct investors are said to have to wait 12–18 months to get projects approved, and to deal with 10 different levels of bureaucracy in as many as six different departments or ministries (Vora 1989:16). After being assured of a project's acceptability and waiting months, the project is rejected. After high-level intervention the project is resubmitted and finally accepted. However, necessary import or operating licenses have expired during the delay. Or the business is caught in the crossfire between a national agency which approved it and a hostile local agency that is withholding some crucial piece of paper. Production is delayed, money is lost. Even the owners of savings accounts have horror stories about spending months, as their tourist visas expire, trying to extricate savings in dollars from NRI accounts where such withdrawals have been explicitly promised. It is not the bank which says no, but the refusal of some tax office to issue the necessary "no objection" certificate.

These kinds of complaints, of course, have been echoed by virtually all other would-be investors in India, whether American, West German or Japanese. Local Indian entrepreneurs also bewail the currency restrictions, the licensing requirements and the maze of tax laws that slow their march toward profit. But if individual entrepreneurs chafe at the inconveniences imposed by an elaborate regulatory bureaucracy, international capitalists and the states that represent their interests have pushed vigorously for a more general opening up of India's labor, consumer and currency markets. Virtually every month some official in the U.S. State Department makes pointed public remarks about the inaccessibility of the Indian economy to foreign investors. In 1990–91, when India faced a serious debt crisis exacerbated by the Gulf war, much of that pressure was channeled through international lending agencies like the World Bank. There is thus a concerted effort on the part of international capital to make India's markets more fully part of a global economic system, accessible to Western and Japanese capital. The "over-regulation" of the Indian economy, which U.S. officials often cite as the stumbling block to increased U.S. trade and investment in India, represents protective barriers which have, historically, partially shielded India from some of the economic penetration and destabilization which has hurt other Third World countries. The Indian government has been reluctant to change the basic premises on which regulatory structures rest. Until recently NRI political pressure for change had little far-reaching effect. Now larger economic and political crises may impell some of the changes NRIs have pressed for.

Meanwhile NRIs continue their own organizing and lobbying efforts. Numerous groups of NRIs have met in the United States to coordinate strategy and to formulate demands on the Indian government. Other, more international, groups of NRI investors also meet and gather regularly in Delhi to press their concerns there. In response the Indian government has created high-level government departments to deal with NRI problems, to mediate their complaints, and to formulate responses to their demands. Some of this NRI lobbying is successful: India and the United States recently concluded a tax treaty which should ease the paperwork, if not the tax burden, on NRIs living and working in two countries. The new foreign investment policies are intended to lower some of the bureaucratic hurdles investors face, for instance by removing the requirement to license certain industries.

One persistent NRI demand is for dual citizenship. Immigrants would find it extremely convenient to retain citizenship in their adopted countries while also having the privileges of Indian citizenship. As Indian citizens, NRIs could own industrial enterprises outright and repatriate profits more freely than they do now, even under the new regulations. They could also spend longer periods in India without having to renew visas or worry about Indian taxation. The other motivation, which NRIs speak about freely, is to gain voting rights and through them, direct leverage on the Indian government (Gopalakrishnan 1989b:30; 1989c:16). The government of India has so far firmly rejected all dual citizenship proposals, pointing out that such a move would probably require a constitutional amendment.

The government is stiffened in its resolve by the hostility of an Indian business class towards competitors who already enjoy significant advantages and by a more generalized public suspicion that NRIs, under the banner of modernity, represent a profoundly destructive force in Indian politics. Indians are beginning to connect NRIs with the price being paid for this kind of industrialization strategy. A politician in the rapidly industrializing state of Maharashtra, for instance, is said to have promised NRI industrialists that unions in the area would be kept on a leash, lest they cause labor unrest or agitation for higher wages. In a country where industrial pollution is already a life-threatening problem in many areas, NRI firms have been identified as among the major polluters in the industrial belt outside Hyderabad (Crossette 1991:A4).

At the same time the large government expenditures on promoting and subsidizing NRI investment are beginning to attract attention. This is a particularly sensitive question at a time when the class bias inherent in modernization is already under hostile scrutiny in India.

A particular focus of rage has been the large, lush NRI medical institutes and hospitals which are springing up, some of them described earlier in this paper. India's stratified health system provides a vivid, concrete vision of class privilege. Many rural dwellers get almost no medical care at all, other than that offered by local folk healers. The urban poor do have access to large public hospitals, where the most basic equipment and medical supplies are frequently lacking. The well-to-do refuse to chance the crowds and dirt of public hospitals but go to private clinics and nursing homes (where relatives nevertheless mount 24-hour guard to make sure patients are cared for properly.)

The very rich go to the few premier medical institutions in major cities which offer the most sophisticated diagnostic facilities. Into this situation have come a number of NRI medical centers and hospitals, again geared to the rich but heavily subsidized by state governments. Commentators point out that these same state governments cannot provide their citizens clean drinking water, let alone maintain adequate public hospitals. Yet public money is being spent on these NRI facilities. Building sites are offered cheaply or for free; water, electric power and telephone connections and access roads are made available. Tax holidays mean revenue foregone while state loans tie up capital which might otherwise finance public services. In short, a number of Indians are beginning to notice that NRI ventures demand a good deal from the public coffer but generate little that is useful to the population at large. Some of these hospitals clearly intend to draw their top staff from among NRI medical personnel, not from among local doctors, so that the employment they offer is also limited. The mounting chorus of indignation has restrained the government, for the moment, from handing out further political concessions to NRIs. It has not, however, derailed the development strategy tied to pursuit of NRI investments.

CONCLUSIONS

The existence of the kind of immigrant overseas investment described here, very different in scope and impact from the more traditional remittances and return migration of earlier groups, necessarily alters how we look at the migration process. Although the last ten years have seen "new immigration" studies which link migration with international flows of capital and labor, there is still a tendency to regard immigrants primarily as workers or petty entrepreneurs, who enter their host societies at the bottom. Along with this is the tendency to see migrants as the passive objects, if not victims, of capitalist forces. This material on Indian immigrants suggests, however, that selective migration processes are creating groups of migrants who are professionally educated and well-off to begin with and who use these advantages after immigration to become active participants in capitalism's thrust toward overseas investment in underdeveloped countries. Furthermore, these migrants are taking an active role in reshaping the national/cultural ideology which impinges on their economic and political goals.

In thinking about immigration we must now consider a more long-lasting link between host and receiving countries; some immigrants now retain a far more compelling and enduring stake in the former homeland. They also gain more power to influence it. The impetus to elaborate transnational strategies in the economic and social spheres, already present before this pattern of investment emerged, is now far greater. The kinds of social and economic contacts from overseas, which alter the host society and foster still further outmigration, are intensified. The Indian example is, at the moment, shaped by particular governmental development strategies which promote NRI investment aggressively. Yet this form of investment by quasi-insiders may not remain unique for long. Other less developed countries in pursuit of industrialization may also begin to look on their own departed migrants as a major resource. There is evidence that China, for instance, is already doing so, despite ideological constraints.

At the same time we have to alter our understanding of class and social mobility among immigrants, and of how and where it is achieved. The outmoded vision of immigrant-as-sweated-worker implied that the second generation crawled into the professional middle classes through education, through business acumen, and through assimilation into mainstream American culture. "Making it" needed several generations and the whole process took place within the framework of the host society and its culture. Neither model holds true for NRI investors. Some have, in a single generation, vaulted from the modest urban bourgeoisie of India to the ranks of wealthy professionals in the West. From there the same individuals have moved into the role of large-scale international entrepreneurs who juggle enormous loans obtained with Indian government assistance and engage in international political organizing among fellow capitalists. The opening up of a sending country's industry to investment by its immigrants creates a whole new arena in which immigrant wealth can be accumulated. Simultaneously it creates a new class to operate within this arena. Social mobility of this type requires an international stage and well-developed social ties in both cultures. It places a premium on retention of cultural identity rather than on assimilation. Inevitably, it also accentuates the internal stratification within sectors of both societies. In the case of India, the emergence of NRI enterprises and the growth of NRIs as a class of new rich is highlighting existing internal class conflicts.

The NRI investment strategy of the 1980s formalized the role of the cultural insider/outsider, an entire group of people who had access to important resources—financial, technical and human—in two societies. Thus the whole phenomenon of dual cultural identities and dual allegiances becomes the subject of symbolic manipulation on the part of both Indian government, the Indian people and Indian immigrants. The old, pure capitalist imperatives of profit and self-interest are no longer enough. Ideologies of nationalism, of common history and of cultural integration, as well as the emotions of love, guilt and ambivalence, are invoked to woo NRIs into participating in an economy they once rejected. NRIs rework the same framework to define their new relationship—partially dependent, potentially coercive—with India. Eventually, of course, the rhetoric of Indian-ness will have to give way to the internationalizing thrust of capitalism itself. The Indian government, which is pursuing a risky strategy to speed up industrialization and development, will eventually find that NRIs can no longer be controlled through appeals to traditional Indian national interests. These too will be redefined.

REFERENCES CITED

Basu, Tarun
1989   Plan for NRI fund for industry. *India Abroad*, July 21:17.
Crossette, Barbara
1991   300 Factories add up to India's very sick town. *New York Times*, February 6:A4.
Dutt, Ela
1989   Boom eases, immigrant mix changes. *India Abroad*, July 7:12.
Ejnavarzala, Haribabu
1986   Political economy of international migration: A study of potential professional emigrants from India. Paper presented at the 11th World Congress of Sociology, New Delhi.
Gopalakrishnan, I.
1989a   Big growth in nonresident deposits. *India Abroad*, July 14:16.
1989b   Dual citizenship urged for NRIs. *India Abroad*, September 22:30.
1989c   More easing of NRI investment seen. *India Abroad*, October 14:16.
Helweg, Arthur and Usha Helweg
1990   *An immigrant success story, East Indians in America*. Philadelphia: University of Pennsylvania Press.
Hindu, The
1989   NRI investment on the rise. *The Hindu*, July 13:9.
India Abroad
1989   SBI helps NRIs raise capital. *India Abroad*, November 10:19.
1990   Prospectus for International Medical City (ad). *India Abroad*, January 26:21–22.
1991a   State Bank of India (ad). *India Abroad*, January 25:7.
1991b   Citibank (ad). *India Abroad*, March 1:15.
1991c   Prospectus for Kalinga Hospital (ad). *India Abroad*, March 1:27.
India Today
1989   NRI entrepreneurs, a mixed homecoming. *India Today*, July 31:90–93.
Jain, R. K.
1987   *Guide on foreign collaboration, policies and procedures 1987–88*. Delhi: S. S. Books Associates for India Investment Publication.
Kim, Illsoo
1981   *The new urban immigrants, the Korean community in New York*. Princeton: Princeton University Press.
Lessinger, Johanna
1986   Research report on Indian immigrant entrepreneurs in New York City. *Research report, the Rockefeller Foundation*, New York, NY.
1990   Asian Indians in New York: Dreams and despair in the newsstand business. *The Portable Lower East Side, special issue New Asia* 7(2):73–87.
1991   NRI investment and India's industrialization drive. In *Anthropology and the global factory*, edited by Michael Blim and Frances Rothstein. New York: Bergin and Garvey.

News India
    1990a Incentives to attract NRI investments in next budget. *News India*, March
           9:22.
    1990b Apollo Hospital Sterling Amhedabad prospectus (ad). *News India*, October
           19:15.
Nowikowski, Susan
    1984   Snakes and ladders: Asian business in Britain. In *Ethnic Communities in Busi-
           ness*, edited by R. Ward and R. Jenkins. Cambridge: Cambridge University
           Press.
Patwardhan, M. S.
    1986   *Oil and other multinationals in India*. Bombay: Popular Prakshan.
Ray, Shantanu
    1989   Professionals seeking visas. *India Abroad*, July 7:15.
Reserve Bank of India
    1985   *Foreign collaboration in Indian industry, fourth survey report 1985*. Bombay: Re-
           serve Bank of India.
    1989   *Annual Report 1989*. Bombay: Popular Prakashan.
Root, Vidya Nayak
    1989   NRIs' direct investment is rising. *India Abroad*, February 3:17.
Sen, Gita
    1991   Talk delivered as part of panel *What are the alternatives for the Third World?*
           At Ninth Annual Socialist Scholars Conference. April 5–7. New York, NY.
Sikri, Aprajita
    1990   Big market for plastic lenses. *India Abroad*, January 12:21.
Tambs-Lynch, Harald
    1980   *London Patidars, a case study in urban ethnicity*. London: Routledge & Kegan
           Paul.
Vora, Batuk
    1989   India a force in world of high tech. *India Abroad*, January 20:16.

Gender, Class, and Migration in the Dominican Republic: Women's Experiences in a Transnational Community

EUGENIA GEORGES

Department of Anthropology
Rice University
P.O. Box 1892
Houston, Texas 77251

Transnational migration has produced effects which have rippled through both "sending" and "receiving" societies, now linked by their incorporation into a single global economy. To negotiate the insecurities of this global economy, transnational migrants attempt to keep open multiple options which include continued participation in their home societies. Thus, although transnationalism is firmly grounded in the daily experiences and social relations of migrants, as outlined in the introduction to this volume, it also touches the lives and shapes the experiences of women and men who have never migrated.

In this paper, I describe some aspects of the experiences of women in one village in the Dominican Republic, Los Pinos, as these relate in various ways to the dense transnational network of social relations that now link the village to New York City, the destination of the great majority of Dominican migrants. In particular, I focus on patterns of gender subordination that characterize women of different social class, generation, marital status, and conjugal ideology. To anticipate, in the wake of some three decades of migration, the division of labor by gender, gender roles and gender identities have not fundamentally changed. Yet the multiple transnational links between the village and New York City have presented some women with possibilities, however limited, fragmented and constrained by larger processes and by asymmetries in prevailing gender ideologies, that they have been able to use to capture some of the opportunities and resources generated by the migration process.

The paper is divided into three sections. In the first, I give a brief synopsis of the historical patterns of Los Pinos' articulation with the changing conditions of global capitalism. This section provides the background to an understanding of the historical development of the increasingly complex linkages

81

connecting the village and New York, linkages which at the same time have given impetus to and have made possible intensive United States-bound migration after 1961. In the second section, I examine the interplay between the Pinero cultural construction of gender and the economic choices available to both women and men as a result of migration. The final section discusses how different women have experienced the transnationalization of their society and describes some of the cultural responses Pinera women have fashioned to the changing circumstances that have emerged.

TRANSNATIONAL MIGRATION FROM LOS PINOS AS A PRODUCT OF GLOBAL CAPITALISM

Los Pinos[1] is a village of some 1000 people located in the La Sierra region of the northern Dominican Republic, an area known for its intensive migration to the United States. Agriculture has always been an integral component of the local economy, but logging, commerce, and handicraft production have also been of great importance. For decades, Los Pinos has served as a commercial entrepôt, as well as a local-level political and administrative center for its surrounding villages and hamlets. Most of the village's inhabitants are linked to each other by ties of kinship, both fictive and real, as well as by the bonds of friendship and neighborliness. Just four surnames, those of the earliest settlers, account for some three-quarters of the village's population and attest to a high level of village endogamy.

By the end of the nineteenth century, Sierran settlements such as Los Pinos had become increasingly drawn into the world economy. First, German capital, which had underwritten the production of low-grade Dominican tobacco for export, trickled along a chain of middlemen to finance tobacco production in Los Pinos. Tobacco became the principal cash crop and the first important nexus to the world economy. Demand for construction materials emanating from the republic's rapidly growing towns and cities also drew Los Pinos into the process of national development as a major supplier of lumber (cf. Hoetink 1981). A combination of tobacco and food crop production and independent logging in the dense forests surrounding the village provided the economic mainstay for Los Pinos' steadily growing population during the early decades of this century.

The first U.S. occupation of 1916–1924 set in motion profound transformations in Dominican society from which Los Pinos' was initially buffered by its relative remoteness. The culmination of years of interference in Domin-

---

[1] Los Pinos is a pseudonym for the village in which I conducted anthropological fieldwork for 16 months in 1980 and 1981, and visited again briefly in 1987. All quantitative information concerning the village is from a census I conducted in May, 1981 after a year's residence in Los Pinos.

ican internal affairs, the occupation was another step toward the expansion of U.S. influence in the Caribbean and elsewhere after the Spanish-American War of 1898 (Calder 1984:xii). Los Pinos was most directly affected by reforms whose goal it was to eliminate political fragmentation and finally centralize the power of the state. To this end, and to facilitate the pacification of popular opposition to the U.S. occupation, a national guard was established. The guard provided the vehicle for the rise to power of Rafael Trujillo, who ruled the republic for the next thirty years.

Trujillo's long-term despotic control of the state apparatus resulted in enormous social and economic change throughout the republic. Remote areas such as Los Pinos experienced not only the shock waves of these transformations, but frequently Trujillo's direct intervention as well. Among the many changes that took place during the Trujillato (1930–1961), three had a particularly devastating impact on Pinero society. Trujillo's expropriation of forests and subsequent monopolization of the local lumber industry abruptly eliminated one of the most important sources of local income. His development of infrastructure, principally roads and bridges, facilitated mechanized transport and the penetration into the region of manufactured goods which quickly outcompeted locally produced items. Many of these goods were the products of new import substitution industries, nearly all monopolies of Trujillo's. Finally, Trujillo introduced the cultivation of a new crop, peanuts, in order to provide the raw material for his vegetable oil monopoly. Peanuts soon became the main cash crop of Los Pinos, but low prices and an absence of measures to improve the productivity of land or labor hastened erosion and depletion of fragile local land resources. These transformations brought prosperity for some, particularly the small merchant elite which profited from the increased commercialization of local life, but the majority of Pineros found themselves pushed to a critical margin. As one Pinero explained to me, "by 1961, Los Pinos had become a pressure cooker ready to explode."

Under Trujillo, strict limitations on population movement off the island were vigorously enforced. This was in part the result of a desire to increase the national population in the face of longstanding geopolitical disputes with neighboring Haiti. But Trujillo was also motivated by the need to insure a stable supply of disciplined and low-wage labor for his project of "development to the inside."

The situation changed abruptly with Trujillo's assassination in 1961, the result of increasing internal opposition and a new U.S. disaffection. Trujillo's assassination was followed by factional struggles for control over the state and its vast assets (Trujillo's former properties). In contrast to the restrictive policies of Trujillo, dominant classes in the Dominican Republic now came to view migration as a partial solution to the social and economic tensions unleashed after Trujillo's death and to the growing problem of unemployment. Indeed, in 1962, Dominican elites requested that the United States speed up the visa process and expand its consular facilities to handle more applicants (Castro 1985:205; Martin 1966). The following year saw a 300% increase in the number of resident visas granted, the steepest seen before or since. A lesser, but still large, peak followed the suppression of the popular revolt of 1965 by a second U.S. occupation of the republic.

United States-bound migration continued to increase in the latter part of the 1960s and early 1970s, despite the phenomenally high economic growth rates the republic was experiencing. Generous concessions to foreign investors (largely U.S. transnational corporations) led to an expansion of manufacturing, extractive industries, and a few other sectors (Gomez 1979; NACLA 1975). High levels of public spending, underwritten by massive international loans, also lent a boost to the economy. However, the capital-intensive nature of most investments meant a comparatively low level of job creation, and the overall level of unemployment during this period remained virtually unchanged. Real incomes of workers declined during this period as a result of rapidly increasing inflation coupled with stagnant wages, held in check largely through repression (Kryzanek 1979). Thus, when Pineros looked for alternatives to deteriorating conditions in the countryside, which were exacerbated even further during this period by the urban bias of state development policies, they could find only limited and generally low-paying employment opportunities in the republic's cities.

The drastic deterioration of the national economy since the mid-1970s has reinforced the conviction held by Dominican elites that migration to the United States is part of a solution, and not problematic for the republic. Global economic recessions and consequent sharp drops in the prices of most of the republic's major exports, severe restrictions of the U.S. sugar quota since the mid-1980s, spiralling inflation, the heavy cost of servicing the foreign debt, and accession to the International Monetary Funds demands for wage and price freezes and currency reforms have all had devastating effects on Dominican society.

United States-bound migration from Los Pinos had begun haltingly in the 1950s when a few of the daughters and sons of the village's largest landholders used their personal ties to the Trujillo regime to secure passports to go to New York. However, it was only after restrictions were removed in the early 1960s that Pineros responded to the dislocations of the Trujillato by migrating in large numbers.

Despite a patriarchal gender ideology that ideally emphasized the role of the husband-father as the breadwinner and decision-maker within the household, Pinera women, like Dominican women generally, have been active participants in the transnational migration process (cf. Gonzalez 1976). From the start, they have migrated in numbers slightly greater than men. Similarly, in Los Pinos in 1981, 52% of the village's 394 migrants were women. The earliest women to leave the village went in spite of criticism and gossip which many attempted to avoid or deflect by traveling in the company of other, older women or married couples. Still, it was sometimes said that they were going to New York to become prostitutes, to cuckold their husbands, and so on, a widespread stereotype that persists today.[2]

From the start, Dominican migration to the United States has been self-initiated and self-financed. While most of the more recent migrants have entered the United States as legal resident aliens under family reunification provisions, the pioneers had to use alternative routes. Migration brokers, whose professional networks reached the village level through local representatives, were critical in channelling undocumented migrants to the United States. These brokers might also help potential migrants arrange usurious loans to meet the high cost of undocumented entry (ranging from about US$1000 in the early 1970s up to US$3000 in the early 1980s). Pineros also have been ingenious in using the family reunification provisions of U.S. immigration law to evade the constraints of U.S. policy and fashion an extralegal system of migration. Loaning residence visas to kin or friends, sponsoring the migration of a neighbor's child as if it were one's own, or marrying a poor cousin were widely used strategies that enabled Pineros to fill cultural expectations to help needy members of their networks (cf. Garrison and Weiss 1979). Such strategies continuously pitted villagers against consular and immigration agents, wily adversaries who were well aware of these practices.

Thus, at the same time as internal forces and the external constraints of integration into global capitalist processes have impinged on and transformed their village, Pineros have used their cultural resources to mount a response to these processes. They have fashioned a complex transnational migration system which, although representing in part an accommodation to the existing global division of labor, has also encompassed resistance to unemployment and limited economic opportunities in the Dominican Republic, as well as to the constraints of U.S. immigration policy. It must be noted, however, that not all villagers participated equally in this system. The high cost of initial undocumented migration screened for better-off Pineros, a trend that was amplified once the pioneers regularized their status and could sponsor the migration of their close kin. Thus, the majority (77%) of migrants came from households with moderate to large-sized landholdings. Migrants were underrepresented from the two extremes of Los Pinos' social hierarchy, the landless poor and the wealthiest merchants, who formed the village elite. In short, migrants originated disproportionately from those sectors of Pinero society which were experiencing severe economic strains and the threat of downward mobility, but which also had the social and economic resources necessary to underwrite

---

[2] Cf. Mones and Grant (1987:46): "Although precise data are not available, international migration of Dominican women, a great many of whom become prostitutes, has increased in the past decade."

migration. The expansion of the extralegal system moderated this selectivity to some extent, but could not eliminate it. The poorest remained behind, where they formed a pool of cheap labor available for tapping by migrants who invested U.S. earnings in the village.

MIGRANTS' INVESTMENTS IN LOS PINOS: GENERATING AND GENDERING NEW WORK OPPORTUNITIES

Since the 1970s, a number of anthropological studies of sending societies have critiqued the premises of modernization theory and its predictions regarding the positive relationship between international migration and economic development. With stunning regularity, these studies have found that migration has rarely led to the productive deployment of investments, the infusion of new skills, or the promotion of equitable growth.[3] Initially, the notion that migrants could effect structural changes in their home societies might have been useful in providing ideological justification for the massive transfer of people to advanced capitalist nations. But after the experience of some three decades, such a notion no longer seems tenable.

Los Pinos was no exception to the general pattern found in other sending societies. Given the constraints of the larger development context, the growth that has occurred has been unsurprisingly shallow, generally of low productivity and, furthermore, intensely dependent upon the continued maintenance of transnational links with New York. Nevertheless, migrants have invested heavily in the village. Like those in many other parts of the world, Pinero migrants regard their village not only as a cultural hearth to which they might return one day, but also as a locus of investment where U.S. savings might be "put to work" to hasten the arrival of that day. Migrants' unique positioning, straddling as it does a single transnational system, allowed them access to opportunities unequally distributed within the global economy. As Portes and Walton (1981:60) have observed, "[o]pportunities for wage earning are often greater in the center, those for investment and informal economic activity are frequently greater in the periphery." In this section, I wish to go beyond generalizations concerning the extent of economic development achieved as a consequence of migration. Instead, I wish to focus on the effects of migrants' investments for the women and men who remain in the village. To fully understand these effects, the asymmetries inherent in the prevailing gender ideology must also be examined (cf. Wilson 1985; Standing 1985). For, as will be seen, this gender ideology has led to an appropriation of the most desirable and better-paying full-time jobs by men.

---

[3] For reviews of the literature, see Kearney 1986; Russell 1986; Swanson 1979; Weist 1979.

The project of the great majority of migrants with whom I spoke was a long-term one: to accumulate sufficient resources to return and securely sustain themselves and their families in the Dominican "middle class" (see also Pessar 1984; Baez Evertsz and D'Oleo Ramírez 1986). For many, this is understandably an illusive goal, given the combination of the low wages characterizing the secondary sector of the U.S. economy where most migrants were found,[4] the high cost of migration and subsequent status regularization for the many who began their sojourn as undocumented migrants, and the expenses of maintaining family members in Los Pinos. Still, migrants used several tactics to enhance their ability to save and return. Among the most important of these was investing savings accumulated by working for comparatively higher U.S. wages in Los Pinos, where a range of informal investment opportunities presented themselves and where a local supply of cheap and, with luck, loyal labor was available.

In a self-reinforcing manner, the large inflow of migrants' remittances underpinned this tactic. An estimated US$200,000 in remittances entered Los Pinos in 1980–1981. Remittances of this magnitude simultaneously exacerbated preexisting tendencies toward the disintegration of local productive activities and the commercialization of daily life, and stimulated the expansion of opportunities for informal investment in commerce and services.

Migrants' investments in Los Pinos differed little from those reported for other parts of the Caribbean, and many other sending societies throughout the world. Migrants have bought land, which is used primarily for raising cattle, and seldom for agriculture; they have purchased jitneys, minibuses and trucks to service the growing demand for transportation to the nation's largest cities; and they have established numerous grocery stores and shops. For example, seven of the village's fifteen grocery stores and shops were migrant-owned, although generally managed by non-migrants, and all relied heavily on migrant household patronage. One return migrant alone had established four small stores in Los Pinos, each one tended by a Pinero with whom he shared *confianza*, a relationship of mutual trust with moral overtones (*cf.* Lomnitz 1977:4), and who, in the usual practice, kept half the profits.

Another important target of migrants' investments is the illegal lottery, which had grown tremendously in recent years. In the illegal lottery, winning numbers are pegged to the legitimate national lottery, but prizes are paid from a fund provided by "local" backers, the majority of whom, in fact, are U.S. migrants. Lottery vendors work for a specific backer for a percentage of the profits. That some twenty to thirty Pineros worked as vendors, most on a full-time basis, attests to the importance of the lottery to the local economy.

---

[4] A recent study based on the 1980 U.S. Census found that Dominicans ranked next-to-last in average annual income among a sample of eighteen demographically important new immigrant populations (Koch 1987).

All of these work opportunities, desirable to the poorest Pineros for their steady and secure incomes, have been filled exclusively by men. Most of the full-time opportunities for women to earn income have derived from the fact that the migration process has contributed to the commodification of previously nonwaged domestic work. When a woman migrated, children might be left behind for a variety of reasons: because they had not yet reached working age, because they would have impeded their mothers' ability to work in New York, or because they had been denied visas. In such situations, the migrant's domestic reproductive labor had to be replaced. Other women, generally close kin, acted as caretakers for the children of migrants; they were sent remittances for their services, a portion of which went to their own household expenses.

Migrants' remittances have also led to greater demand for domestic servants. In the past, only the wealthiest merchants employed servants. Now many migrant households employ women from the poorest households to clean house, wash clothes, and care for children. Domestic service, however, was low-status work characterized by extremely low pay and poor working conditions.

The wage differential in women's and men's work opportunities generated by U.S. migrants was considerable. Servants, for the most part young, unmarried women, worked under highly supervised conditions for ten or eleven hours each day, six days a week, and, in 1981, earned only DR$30 to $40 a month, plus three meals a day. In contrast, a man who worked full-time as a lottery vender or jitney driver made between DR$120 and $160 a month, and even more in a few cases (the official minimum urban wage in the early 1980s was DR$125 a month). The hours were long, but often flexible, and the work was generally unsupervised.

Why the more stable and higher-paying new work opportunities were filled by men and why women have been confined largely to domestic labor and childcare can only be understood by examining the basic features of Pinero gender ideology and women's subordination in particular, features that characterize the rural Dominican Republic more generally (Rosado, Fernández and Hernández 1987).

Pinera women's subordination rested on a combination of ideological and material foundations. Although practice varied considerably according to class, as will be seen below, the division of labor in Los Pinos reflected a gender ideology that ideally defined women as housewives and men as breadwinners. Women are identified with the house and its environs (*la casa*), and are primarily responsible for tasks revolving around the reproduction of the household. Men are symbolically identified with the street (*la calle*) and are perceived as primarily responsible for the family's livelihood. Additionally, women are generally regarded as best suited for "weak" work (*trabajo débil*) because of their assumed constitutional weakness, and men as apt for "heavy" work (*trabajo pesado*). Into the latter category fell most aspects of agricultural labor, with the notable exception of harvesting, which was often performed by women from poor households. When women conformed to this ideal, they were called "serious" (*seria*). Such women generally belong (or belonged, if widowed) to stable nuclear families.

The opposite of a serious woman was a woman "of the street" (*de la calle*) – the spatial domain of men and boys. The latter term had a sexual connotation as well. The sexual behavior of the domesticated "serious woman" who remained closely confined to house and patio was presumed to be under greater control than that of the woman who symbolically was associated with the domain of men, whose sexual behavior was normatively allowed much greater berth. Older women might derive satisfaction and status by conforming to norms of respectability, but the proscriptions on women's habitual movements within the village fell heavily on young women who were caught in the contradictions of social change. New roles and work aspirations, fashionable clothes from U.S. kin intended for display, and frequent parties and dances in the local bars and social clubs all enticed girls to be more visible in the community; yet they were criticized if they appeared "in the street" too often.

When I asked one Pinero man, a farmer in his 50s, why men and not women worked as drivers and lottery venders, he replied:

> The man is dedicated to searching for the maintenance of the house, the household needs. Work at the level of the street is more for a man than a woman. A woman lottery vender? That would look very bad. In her house, that's another thing . . . There is a woman driver in Santiago who takes children to school in her car. That looks good. But not a woman [jitney] driver. Because of her nervousness [*nerviosismo*], people would be afraid of accidents.

This response exemplifies the ideology which assigns to women tasks symbolically associated with the domestic sphere, even in the face of new work opportunities. In this man's opinion, a woman's *nerviosismo*, a manifestation of her putative weakness, precludes her from driving adults in a jitney; nonetheless, it is not regarded as affecting her ability to chauffeur small children to school.

In addition to the full-time jobs described above, migrants' investments have also increased the number of irregular income-generating opportunities in the village's growing informal sector.[5] This sector, composed of disparate economic activities including both the small-scale production and circulation of goods and services, has most frequently been described as a development

---

[5] In this, the village mirrored the national trend toward expansion of the informal sector of the economy, which had become a major source of employment for Dominicans in the 1980s (Lozano 1987). However, in Los Pinos international migration no doubt intensified this trend.

of peripheral urbanization, the cumulative outcome of the options of rural migrants with scant employment alternatives in the cities. But when agriculture has been severely undermined and no wage labor market of significance has emerged in rural areas, the informal sector may become critical to the survival of many poor households there as well. Such was the case in Los Pinos, as in many other villages of the Dominican Republic (Bendezú Alvarado 1982).

Both women and men participated intensively in informal petty trade. Women sold fruits out of their homes, peddled homemade sweets in the schoolyard at recess to children who often received their allowances from kin in the United States, or operated small stands to sell prepared food. Men often plied a broader array of items, and ranged more widely in the community and beyond.

While confining their business activities largely to their homes, some poor Pinera women nevertheless managed to deploy their networks energetically in order to tap into the spinoffs of migration. The example of one such woman, Blanca Rodríguez, a widow in her mid-60s, illustrates. Blanca Rodríguez was the sole support of four grandchildren. Her principal source of steady income was the daily sales of milk and gasoline she made from her home. Blanca convinced one nephew, a prominent cattleman who managed his migrant siblings' large herds and was married to Blanca's granddaughter, to give his milk exclusively to Blanca to sell. In partial exchange, one of her grandsons performed odd chores on her nephew's ranch. Her principal source of income, however, was the sale of gasoline. The nearest gas station was located in the municipal seat, and Blanca was one of two Pineros who sold gas locally. Until 1980, she could only afford to buy ten gallons a week to resell. Then another, more distantly related nephew (her father's brother's daughter's son) sold his bodega in New York and returned from the United States to Santiago, where he bought a gasoline station. As a favor to his aunt, and to increase his own sales, this nephew advanced her the money to expand her gasoline purchase to 62 gallons a week. Making a net profit of approximately DR$.50 per gallon, Blanca was able to enjoy a substantial increase in income as a result of this collaboration.

Both the examples of Blanca Rodríguez' informal trading and those of more substantial investments in shops, jitneys, illegal lottery pools and land, underscore the importance of maintaining transnational social networks for both migrants and the Pineros who stay behind. But however ingeniously these networks were deployed, and however intimately Pinero women and men became articulated with the global economy via the migration process, recruitment of women and men to fill the new income-generating opportunities nonetheless conformed to culturally appropriate notions of the gendered nature of work. A few women, like Blanca Rodríguez, were able to use their networks creatively to gain a substantial boost in income while still conforming to norms of respectability. However, the prevailing gender ideology generally led to an appropriation of the most desirable and better remunerated full-time jobs by generally poor Pinero men who were members of migrants' networks. Although access to these new work opportunities by a few poor men may have modestly reduced inequalities among Pinero men, it probably had exacerbated inequalities between Pinero men and women. Poor women were restricted to boosting their incomes by peddling food to better-off households, many of them dependent on migrants' remittances, and more frequently, by performing domestic labor. As will be seen in the following section, some women were able to achieve a more substantial lien on the benefits of migration by establishing personal ties with U.S. migrant men and with their extended families in the Dominican Republic.

GENDER RELATIONS AND WOMEN'S STATUS

In a small, endogamous village such as Los Pinos, migration-related social and economic transformations have directly or indirectly affected most women. But women's experiences of, and responses to, these changing circumstances have been influenced markedly by their position in the local class structure, stage of the life cycle, marital status, and the nature of the conjugal ideologies that characterized their relationships with men. In this section, I examine the interplay between international migration and gender relations for two categories of Pinera women: 1) those married to U.S. migrants or with migrant offspring in the United States, that is, those who belong to "migrant households"; and 2) those women who headed their own households and had no household members in the United States. Largely as a consequence of the remittances they received, members of the first group often fell into what might be called the village's transnational "middle class"; the latter group included some of the poorest members of the community.

When husbands migrated to New York first, as was often the case, the household entered a transnational stage which might endure for years. Even if a man migrated with proper documents, long delays in reuniting the family might still occur because of bureaucratic backlogs. During this period of separation, migrants were said to "behave well" (*portarse bien*) if they conformed to cultural expectations to send remittances to household members. In general, migrant husbands often do behave well, with the majority sending remittances at or above the minimum required to cover basic household expenses (Georges 1990).

The continued receipt of remittances also depends on wives' "behaving well." During the period of separation from their husbands, many wives thus became *more* constrained in their daily movements. In some cases, Pinera women living in Santiago or Santo Domingo returned to Los Pinos to live with their own or their husbands' parents after their husbands migrated. In part, these returns had an economic motivation. It was simply cheaper to collapse households and to live in the countryside. But such returns also occurred because it was believed that a wife's sexuality would be under greater control if she resided with kin in Los Pinos than if she were left alone in the city. For instance, one woman moved from Santiago to her husband's parents' house after he received an anonymous letter in New York alleging that his wife had been unfaithful. To quell the rumor and forestall the separation that her husband threatened, she returned to Los Pinos with her children.

In general, women directly received and managed the remittances sent by their migrant husbands. However, in the majority of households these were just sufficient to cover basic expenses. Only 31% of all migrant households reported regularly having a surplus left over after meeting these expenses, and this surplus was generally quite small. Pegging remittances at, or just under, the basic subsistence requirements of the family in Los Pinos was one way migrants avoided obligations to share resources among tightly knit social networks. But the sending of subsistence-level remittances also deprived most wives of all but a kind of "pseudo-choice" in deciding how to spend remittance income and ensured that they were totally, or almost totally, dependent on husbands' remittances to maintain their families.[6]

In short, women in patrifocal, stable marriages with U.S. migrants were able to conform more readily to prevailing ideals of respectable feminine behavior. For many Pineras, as noted earlier, there was the satisfaction that their respectability and reputation for propriety were enhanced by the ability to conform to community ideals. Such respectability was buttressed too by the status the household derived from its remittance-subsidized patterns of consumption, especially of improved housing and consumer goods. For some of the younger women, however, conforming to these ideals was often a chafing obligation observed at least in part out of fear of gossip.

On the other hand, some evidence also exists that transnational migration may reinforce a potential direction for change *across* generations of women. As appeared to be occurring in other rural areas of the Dominican Republic (Rosado *et al.* 1987), household resources were often concentrated on girls' educations, precisely because they were perceived to be at a disadvantage in the rural labor market. Providing an education was one means of attempting to ensure that girls would later be able to "defend themselves." In Los Pinos, children in migrant households were more likely to be in school than children in non-migrant households, and a greater proportion eventually attended secondary school. This was equally true for girls and boys. Thus, it is possible that the next generation of women may experience a wider range of work op-

---

[6] See Brouwer and Priester (1983) for similar findings for rural Turkish women married to migrants.

portunities and possibly greater autonomy than their mothers. Insofar as remittances subsidize girls' educations, transnational migration may be helping to promote this process.

For older women, who were generally widows, reliance on the remittances sent by adult sons or daughters meant that household authority passed from husbands to offspring, who might now make most or all the major decisions affecting these women's lives. For example, migrant sons or daughters might decide to sponsor a mother's migration for several reasons: so that she could take care of their children while they worked; because they wished her to work in the United States in order to eventually qualify for Social Security; or because they wanted to avoid making costly visits to Los Pinos to see her. Since these older women were often totally dependent on their children's remittances for survival, they seldom felt they could refuse the children's wishes. One grandmother in her seventies preferred to stay in the village, but told me she was nonetheless moving to New York because "I must go where they want me." It is important to note that, even where fathers were present, the economic dependence of aging parents on children's remittances often gave migrant offspring (including migrant daughters) the most important decision-making voice in the household.

As noted above, when parents migrated and left behind younger children in the village, women who remained assumed the caretaking role. Grandmothers, and sometimes migrants' sisters, particularly if they were poor, often took in these children. While the guardians welcomed the additional income, such *in loco parentis* duties could be quite burdensome for older women. One woman in her sixties was left with her six grandchildren, ranging in age from five to fourteen. She complained to me that "when my daughter is in New York, I am a prisoner. I don't see my other daughters until she returns and takes back her children." Some of these grandmothers were able to hire poorer women to help with domestic chores. But being a guardian also entailed a considerable amount of responsibility. For example, another grandmother in her mid-seventies felt obliged to keep a strict vigil over her teenage granddaughter whose mother was in New York. Keeping the girl "off the street" to maintain her reputation was a heavy responsibility this woman was glad to shed when her granddaughter finally migrated. Thus, as women absorb a variety of new members into their households, their work and responsibility loads are often increased, sometimes considerably.

Occasionally, however, having migrant offspring provides an older woman with an alternative to subordination, particularly when relations with her spouse have become especially vexed. In such instances, migrant offspring offer a woman the means of subsisting independently of her husband and of escaping a painful situation. For example, one migrant Pinera woman learned that her mother in the Dominican Republic had become very distressed because of a secondary union her father had established with another woman.

Being a U.S. citizen and thus able to sponsor a parent's migration, she responded by bringing her mother to New York to live with her, thus effecting a *de facto* separation between her parents.

The normative division of labor by gender is more difficult to achieve in poor households where, out of necessity, women must participate more widely in arenas outside the household. Some poor women who headed their own households also differed from women in patrifocal migrant households in the nature of their conjugal ideologies. In the Dominican Republic, the ideal pattern of mating and family organization is the single mate pattern. A second pattern is also found, however, in which women tend to form serial relationships and have children with more than one man (Brown 1975; Gonzalez 1976; Pessar 1984). While the ideal pattern generally characterizes the middle class, and many poor families as well, the second pattern clusters among poor women (Brown 1975).

Work outside the home, generally in domestic service and the informal sector, and serial unions with multiple partners were important to the economies of many poor women throughout the Dominican Republic. In Los Pinos, the transnational process had also made available new sources of income and mobility (U.S. remittances and savings) and new kinds of social resources (the migrants themselves and their extended families). With their continued membership in the community, U.S. migrants became resources to whom poor women attempted to gain access through a variety of tactics in order to support their families.

Most obviously, migrants were desirable as mates, whether in casual, noncoresidential relationships or in more stable unions. Casual relationships established by migrants with poor women on holiday visits to the village in part represented a kind of conspicuous consumption in which some men engaged, and in part reflected a redefinition of the village as a "migrant resort," among other things. Women received cash and gifts, generally only for the duration of the holiday. Other women established longer-term liaisons, generally with older, sometimes married, migrants who might send remittances ranging from sporadically to quite reliably. One woman in her thirties from one of the poorest families in the village, Teresa Rodríguez, regularly received US$130 a month from a much older migrant in New York who visited her once or twice a year. She was able to save enough from this stipend to upgrade her house and establish a small lottery fund. Women in such relationships enjoyed not only an improved income for the duration, they also appeared to have more autonomy in their daily lives than women in respectable unions.

Most women involved with migrants received much less than Teresa Rodríguez, yet for some, ties with migrant men were nonetheless important to the support of their households. Women who had children with men who subsequently migrated sometimes received small amounts of cash intended to cover the children's basic subsistence expenses. In general, as Pineras put it, this was money *"para la leche,"* enough only for the childrens' milk. But because migrant Pinero men had access to greater and more secure wages than they would have had in the Dominican Republic, they were more likely to conform to expectations to provide some child support, even if quite modest amounts in many cases. More importantly, the men's extended families often continued to reside in the village and represented another potential source of support for poor women. As in other parts of the republic (Walker 1972), when unions resulted in children, affines remained part of a woman's network even after the relationship had ended. Because the migrant's extended family, particularly his parents, were likely to be receiving remittances and gifts, a woman could attempt to lay a claim to some share, even if affines were sometimes reluctant.

Some women also devised ways to use Pinero cultural models of U.S. immigration policy to their advantage in attempting to convince men to live up to cultural expectations to provide support for their children. There is a belief in Los Pinos that breaking the law, whether Dominican or U.S., can potentially result in the loss of one's legal resident visa. United States immigration law[7] does state that conviction of "a crime involving moral turpitude" might exclude a person from admission to the United States. Because under Dominican law, fathers must provide support for their minor children, some Pinero women have attempted to use such beliefs strategically to force fathers to make payments. They have done this by threatening to report fathers who refused to provide child support to U.S. consular officials in Santo Domingo.[8] Other women threatened to expose undocumented migrants to deportation by reporting them too. Although it seems unlikely that a woman lodging such complaints to the U.S. consulate in the Dominican Republic would actually succeed in jeopardizing a migrant's legal status in the United States, or lead to his apprehension and deportation if undocumented, the fear that this was at least possible was sufficiently widespread that such threats sometimes worked. The following story of one woman, Sandra Pérez, illustrates how this tactic can help some poor women secure a lien on migrant men; it also shows that success is not inevitable.

Sandra Pérez, in her mid-30s, headed one of the poorest households in Los Pinos. When she was 16, she became involved with Santos Morales, the son of fairly well-off Pineros, and bore a son. Shortly thereafter, in 1964, Santos Morales migrated to New York, where he subsequently married. Three years later, Sandra became involved with another man, Manuel Santana, from

[7] 8 U.S.C. 1182 (a) (9).

[8] A variation on this theme is the recent case of a Dominican who plays major league baseball in the United States. Because of a child support lawsuit filed against him in the Dominican Republic, the Dominican government denied him exit from the country and he could not return to the U.S. in time for the start of spring training (Martinez 1990). I am grateful to Glenn Peterson for calling this case to my attention.

a nearby village. She bore a daughter, and again, shortly thereafter, Manuel Santana also migrated to New York. She later entered a consensual union with a landless day laborer which lasted until 1979 and produced three children.

Over the years, Sandra Pérez barely kept her family fed by working as a servant in a succession of migrants' and others' households in Los Pinos. In 1975, when her eldest son turned eleven, she found she could no longer afford to clothe him and keep him in school. She went to Santos' parents to ask their help, but was rebuffed. Sandra then threatened to report Santos to the U.S. consulate for violating Dominican Law 2402 if she did not receive some support. Santos and his parents relented. Sandra's son moved into their house and Santos began to send money for his expenses. Over the years, as Santos visited his family of origin in Los Pinos, he became attached to the boy, and decided to adopt him legally so that he could sponsor his migration to the United States. After the son went to New York, he began to send money sporadically to his mother.

Sandra attempted to use the same strategy to force her second partner, Manuel, to support their daughter. This time her bluff was called; Manuel refused to send remittances, and Sandra did nothing. However, Manuel's father, a return migrant who lived comfortably from his Social Security check and his children's remittances, took the child into his household. Her grandfather paid her school expenses, and after school the girl performed the bulk of his household chores. In 1980, Sandra entered a semi-clandestine visiting relationship with a much older married migrant, who provided roughly half of her total household expenses of DR$950 for the year.[9] By 1981, the relationship had ended and she was once again the sole support of her youngest three children.

Sandra Pérez is typical of the Dominican women who lodge complaints against ex-spouses under Law 2402. Such complaints are generally made by extremely poor women who have had children by men who are better educated and in a better economic position than they (CIPAF 1985). Living in a transnational community, Sandra was also able to negotiate aspects of the migration system, and in particular, local cultural models of this system, to secure some benefits for herself and her children.

Of course, such tactics are not without cost. Sandra Pérez, like other women who have had short-term relationships with migrant men, has very low social status in Los Pinos; such women may also be the objects of gossip, general social disapprobation and on occasion, violent hostility.[10]

---

[9] During the period of fieldwork, the U.S. dollar was valued at approximately DR$1.23.

[10] Four years after I recorded Sandra Pérez' life history, her eight-year-old daughter was raped by a neighbor's teenaged son.

CONCLUSION

This paper has described some of the changes that have been set in motion by the incorporation of one Dominican village into the global economy through the process of transnational migration. As the locus of many migrants' investments, the village of Los Pinos has experienced a modest growth in the number of full-time jobs paying somewhat above the minimum urban wage and in opportunities for a variety of petty entrepreneurial activities. In a self-reinforcing fashion, these economic activities tend to depend heavily on the patronage of migrant households, themselves heavily subsidized by remittances from the United States. In conformity with local conceptions of the gendered nature of work, all of the desirable new jobs have gone to men. Jobs filled by women are concentrated in domestic service and childcare, and paid about one-fifth of what a man could earn driving a jitney or hawking lottery numbers. When migrant husbands remitted regularly, married women generally conformed to the strictures of established gender roles, thus ensuring that husbands continued to "behave well" by sending money in the future. Women who followed a serial mating pattern, including some of the village's poorest, were able to gain access to the benefits of migration (higher income, consumer goods, visas) through the informal ties they established with migrants and their kin. The articulation of the village into a single social field with New York City had thus allowed some poor Pinera women some spaces in which to actively negotiate access to resources generated by the migration process for themselves and for their children. For both groups of women, however, prevailing gender ideologies appear to have played an important role in channeling the social and economic changes stemming from the transnational process into directions compatible with Pinero practice.

ACKNOWLEDGMENTS

This research was made possible by funding from the Inter-American Foundation, the National Institute of Mental Health and the American Association of University Women, whose support I gratefully acknowledge. I also wish to thank Nancy Foner, Nancie Gonzalez, and Karin Tice for thoughtful comments on an earlier version of this manuscript.

REFERENCES CITED

Baez Evertsz, F. and F. D'Oleo Ramírez
  1986 *La emigración de dominicanos a Estados Unidos: determinantes socio-económicos y consecuencias.* Santo Domingo: Fundación Friedrich Ebert.

Bendezú Alvarado, G.
1982   La realidad campesina dominicana y sus posibilidades de desarrollo. *Forum* 3:93–138.
Brouwer, L. and M. Priester
1983   Living in between: Turkish women in their homeland and in the Netherlands. In *One way ticket: Migration and female labour*, edited by A. Philzacklea. London: Routledge & Kegan Paul.
Brown, S.
1975   Love unites them and hunger separates them: Poor women in the Dominican Republic. In *Toward an anthropology of women*, edited by R. Reiter. New York: Monthly Review Press.
Calder, B.
1984   The impact of intervention: The Dominican Republic during the U.S. Occupation of 1916–1924. Austin: University of Texas Press.
Castro, M.
1985   Dominican journey: Patterns, context and consequences of migration from the Dominican Republic to the United States. Ph.D. thesis, University of North Carolina at Chapel Hill.
Centro de Investigación para la Acción Feminina (CIPAF)
1985   *Paternidad responsable (un estudio sobre la ley 2402)*. Santo Domingo: Taller.
Garrison, V. and C. Weiss
1979   Dominican family networks and United States immigration policy: A case study. *International Migration Review* 13(2):264–283.
Georges, E.
1990   *The making of a transnational community: Migration, development and cultural change in the Dominican Republic*. New York: Columbia University Press.
Gomez, L.
1979   Relaciones de produción dominantes en la sociodad dominicana, 1897–1975. Santo Domingo: Alfa y Omega.
Gonzalez, N.
1976   Multiple migratory experiences of Dominican women. *Anthropological Quarterly 49(1)*:36–44.
Hoetink, H.
1982   *The Dominican people: 1850–1900*. Baltimore: Johns Hopkins University Press.
Kearney, M.
1986   From the invisible hand to the visible feet: Anthropological studies of migration and development. *Annual Review of Anthropology* 15:331–361.
Koch, J.
1987   The incomes of recent immigrants: A look at ethnic differences. *Social Science Quarterly 68(2)*:294–310.
Kryzanek, T.
1979   Diversion, subversion and repression: The strategies of anti-regime politics in Balaguer's Dominican Republic. *Caribbean Studies 19(1 and 2)*:83–103.
Lomnitz, L.
1977   Networks and marginality: Life in a Mexican shantytown. New York: Academic Press.
Lozano, W.
1987   *Desempleo estructural, dinámica económica y fragmentación de los mercados de trabajo urbanos: el caso dominicano. Documento Base*. Santo Domingo: Fundación Friedrich Ebert.

Martin, J.
  1966   Overtaken by events: From the death of Trujillo to the civil war. New York: Doubleday.
Martinez, J.
  1990   A Child-Support Lawsuit Keeps Perez Out of Camp. *New York Times*, March 27.
Mones, B. and L. Grant
  1987   Agricultural development, the economic crisis, and rural women in the Dominican Republic. In *Rural women and state policy: Feminist perspectives on Latin American agricultural development*, edited by C. Deere and M. Leon. Boulder, CO: Westview Press. Pp. 35–50.
North American Congress on Latin America (NACLA)
  1975   Fruits of the invasion: U.S. interests in the Dominican Republic ten years later.
Pessar, P.
  1984   The linkage between the household and workplace in the experience of Dominican immigrant women in the United States. *International Migration Review 18*:1188–1211.
Portes, A. and J. Walton
  1981   Labor, class and the international system. New York: Academic Press.
Rosado, T., B. Fernández, and I. Hernández
  1987   Ideología y subordinación. In *La mujer rural dominicana*, edited by F. Pou, et al. Santo Domingo: CIPAF. Pp. 197–207.
Russell, S.
  1986   Remittances from international development: A review in perspective. *World Development 14(6)*:677–696.
Standing, H.
  1985   Resources, wages and power: The impact of women's employment on the urban Bengali household. In *Women, work and ideology in the third world*, edited by H. Afshar. London and New York: Tavistock Publications. Pp. 232–257.
Swanson, J.
  1979   The consequences of emigration for economic development: A review of the literature. In *The anthropology of return migration*, edited by R. Rhoades. Norman: University of Oklahoma Press. Pp. 39–56.
Walker, M.
  1972   Politics and the power structure: A rural community in the Dominican Republic. New York: Teachers College Press.
Weist, R.
  1979   Anthropological perspectives on return migration: A critical commentary. In *The anthropology of return migration*, edited by R. Rhoades. Norman: University of Oklahoma Press. Pp. 167–188.
Wilson, F.
  1985   Women and agricultural change in Latin America: Some concepts guiding research. *World Development 13(9)*:1017–1035.

Transnationalism in the Construct of Haitian Migrants' Racial Categories of Identity in New York City[a]

CAROLLE CHARLES

Department of Sociology/Anthropology
Baruch College
City University of New York
New York, New York 10010

More than a single movement from one place to another, international migration is a process of network building, of network ties, of relationships between groups and social agents distributed across different places, maximizing their economic opportunities through mutual and multiple displacements (Portes and Walton 1981:31). One of the most important features of recent international migration is that the movement takes place within a social setting and space that engulfs these new kinds of relationships and processes, linking both societies of origin and destination. In that sense, international migration can no more be conceptualized as a process external to the country of origin and has forced a rethinking of studies of international migration (Larose 1984; Glick Schiller, Basch, and Blanc-Szanton, 1992).

Analyzing international migration from a transnational perspective implies a redefinition of social context. It has been common in most analyses of international migration to posit the state as the boundary and to equate the concept of the state to that of the social formation. Yet, as Larose (1984) points out, because of transnational networks, more and more immigrant workers are embedded and inscribed in two social formations. Haitian immigrant workers for example are not only being incorporated into the U.S. labor force but are also active participants in the reproduction of labor in Haiti. In addition, the existence of transnational networks are one of the most important ideological expressions of the intensity of the ties of the social agents with the country of origin.

[a] This is a revised version of the paper presented in May 1990 at the New York Academy of Sciences.

Though international migration involves primarily a relationship of labor to capital, and thus is part of the process of production and reproduction of class relationships, it also encompasses other forms of social relations of domination. And the multiplicity of these social relations of domination and inequality determine and/or inform a multiplicity of positionalities of the social agents that participate in these processes and relationships. In that regard, international migration is not simply a socio-economic phenomenon but is also political and cultural. On one hand, it implies the making of a subject, a subject constructed by race, ethnicity and/or gender for a more effective control of labor by capital (Thompson 1963). On the other hand, migrants as labor and people bring to their relationships their own conceptions and meanings that inform their "subjectification."

Cultural and physical differences among people are complex phenomena. On the one hand, they can be transformed into structures of inequality and domination in the process of the subjectification of labor. They also inform consciousness and identity. Cultural and physical traits are important elements of the formation of the self. They are part of the way in which one apprehends and assesses historical experience and a way of life. In that sense they inform the way in which people express and organize their social relations. Both dimensions are part of a complex social, political, and historical process. Thus, a person's subjectivity or identity is not constructed only on the basis of his/her position in the relations of production and domination. Rather this identity is itself shaped by the multiple possible constructions according to different discourses about and the different meanings given to the position.

This paper argues that the multiple racial identities which Haitian migrants to New York City display in their organizations and in their public discourse is not expression of an ambiguity and/or denial of a racial consciousness and of racial identity. It is rather an expression of the different meanings of blackness that inform the consciousness and identity of Haitian immigrants.[1] These different meanings of blackness rooted in Haiti become embedded in a transnational network of social relations. In their experience of the migration process (which also involves their form of incorporation) Haitian migrants as historical subjects transformed the meanings of these categories of social relations in building their identities. In that process of the creation and recreation of identities, the tendency is towards a disaffiliation with black Americans. As we will further argue, the dynamics of this differentiation stems from: (1) a rejection of U.S. racial categories of identity that are used as axes

---

[1] Some scholars have attempted to explain this apparently "peculiar Haitian racial behavior" because it is multidimensional. For example, Buchanan (1987) speaks of a conflict of identity. Fontaine (1976) elaborates a concept labeled "autarkic behavior" where there is a complete ignoring of the host society's racism, while Verdieu (1973) speaks of the estrangement of Haitians from racial issues in the United States.

of racial hierarchy and inequality; (2) a reconstruction of the meanings of blackness from their home society; and finally (3) the perception and meanings given to the immigration experience.[2]

THE CONSTRUCT OF A RACIAL SUBJECT

Social categories like class, race, ethnicity, or gender are always characterized by their bi-dimensional meanings in their social usage. On one hand, they are socio-cultural constructs that express and justify relations of domination, exploitation, and subordination. On the other hand, they are categories of identity, a product of social relations, and an expression of social consciousness. In contrast to the category class, whose presuppositions are embedded in production relations and are thus more linked to the economic arrangements and the forms of control of surplus, the presuppositions of categories like race, ethnicity, and gender are generally expression of relations of power. Moreover, these latter categories tend to be arbitrary and more subjective. They are created from the selection of some visible physical and/or cultural characteristics and traits of groups and individuals which are given meanings that are translated and used as axes of relations of social inequality and as dimensions in a hierarchic structure of social positions.

Scientifically speaking, race, as a category which expresses distinctions between human groupings with phenotypical differences or with definite biological characteristics, is not a fixed attribute. Neither does it define behavior. There is rather a continuous alteration of these biological characteristics among human groups and there is no fixed genetic definition of a pure race. Within one population grouping there may exist such a variation of phenotypic features that classification of fixed racial boundaries is difficult. Likewise, it is preposterous to argue that social characteristics and/or cultural forms displayed by a distinct racial grouping are biologically programmed. A given "race" can create quite contrasting cultures in different geographical locations. A case in point is the development of distinct religious and musical practices among people of African descent in the New World.[3] Thus social customs and patterns of behavior attributed to a racial group are not predetermined. Rather, they emerge within a social context and express definite social relations. Attitudes and meanings given to race vary according to time and place.

Race is always constructed, defined, and perceived in an historical, social, and cultural context. Often, the content and reality of racial relations are not

---

[2] A full version of the argument is found in my Ph.D. dissertation, *A transnational dialectic of race, class, and ethnicity: Patterns of identities and forms of consciousness among Haitian migrants in New York City.* (SUNY–Binghamton), 1990.

[3] Two concrete examples come to mind. The first is part of the religious experience in Haiti as expressed in voodoo. The second is the development of jazz in the United States.

necessarily the ones that racial definition or racial taxonomy addresses. In that sense, the meanings of race and of racial hierarchy are not always physical be-cause they are closely connected to other social relations. Thus, any analysis of race must move at the level of objective reality and of that of meanings and appearance. The latter dimension, which expresses the subjective reality of race, is the most important dimension in the process of formation of identities.

Racial meanings are not fixed and unitary, but neither are they purely ideo-logical phenomena rooted in the historical development of former slave-based colonial societies like the United States or Haiti. They are more than a residue of past "history" reified into culture. Rather, they are the expression of both objective and subjective dimensions of social relations and praxis and are con-tinuously being redefined and reconstructed through historical struggle.

Racial Construct in the United States

In the United States, race and in particular the perception of and meanings given to race are important organizing principles defining relations of in-equality and social stratification. They are also important elements of the ascription of position in the U.S. social structure. In spite of the diversity and multiplicity of subordinated racial and ethnic groupings in the United States, and even though U.S. society has confronted each of its racially or culturally defined minorities with unique forms of domination and degradation, for his-torical reasons it is the relationship between the dominant white racial group and one particular dominated group—blacks—that has dominated the dy-namics of race relations and perceptions of race in the United States (Wilson 1979; Omi and Winant 1987; Farley 1979; Pettigrew 1980).

Because of the significance of race in the social fabric of U.S. society, per-ception of the U.S. social structure tends to take the form of a polarized so-ciety organized primarily along racial lines in which the subordinated pole— the bottom—is filled by blacks (Ossowski 1967; Myrdal 1944; Kerner Report 1988). The persistent perception of a subordinated place for blacks does not, however, mechanically reflect the real socio-economic position of all blacks. Indeed, for an important segment of the black population there have been some significant changes (Wilson 1979; 1987). Rather, this perception is part of a symbolic translation of racial meanings of "blackness" at all levels of the society. These meanings of race allow for a constant reassertion of a subordi-nated place assigned to blackness.

It is to these meanings of blackness that many African-American writers refer. It is what Baldwin (1961) calls "the bottom." He writes, "Blacks define the limits where one, cannot fall" (Baldwin 1961:61). In Baldwin's statement, this notion of the bottom is a mythical bottom yet it refers to the notion of a subordinate place. Hurston (1945) had previously made the same remark when she commented that sometimes a black can be perceived as being as brilliant as any white yet there is always the potential to dehumanize him. In *Crazy for that democracy*, she writes that the notion of a "place" for blacks has a double-edged character. It is physical but also psychological. It can be a back seat or the conviction of a white child that he is "first by birth, eternal and irrevocable like the place assigned to the Levites by Moses." She continues: "All physical and emotional things flow from this premise. It perpetuates itself for it is the unnatural exaltation of one ego, and the equally unnatural grinding down of the other" (Hurston [1945] 1979:168).

The constellation of different meanings of blackness in that notion of a "bottom," a subordinate place, is, on the one hand, a testimony to prevailing patterns of racial domination and social inequality which effect blacks in U.S. society. It is part of the social reality. On the other hand, because it is also the result of what people make of physical differences, it has become part of "folkways," of culture. "Place" establishes in the popular mind real and imaginary boundaries that separate one from the other, the other being in particular, black.[4]

The various meanings of blackness as they have developed over time are informed both by perceptions of race in the U.S. social structure and by the reality of race relations (Omi and Winant 1986; Takaki 1979; 1987). To quote Omi and Winant (1986:63), "Skin color differences are thought to explain perceived differences in intellectual, physical and artistic temperaments, and to justify distinct treatment of racially identified individuals and groups." These beliefs are reinforced in periods of economic crisis and rapid social change. Because of continuing changes in the meaning of blackness which inform the subjective definition of place, boundaries of place are constantly transformed and redefined.[5]

[4] Perceptions of blackness existed in the world view of European colonists and conquerors who came to the Americas. Yet it was with the development of slavery that blackness came to be associated with the bottom. Blacks were defined as the antithesis of whites, and the racial uniqueness of whites was posited through an inverted image of blacks. In that construct, all Africans, and thus all blacks, were incorporated into a single category, without distinguishing among them. Thus at the onset, the definition of blackness became, because of its total dimension, the source of a vast array of imagery upon which racism, class, culture, and ideology could play. Over time blackness would encompass a wide range of myths, stereotypes and beliefs. Meanings of blackness in U.S. society have varied, from an original definition of Africans as apes, to one of slaves as savages and heathens, or as lacking mental and intellectual capacities. Blackness has also been associated as a color with filth, dirt, malignancy, disaster, and ugliness. It has indicated censure, disgrace, and punishment. Blackness came to mean ingratitude, unfaithfulness, disloyalty, treason, and laziness (Davis 1974; Jordan 1968; 1987; Genovese 1972; Takaki 1987; Omi and Winant 1986; Williamson 1971; Frederickson 1971; Wynter 1979, *etc.*).

[5] The shift in boundaries of place has benefited some segments of the black population. It is the basis of Sowell (1981) and Wilson (1980) argument. Yet in spite of their thesis on the declining significance of race in defining place, racial meanings still continue to influence location of blacks and affects patterns of class and groups formation, forms of social consciousness and identities in U.S. society.

For a detailed account on the controversy that has arisen from the Wilson and Sowell position, see the opposite views of Thomas and Hughes 1986; Willie 1979; Edwards 1979; and Blauner 1972.

The construction of a subordinate place for blackness, while defined and informed primarily by race, expresses the dynamic of class conflict and other antagonistic social relations within U.S. society (Kousser and McPherson 1982; Rollins 1985). Moreover, in a social context where race, class, culture, and gender are confounded, the notion of place crystallizes all these relations and points out the interconnectedness of these various forms of domination. In the United States, the notion of a place for blacks is thus a social construct informed primarily by race that stands in the intertwined realm of ideology and culture, yet its presuppositions are also real socio-economic relations.

It is this notion of place that Haitian immigrants also come to perceive. It is well illustrated in the following statement of a Haitian student.

> The Haitian dreams of coming to New York. He comes to New York, But He'll never be an American. Why? He is an entity. He has a cultural background. He is somebody. He won't deny his past, because his past belongs to the greatest of Occidental nations. We were the first ones to vanquish Napoleon (*New Yorker* March 1975).

Underlying this evaluation of the Haitian student is a different construct of Haitian racial meanings which inform Haitian identities. Indeed, Haitians do not come into the United States as a "tabula rasa" a generic "immigrant labor group." Instead, they bring with them an understanding of class, race, and ethnic relations that differs from that conventionally used in the United States. Their process of incorporation and adaptation thus entails a recreation and redefinition of the meanings of these relationships.

The previous student statement might be taken as exceptional and sophisticated. Yet it expresses a sentiment common to Haitians across race, gender and class lines. Pride in the Haitian Revolution is part of the cultural and ideological make-up of the Haitian social fabric. There is no Haitian political and social statement that does not make reference to Haiti's independence. The Haitian revolution of 1791–1804 is the basis on which Haitians define themselves, perceive and evaluate others, and create their identities.

Haitian Racial Meanings

Categories of class, race, gender, and ethnicity are also part of the social make-up of Haitian life. Like the United States and like other Caribbean societies, Haiti is a former slave-based society and race has played an important role in its historical development. In the Caribbean and Haiti, however, although race affects social location, consciousness, attitudes, and identities, the fluidity of class, ethnic, and race relations force a constant redefinition of the boundaries of all of these categories, and of race in particular. The distinctiveness of race relations in the social structure as well as in the perception of that structure has to do, in my view, with the development and transformation of Caribbean slave societies. In this region, the evolution of these slave-based societies resulted in the creation of a social context where class/race or class/ethnicity tend to be confounded.

In Caribbean societies, the construction of racial/color categories is complex. The phenotypic variety is so great that it becomes necessary to use socio-economic referents in the ascription of color. Race/color is not constructed into mutually exclusive bipolar categories of black/white. Rather there is a continuum, conceptualized as a gradation along the lines of color. The development of a color system of differentiation does not mean, however, the absence of racial stratification. Indeed, differentiation and gradation of color presupposes the existence of poles of reference. Class, politics and culture modify significantly the color gradation as well as the poles. As a result, the meaning of blackness is clearly connected to the internal dynamics of social relations, with a tendency toward the overlapping of class and race categories. While blackness mediates class, class always qualifies race/color. Poverty, as an affect of class position, is equated with blackness and affluence is associated with light skin. Thus racial category and racial meaning have a social character. Although whiteness is still perceived as affluence and superior status, money and power act as qualifiers and provide grounds for the development of different variants of blackness. Thus blackness is not a fixed category defined primarily by physical traits. It is rather a situational position and identity.

In most Caribbean societies, including Haiti, there is no official classificatory system of race relations, no bipolar ranking based on racial stratification.[6] Therefore, ascription of racial categories of identity is based on a perception of race/color which itself is conditioned by class and culture. Although Haiti has had a historical experience similar to that of other Caribbean societies, because of its political history, race/color differentiation exhibits some specific characteristics.

In most analyses of Haitian social structure, race is conceived either as an ideology of domination (Labelle [1976] 1986; Dupuy 1989) or as the pure manifestation of class strife between dominant groups (Nicholls 1979; 1985;

[6] In the Caribbean race has not, as it has in the United States, taken on an important role in defining a subordinated place for blacks. The presence within these societies of different racial groups that stand in an antagonistic relationship to each other is not translated into a structure of exclusion and hierarchy. There is no dichotomic vision of the social structure with black and white occupying mutually exclusive positions. Consequently, social consciousness and patterns of racial identity are not exclusively shaped and conditioned by the ascription of a subordinated place defined primarily by race. In all representations of the social structure, the realities of race and class and/or ethnicity have become so intertwined that race mediates class relations and class qualifies race relations. A full analysis of Caribbean racial stratification can be found in the work of many scholars (Harris 1964; Patterson 1982; Kuper 1977; Giraud 1983; Sudama 1983; Hoetink 1985; Hall 1977).

Paquin 1983; Dupuy 1989). In both perspectives, race is seen as a residual category. Yet race is a matter of collective praxis, thus of both social relations and of individual identity. While in the former case it participates in the creation and ascription of place, in the latter it is a matter of identity formation manifested in taste, networks of friends and clients, strategies of reproduction through marriage, and self-identification, as well as in other ways (Omi and Winant 1986; Hall 1977). In Haiti, the race/color hierarchy, coupled with class differentiation, is manifested at all levels of the society. Moreover, racial identity and racial awareness are so salient that one can hardly separate the two.

All Haitian perceptions of race have been shaped by the dynamics of the country's political history, and over time blackness has taken various meanings. First, with the creation of the Haitian state, an outcome of the slave revolution of 1791–1804, race became the unifying theme for the formation of nationhood. The equating of race and nation permitted the use of blackness as a means to legitimate power and to establish a political compromise between two racially differentiated fractions of the ruling elite. The equating of nation and race also provided the ruling elite with the means to exercise its hegemony over the masses by building popular consent on the basis of racial pride. Moreover, the equating of race and nation conveys a sense of race-pride. Blackness is the basis for a cultural nationalism in Haiti, and the Haitian revolution symbolizes the dignity and pride of the black race. Nevertheless, the equating of blackness with race-pride is complex and contradictory. While such a claim is the vindication of the race, it also disaffiliates itself from Africa and praises its ties to Western culture. At the same time, the Haitian revolution, the source of that race-pride, makes Haitians equal to whites.

Blackness in Haiti is also a conceptualization of class interest in the language of race. It is a racial symbol whose meaning hides class conflicts, in particular between those dominant groups. Race is equated to class and is used as a means to promote and formulate class interest. It is racial capital.[7]

The fluidity of Haitian perceptions of blackness—a fluidity closely connected to the dynamics of class relations—is part of a collective memory, of a social consciousness and identity. Yet, because of the multidimensional nature of the meanings of blackness, the formation of an Haitian identity is not informed primarily by race. However, in the United States, blackness does in-

---

[7] The concept of "racial capital" is developed more fully in the work of some French Caribbean scholars. It is a concept closely linked to that of "cultural capital" formulated by Pierre Bourdieu (1977). For a more extensive analysis of the concept of racial capital see Giraud (1983) and Sudama (1983).

The category of cultural capital has been developed by Bourdieu. It can be broadly defined as the accumulated knowledge of cultural taste, manners, attitudes and information transmitted from parents to child. It is the intergenerational transmission of the socialization of cultural attitudes, motivations and knowledge of a dominant culture which works to reinforce and reproduce social inequalities.

form consciousness and shape identities, in particular racial identity. Yet it is an identity that shuns any fixed category of racial ascription as expressed in the distance from any total identification with African-Americans. This distance became reinforced by the politicization of most cultural and social activities that praise the maintenance of a cultural nationalist identity.

THE IMMIGRATION EXPERIENCE

Black immigrants from the Caribbean are a large part of the immigrant labor force currently settled in the United States, and in particular, in New York City.[8] These immigrants are part of a new wave of immigration which began since 1965. The flow comprises a large Haitian component. More than half of the new immigrants are female (Sasseen-Koob 1983; Foner 1987). This wave also contains many undocumented aliens, political refugees, and professionals (Portes and Bach 1985).

The early Haitian immigrants in New York City found jobs mostly in factories (Laguerre 1984; Paquin 1983). Over time, with more knowledge of English and more experience of the labor market, some began to move into white collar jobs starting at the lowest positions. Many financial and service institutions on Wall Street hired them. A few others went into business on their own, opening gas stations, or working as electricians, cleaning contractors, or grocers. The women went to work in hospitals and nursing homes as nurse's aides and increasingly as registered nurses. Many worked as maids. By the 1960s many were employed as secretaries in private firms and a few in African missions to the UN (Laguerre 1983). By 1980, while the bulk of Haitian migrants concentrated in manufacturing and services as semi-skilled and unskilled labor, about 35% hold white collar and clerical jobs (Leavitt and Lutz 1988; Bogen 1987).

For both legal and undocumented immigrants, information about labor markets tends to come from friends and relatives. Haitian churches and community centers are also active in locating jobs. Even in white collar and clerical positions, the ethnic network operates. It assists new arrivals in all stages of the migration process but, more importantly, in recruitment and placement in the labor market. In many industries, obtaining jobs through an in-

[8] New York is appealing because of the availability of employment opportunities and because of the existence of family and household networks. The city has traditionally attracted Afro-Caribbean immigrants because of the diversity of racial and ethnic groupings. The 1980 U.S. Census estimates the total black population in New York City at 24% of the total population. Native-born blacks account for 25.7% of that percentage. Similarly, between 1975 and 1980, foreign-born blacks total 23.4% of the total immigrant population. These figures exclude blacks of Hispanic origin (Bogen 1987:40).

formal network is widespread regardless of whether the workers employed are undocumented.

Although there are economic opportunities, most of the positions available to Afro-Caribbean immigrants are in the secondary sectors of the labor market (Piore 1979; Edwards 1979; Sasseen-Koob 1978; Marshall 1987). For many Afro-Caribbeans, and in particular for Haitians, New York also marks their first exposure to overt racial inequality and blatant racist exclusion.

For the majority of Haitian immigrants, incorporation into U.S. society has a twofold character. First, most Haitians are integrated into the secondary sector of the economy. In terms of economic reward, this means they have a weak position in the labor market structure. Second, as a black immigrant population, the significance of any ascribed status, in particular of race, is important for it implies differential access to resources and skills because of race. The strategies of resistance and accommodation put forward by Haitian migrants to supersede the economic constraints and to circumvent limits and/or obstacles to access to resources and rewards are manifold. One of the most important manifestations of these strategies is the multiple forms of identity displayed. In searching to achieve economic or social mobility, political power or civil rights, Haitian immigrants in New York City differentiate themselves from the black American population.

The Creation of Transnational Networks

The migration of Haitians to the United States is not a unidirectional process. Indeed, one striking feature of the Haitian migration experience is the extent and scope of their transnational networks. The household strategies of Haitian families are illustrative. Indeed, resettlement of Haitian immigrants in New York involves the interaction among household members living in North America and Haiti as well as friends and other relatives in other parts of the United States and in Canada.

The migration of a member of a household, particularly one of rural or working class background, is likely to produce a chain of migration. Once here, the migrant often sends for other members of the household. Family reunification may take several years depending on economic resources. In fact, for families of middle class and upper-middle class background, conditions of migration differ. Often children are left in Haiti for later reunification while both parents migrate. Nonetheless, for the majority of Haitian migrants, the pattern tends to be that one member of the household migrates first. Generally a woman, she immediately becomes the broker for initial reference point and orientation source (Laguerre 1984; Labelle et al. 1987).[9]

[9] One of the most important features of the new migration movement in the U.S. compared to the old migration of Europeans is that males do not outnumber females. Rather since

Specific to the Haitian family is its form of integration into transnational migration networks. This has important consequences for the household and the mobility of members depending on the class origin of migrants. Peasant or working class immigrants are more prone to have the remainder of their family and household in Haiti. A reverse situation exists for many middle class immigrants. Extended members of the family and the household may or may not reside in Haiti. The effects on the reproduction of a migration chain and on the obligations toward other members of the family therefore differ.

Both Larose (1984) and Labelle (1987) have surveyed the extent of the transnational household structure of the Haitian family. Some of the examples presented in their survey illustrate well how networking differs by class. Yet, their data also indicate that all Haitian families participate at a level in building transnational networks. For example, a middle class family in New York may send its children to an aunt living in Montreal to receive a "French" education. Often, mother and father of migrant families of middle class background, come from Haiti to visit with a specific goal, to help temporarily in domestic tasks and child nurturing (Larose 1984). In contrast, a divorced woman garment worker in Montreal sent her child temporarily to her sister in New York. An unemployed worker in Montreal comes illegally to New York where his cousin helps find him a job. The brother of a U.S. immigrant in New York is advised to migrate to New York rather than Montreal because of the high unemployment rate in Canada and because there is a larger undocumented population in the United States. U.S. residents with relatives in Canada, visit Montreal to benefit from the free health care system. Children are sent to Haiti for schooling.

Examples thus abound of an intense network and communication with parents and relatives in New York, Montreal, Miami, and Haiti. Communication is by visit, letter, telephone conversation, and remittance (Larose 1984: 229–230). The network involves not only economic exchanges (DeWind 1987) but also information about labor market and other important conditions related to settlement. It also operates for exchange of services, mate matching and sharing of domestic tasks.

Transnationalism is also manifested in the formation of voluntary organizations among Haitian migrants. Haitians, like other Caribbean immigrants in the United States, have created various voluntary associations which for many people reinforce the experience of belonging to the same group. These associations vary according to their own specific goal: some are oriented toward maintaining both cultural and social links with Haiti, others are eco-

---

1945, more than half of the new legal immigrants are female. Moreover studies on Haitians, Jamaicans, and Dominicans in New York City show an unusual pattern where single women tend to migrate or where they often precede spouses in the process (Nash and Fernandez-Kelly 1983; Sassen-Koob 1983; Foner 1987; Marshall 1987; Buchanan 1981; Labelle et al. 1987).

nomic and political organizations, some strive to meet the spiritual and religious need of their members, and others are geared toward defining a form of integration into U.S. society that does not imply complete assimilation. The role of politics was crucial in that process. Indeed, for many, membership in these associations was their way of responding to pressures created by political groups whose strategies focused almost exclusively around Haiti. Politics has played a significant role in defining identity and in forcing Haitians to create alternatives to assimilation (Charles 1990a; Laguerre 1984; Fouron 1983; Glick Schiller *et al.* 1987).

The Role of Politics

One cannot understand the pattern of incorporation of Haitian immigrants, their conception of the U.S. social structure, their level of consciousness and patterns of identities without reference to the impact of politics and of political ideas on the Haitian migrant population in New York. The role of the first settlers is crucial in that process. For most of the first Haitian migrants, in their majority political exiles, the migration process was always perceived temporarily. New York was a place of transit, a place to come and organize opposition against the Duvalier regime.[10] This was expressed not only in the proliferation of political groups and the multiplicity of political activities but also in the political discourse that explained the causes of Haitian migration only through politics. Paquin's (1983) testimony on the political mobilization in the community during its first years of formation is illustrative as the following quote reveals:

> Apartment 15-B in the hotel Alexandria, located at 103rd and Broadway in Manhattan, was the headquarters of the opposition. It also became a screening and orientation center, a kind of Ellis island for new Haitian refugees between Papa Doc country and the U.S. unknown (Paquin 1983:162).

Political activities took different forms, from organization of raids to cultural events (Jumelle 1973; Paquin 1983). The process began with the transfer from Haiti into the New York scene in 1957, of political confrontation among political leaders. All the main political actors who opposed Duvalier in the 1957 election settled in New York. Magloire, a general of the army who held power between 1949 and 1956, lived first on the East Side of Manhattan and later moved to Jamaica Estates, an affluent neighborhood in Queens. Dejoie, the mulatto and bourgeois candidate resided with his group on Manhattan's

---

[10] It was almost impossible for the Duvalier regime to organize support groups in the various communities of the diaspora. The opposition really controls all political activities. Anyone with official ties with the Haitian government was systematically denounced and scorned.

upper West Side. Fignole, the populist candidate but also an interim president in 1956–1957, was based in Brooklyn (Paquin 1983).

The presence of these political actors, and their active interaction with the community, set the political context for any politics oriented toward integration. The political agenda clearly defined the priority. It was national politics. Paquin's account of the first invasion launched in New York in 1958 is revealing.

> At Roger's two room apartment on Broadway and 103rd street, there was pandemonium. People all around were talking at the same time. No Haitians went to work this morning of July 29th 1958. They were all relishing the idea of going to their last pay check, and showing their revulsion and hostility for "le blanc" who had squeezed their labor to the very last cent of the minimum wage or even far less, since most of them were illegal, thus helpless. They were all going back to Haiti by the first available plane (Paquin 1983:163).

This tendency for Haitians to see themselves as transient migrants in their first phase of settlement is not a uniquely Haitian phenomenon (Pastor 1985). Yet the specificity in the Haitian case is that perception was reinforced by politics. The migration process was perceived as transitory and New York was defined as a transient place. Yet it was not a mere transit point, rather it was a place to organize political opposition to the Duvalier regime. Such political perceptions of the migration process would permeate all dimensions of cultural life in the community. From the early 1960s up to the uprooting of the Duvalier regime in 1986, no single activity could escape political scrutiny. The strong influence of a political and ideological discourse that went against any full assimilation and integration into U.S. social life, even affected groups, like the Haitian Unity Council, that promoted integration and participation in U.S. politics (*Unity* 1976, 30:3). Their discourse was always mediated by their reference to the Haitian revolution.

The decline of traditional politics during the 1970s and the emergence of progressive groups in the political arena did not change the prevailing conception of the immigration experience. Thus, up to 1986 the migration process was perceived of and experienced as transitory. New York had become an extended arena of Haitian politics. The task adopted by many leaders protected Haitian identity against any form of integration that might lead to assimilation, thus to a betrayal of a nationalist commitment.

With the increase of immigration in the 1970s, social differentiation increased within the community. The new waves of immigrants primarily from working class backgrounds came to the United States to "make it," using the migration process as a way to resolve problems of survival and economic mobility. New York was then perceived primarily as a place to work, where opportunities are more promising than in Haiti.

Two perceptions of the United States have thus shaped incorporation and identity of Haitian migrants in New York. Most Haitian migrants see the United States as a place to work and to earn money. For many, and in particular for Haitians of working class background, gaining a better economic position tends to be the most important parameter in their perception of the immigration experience and consequently of their assessment of the U.S. reality. All their problems revolve around work and on how to survive and create better opportunities for children and relatives in Haiti. So long as Haiti is the primary reference point, there is no need to be assimilated as Americans and less as black Americans for they already have a country of socio-cultural identity. However, this does not prevent Haitian workers from using U.S. citizenship to facilitate family immigration and access to employment (Leavitt and Lutz 1988). Moreover, the nationalist discourse of the left has reinforced workers' racial and national pride in Haiti's history. In that sense the United States is also perceived as a country of whites, and Haitian workers cannot understand how black Americans have accepted such conditions of oppression. Up to 1986, the primary political concern of most Haitian leaders was how to maintain and promote a Haitian identity that shuns integration in U.S. society and its capitalistic values. The answer was political action oriented to Haiti. As Verdieu (1973b:46) stated, "une expérience politique dans le milieu de vie de l'émigration constituerait ainsi une aide précieuse pour un engagement politique éventuel demain en Haïti."[11]

Nonetheless, in both perceptions the absence of a racial discourse is striking. What is rather at play is a nationalist preoccupation which fosters the creation of a separate identity from black Americans and the explanation for such a behavior is both historical and cultural. Indeed, Haitians place a high value on the west; yet, they also see themselves as belonging equally to that western world. As the student stated, they defeated Napoleon. That defeat evidences their power as a people and as a race and serve in the making of their identity. It is a consciousness expressed in a race-pride based on their historical experience. The collective memory of that unique experience coupled with a limited incorporation into the U.S. social structure as workers, make them cognizant of racism, but at a distance. As foreigners they have nothing to fear, they are external to the U.S. racial conflicts. The reality of racism thus does not become crucial in their lives. When they become victims of racism, it is incomprehensible, for Haitians are different and not fully a part of U.S. society. And it is that uniqueness that Haitians highlight as expressions of their identity.

The tension in the dynamics of the process of settlement stems from a contradiction between two perceptions of the migration process: as tempo-

---

[11] It is interesting to note that Verdieu was the minister of Social Affairs of the Aristide-Preval government in 1990.

rary means to an end or as an end in itself. Yet, rather than resulting in conflict, there is coexistence and interdependence between the two visions. On one hand, political life in the community has created a context for the development of alternative forms of integration and has helped to define new identities. On the other hand, strategies of survival for the majority of the immigrants and their extended households provides a foundation for national politics to predominate. Haitian workers in defining the United States and New York as a work place, could separate their activities as laborers from their social and cultural lives.

While in Haiti, variables like education, wealth and income, and family background are linked together in defining class and status position, in the United States these variables do not operate on the same dynamics. For the majority of Haitian immigrants, the goal is not to achieve social status but to have a better economic position and more importantly to save. Therefore, it is possible to separate position in the work place, which gives access to economic betterment, from their social and cultural life, which takes place primarily in reference to Haiti. All values and norms that signify status and social mobility are in reference to the Haitian social structure. This can be more clearly understood when a working class immigrant works hard to pay for a month's vacation in Haiti. The dominant motive is to arrive and to display the acquired new wealth. The same behavior is also present among members of the middle class who own a luxurious house in Haiti that they can maintain only with their employment in the United States.

DISPLAY OF MULTIPLE IDENTITIES: THE 1973 AND 1985 SURVEYS

In 1973, the Haitian journal *Sèl* surveyed 131 college and high school Haitian students in New York City to determine their degree of satisfaction with U.S. life (*Sèl* July 1973, 10:20–27). Most of these students were the children of first generation immigrants. On an average, they had resided in the United States for more than three years. More than 70% answered the questionnaire in English, showing fluency in the language. Three questions alluded to their perception of the U.S. social structure. The first question was to name two important things that brought satisfaction and reward in New York. The results were as follows: 19% of the students said everything, 15.5% "freedom," 15% money, 14% schooling, 10% leisure time, and 8% dating. Fourteen percent did not answer and 4% did not like anything. The second question was about problems and difficulties they encountered in New York. Again the results were revealing: 13.5% stated they had no problems, while for the rest 16.4% mentioned English, 14.1% U.S. society, 10% money, 9.4% work, and 8.8% school. Around 15% did not answer. The remaining 10% was divided between those who found that life was dangerous and those who had conflicts with their families. This conflict especially characterized the problems of the girls whose parents imposed traditional restrictions.

The third question had two dimensions. First, the students were asked about their future commitment to Haiti and second if they wanted to return to work in Haiti. Seventy-two percent answered they were committed to Haiti's future but, with respect to returning to work in Haiti, 30.6% said yes, 16% said no, and 49.6% said they did not know. Four percent did not answer.

Interestingly, the students never mentioned race or racism in their answers. Their perception of U.S. life was informed mainly by the belief that, as immigrants, they had the same life chance opportunities as anybody else. Though the issue of discrimination in employment was not directly posed, some students mentioned the racist structure of U.S. society. Yet, the majority stressed possibilities for economic success in the United States.

That Haiti was a political concern to 70% of the students, illustrates their level of national consciousness and reflects the impact of political groups that emphasized commitment to Haiti. That about 50% of the students were undecided about returning to Haiti, even though a relatively large proportion—30%—posited return as an alternative, reflected the gap and tension between the agenda of nationalist political groups and the students' interests in their immediate community. The students did not want to assimilate, yet they aspired to some form of integration into U.S. society as new immigrants. That tension has always existed among Haitian migrants. It is a tension informed on one hand by nationalism, cultural heritage, and different racial meanings, and on the other hand by a dual conception of the United States as a work place and an arena of Haitian political struggles. Comments of Haitian workers reflect the tension between pro-U.S. and nationalist orientations. A female worker stated:

> Here, I can work, earn more money than I did in Haiti, and give my kids a better chance in life. They can become anything they want to be. When I am able, I want to improve my English, get a High School Equivalency diploma and then a teaching certificate or a nurse license (Buchanan 1979:22).

In contrast, the same worker evaluated her own socio-economic status and her place in the United States differently.

> The job I do is for an animal. It's the same day after day. No matter how fast I work, my boss always complains about my slowness. He speaks to me disrespectfully because I am black and foreign. He knows I don't have an alien card and won't argue with him. He might report me to immigration or fire me. Before I even get here, I am tired from the pushing and shoving on the train. We only have a half hour for lunch so I'm rushed there too . . . I used to be a schoolteacher in Haiti. Now, I am doing a job that doesn't even require me to think (Buchanan 1979:22).

Though most Haitian workers could not formulate their perception of race and class through an assessment of their relative status in Haiti and in the United States, hers is a widespread perception. Compared to Haiti, the United States offers more economic opportunities. There seems to be no awareness of major obstacles to improving one's own or one's family's standard of living, not even race. At the same time, because of their historical experience, particularly of race and nationalism, Haitian immigrants despise the position of blacks in this society.

In the same vein, in a 1973 article on the cultural dimensions of Haitian emigration, Ernst Verdieu, a member of *Sèl* stated,

> Pour que les Haïtiens connaissent réellement un affrontement racial, il faudrait qu'ils montent sur le terrain, qu'ils s'intègrent ou cherchent à s'intégrer et qu'ils rencontrent alors les barrières. Mais dans la mesure ou ils ne sont pas concernés, ils se contentent d'assister à cet affrontement sans y prendre part (Verdieu 1973b:50).

As clearly shown in that statement, the issue of race was conditioned by the issue of integration. In that perspective, the incorporation of Haitians into the U.S. labor market was not seen as a form of integration because in Verdieu's conception, integration meant a loss or redefinition of identity. To confront issues of racism would only be possible if Haitians defined themselves as black members of U.S. society. But, Haitians defined themselves mainly as observers. The absence of any reference to race in the actions of groups that aimed toward the politicization and mobilization of Haitian immigrants clearly indicates that class, nationalism, and a different meaning of blackness have been the main parameters through which Haitian identity has been formed in the United States. Such a pattern of behavior also tends to prevail in the 1985 survey.[12]

Analysis of the 1985 survey also indicates the significance and interconnectedness of race, class, and culture in informing Haitian social and cultural practices. One of the most important dimensions of that interconnectedness is revealed in the tendency towards a disaffiliation with black Americans. Yet the data also show that that distance did not mean a denial of blackness or the absence of a racial consciousness. Being Haitian is also being black, yet this blackness is linked to Haitian history through Africa and not through the

---

[12] The research was conducted by a team at Columbia University investigating 91 Haitian organizations composed primarily of Haitian immigrants. Between 1985 and 1987 leaders and/or prominent members of 91 Haitian and 50 U.S. organizations located in the New York metropolitan area were interviewed. The research was funded by a NICHD (grant #HD18140) to Josh DeWind and Nina Glick Schiller, who conducted the research with a team including the author of this paper. Three forms of data collection—extensive interviews, participant data observation, and documents—were used in order to create an ethnographic record of the Haitian immigrant's incorporation and adaptation.

United States. Thus efforts to organize around a Haitian identity with different levels of meaning and the various statements of social distance displayed in the survey are modes of resistance to ascription into the low status that is generally allocated to black Americans (Charles and Glick Schiller 1987; Glick Schiller *et al.* 1987).

For many Haitians, to accept a racial identity that conveys confinement to a surbordinate place leaves no space for social mobility to operate. Rather, they tend to reject the use of race to ascribe limits to class mobility. And such practices tend not only to deny the uniqueness of being Haitian but also to create more constraints in their incorporation as an immigrant group which happens to be black.

In their assessment and evaluation of the different places assigned to differentiated groups of people in the U.S. social structure, Haitian leaders and organizations interviewed developed two main strategies. All these strategies reflect different levels and forms of social consciousness which are expressed in the pattern of identities.

One strategy has been to accept partially or totally racial and ethnic ascriptions imposed by U.S. society and to use them as identities around which to organize in order to obtain resources. It tends to lead to participation in interest group politics in conjunction with black American and/or Caribbean politicians. This has proved to be a path of individual mobility for the leadership. Another strategy has led some Haitians to maintain ties with Haiti. They continue to identify with Haiti or with a particular town, strata, or class in Haiti. Other Haitians continue to look toward Haiti as a place to obtain status, or as a place where they could obtain political power. During the 1970s and 1980s some aspired to replace Duvalier, while others struggled for fundamental and lasting changes.

These strategies in both their individual or collective form, tend to challenge and resist the structural position assigned to black people in the United States and thus were expressions of a level of social consciousness and pattern of identities.

The tendency among Haitian leaders to reject any fixed ascribed identity, which may be the basis for a fixed location in the U.S. social structure, is informed, as we have been arguing, by multiple processes. For example, although blackness is part of their social experiences, race does not become the prime mover in their quest for a social identity. Moreover, because of the role of race in defining social location in the United States, they tend to distance themselves from those who symbolize blackness in U.S. society. The rejection is also informed by their perception of the intricate relationship of ethnicity to race and class. On the one hand, to accept a U.S.–defined ethnic identity may result in being defined and perceived through some physical characteristics where ethnicity becomes equated to a distinct meaning of blackness and of race. On the other hand, the acceptance may also lead to negation of class differentiation among different groups of Haitian migrants.

Economic mobility is something strongly desired by Haitian immigrants. In the United States, social mobility generally operates through education or wealth. Race, however, does impose constraints and does mediate that process. In the United States, race as a phenotype manifested in color, becomes a socially defined reality where blackness is a marker for a location at the bottom. Haitians tend to see that location as a limit imposed and to some extent accepted by black Americans.

Although the process of evaluation of U.S. social structure and of the significant role of race in that structure has informed the pattern of identities and forms of incorporation of Haitian migrants, the fluidity of racial meanings in Haiti, and its close relation to class position, also affects that perception and informs identities. While in the United States perceptions of race are expressed in a permanent, fixed attribute that defines social location, in contrast, such is not the case in Haiti.

CONCLUSION

I have argued that the creation of Haitian identities is rooted in three processes embedded in a transnational social context: 1) the use of meanings of race and class based on experiences in Haiti; 2) the capturing, through the symbolic notion of place, of the perceived racial status and class position ascribed to blacks in the U.S. social structure; and 3) on the dual perception of the immigration experience. In creating identity, the tendency is to negate the U.S. meaning of blackness, yet at the same time, race, class, and culture are reaffirmed. In particular, Haitian perceptions of the U.S. racial reality are not the product of false consciousness or of any conflict over racial identity. They are rather a way to apprehend the concrete, objective reality of class, ethnic, and race hierarchies in the United States. They are part of a consciousness informed by a different socio-political experience. Because of that specific experience, the assessment does not separate relations of race, class, or ethnicity into isolated spheres of life, but sees them as interconnected. It is particularly in relation to the perception of a subordinated place ascribed to blacks in the U.S. social structure that Haitian immigrants construct their own identities.

The awareness of social stratification organized around racial status entails a continuous rejection of meanings of blackness that signify dehumanization and constraints/obstacles to social mobility. However, Haitian strategies and responses are crystallized in the forms of identity displayed, but are only in part informed by their experiences of incorporation into U.S. society. These forms of identity are also informed by their past experience of social relations in Haiti, as well as by their continuing interaction in social processes still occurring in their home society. Important in that dynamic is the role of culture, of collective memory, of structured experiences of race, class and nation. That shared experience forms a common thread, sews together these different views into the fabric of a community. This shared past also permits Haitian immigrants to maintain a racial identity that emphasizes their uniqueness and difference in a society that perceives few racial differences. The ways in which uniqueness and difference are part of the Haitian social consciousness are expressed in a multiple form of identities.

REFERENCES CITED

Archipelago
  1983   Race et classe dans la Caraibe. Paris: Editions Caribennes.
Baldwin, James
  1961   *Nobody knows my name.* New York: Dial Press.
Blauner, R.
  1972   *Racial oppression in America.* New York: Harper and Row.
Bogen, E.
  1987   *Immigration in New York.* New York: Praeger.
Bourdieu, P.
  1977   *Reproduction in education, society and culture.* Beverley Hills: Sage.
Buchanan, Susan
  1979   Language and identity: Haitians in New York City. *International Migration Review.* 13(2):298–313.
  1981   Profile of an Haitian migrant woman. In *Female immigrants to the United States: Caribbean, Latin American, and African experiences*, edited by Delores Mortimer and Roy Bryce-Laporte. *RIIES Occasional Papers No. 2.* Smithsonian Institution, Washington D.C.
Charles, Carolle
  1990a *A Transnational dialectic of race, class, and ethnicity: Patterns of identities and forms of consciousness among Haitian migrants in New York City.* Ph.D. dissertation, SUNY–Binghamton.
  1990b Different meanings of blackness: Patterns of identity among Haitian migrants in New York City. *Cimarron 2(3)* Winter.
Charles, C. and Nina Glick Schiller
  1987   On not being black twice. Paper presented at the CUNYACS Conference. Brooklyn College. New York, March.
Davis, David B.
  1974 [1967]   The problems of slavery in Western culture. Ithaca, NY: Cornell University Press.
Dewind, Josh
  1987   The remittances of Haitian immigrants in New York City. A Citibank Report. New York, November.
Dewind, Josh and David Kinley
  1988 [1986]   *Aiding migration: The impact of international development assistance on Haiti.* New York: Westview Press.
Dupuy, Alex
  1989   *Haiti in the world economy: Class, race, and underdevelopment since 1700.* Boulder, CO/London: Westview Press.

Edwards, R.
1979   *Contested terrain: The transformation of the workplace in the 20th century.* New York: Basic Books.
Foner, Nancy, Ed.
1987   *New immigrants in New York.* New York: Columbia University Press.
Fouron, Georges
1983   The black dilemna in the U.S.: The Haitian experience. *Journal of Caribbean Studies 3(3):*242–265.
Frederickson, G.
1971   *The black image in the white mind.* New York: Harper Torchbooks.
Genovese, E. D.
1972   The slave states of North America. In *Neither slaves nor free,* edited by D. Cohen and J. P. Green. Baltimore: John Hopkins University Press. Pp. 258–278.
Giraud, M.
1979   *Races et classes la Martinique.* Paris: Anthropos.
Glick Schiller, Nina, Linda Basch, and Cristina Blanc-Szanton, Eds.
1992   *Migration in transnational perspective: Rethinking race, ethnicity, nationalism and class. Annals of the New York Academy of Sciences Volume 645.*
Glick Schiller, Nina *et al.*
1987a   All in the same boat: Unity and diversity in Haitian organizing in New York. In *Caribbean life in New York City: Sociocultural dimensions,* edited by Constance Sutton and Elsa Chaney. Staten Island: New York Center for Migration Studies.
1987b   Emigrant, ethnic, refugee: Changing organizational identities among Haitian immigrants. *Migration World XV,* no. 1.
Gordon, D., M. Reich, and R. Edwards
1973   *Labor market segmentation.* Lexington, MA: DC Heath.
1982   *Segmented work, divided workers: The historical transformation of labor in the US.* New York: Cambridge University Press.
Hall, Stuart
1977   Pluralism, race and class in Caribbean societies. In *Race and class in postcolonial societies.* UNESCO. Pp. 150–182.
Hurston, Zora N.
1979 [1945]   *I love myself: A Zora Neale Hurston reader,* edited by Alice Walker. New York: Feminist Press.
Jarvis, Anderson
1975   The Haitians in New York. *New Yorker.* March, 50–75.
Jordan, Winthrop D.
1968   *White over black: American attitudes toward the Negro, 1550–1812.* New York: Norton.
1987   First impressions: Libidinous blacks. In *From different shores,* edited by R. Takaki. Pp. 43–53.
Jumelle, Julien
1973   L'opposition politique dans l'émigration haïtienne. *Sèl 10:*38–51.
Kousser, J. M. and M. McPherson
1982   *Region, race and reconstruction.* New York/Oxford: Oxford University Press.
Kritz, Mary M., Ed.
1983   *US immigration and refugee policy.* Lexington, MA: Lexington Books.
Labelle, M.
1986 [1976]   *Idéologies de couleur et classes sociales en Haïti.* Montreal: CIDHICA.

Labelle, M., Geneviève Turcotte, Marianne Kempeneers, and Deirdre Meintel
    1987   *Histoires d'immigrées*. Montreal: Editions Boreal
Laguerre, M.
    1984   *American odyssey. Haitians in New York City*. Ithaca, NY: Cornell University Press.
Larose, Serge
    1984   Transnationalité et réseaux migratoires: Entre le Québec, les Etats-Unis et Haïti. *Cahiers de Recherches Sociologiques 2(2)*:115–138.
Leavitt Roy and Mary E. Lutz, Eds.
    1988   *Three new immigrant groups in New York City. Dominicans, Haitians and Cambodians*. New York: Community Council of Greater New York.
Marshall, Adriana
    1983   *Immigration in a surplus worker labor market: The case of New York*. Occasional Papers Series #39. New York: Center for L.A. and Caribbean Studies, NYU.
    1987   New immigrants in New York's economy. In *New immigrants in New York City*, edited by N. Foner. New York: Columbia University Press. Pp. 79–102.
Myrdal, Gunnar
    1962 [1944]   *An American dilemma. The Negro problem and modern democracy*. New York: Harper and Row.
Nicholls, David
    1979   *From Dessalines to Duvalier*. New York: Cambridge University Press.
    1985   *Haiti in Caribbean context*. New York: St. Martin's Press.
Omi, M. and H. Winant
    1986   *Racial formation in the United States*. London: Routledge and Kegan Paul.
Ossowski, Stanislas
    1967 [1954]   *Class structure in the social consciousness*. New York: The Free Press of Glencoe.
Paquin, Lyonel
    1983   *The Haitians: Class and color politics*. New York: Multi-Type.
Pastor, Robert
    1985   *Migration and development in the Caribbean: The unexplored connection*. New York: Westview Press.
Pettigrew, Thomas, Ed.
    1980   *The sociology of race relations*. New York: The Free Press.
Piore, Michael
    1979   *Birds of passage*. New York: Cambridge University Press.
Portes, Alejandro and J. Walton
    1981   *Labor, class and the international system*. New York: Academic Press.
Portes, A. and R. Bach
    1985   *Latin odyssey*. Berkeley: University of California Press.
Reich, M.
    1981   *Racial inequality: A political-economic analysis*. New Jersey: Princeton University Press.
Rollins, Judith
    1985   *Between women: Domestic workers and their employers*. Philadelphia: Temple University Press.
Sassen-Koob, Saskia
    1978   The international circulation of resources and development: The case of migrant labor. *Development and Change 9(4)*:509–547.
    1983   Labor migration and the new industrial division of labor. In *Women, men and the international division of labor*, edited by J. Nash and P. Fernandez-Kelly. Pp. 175–205.

Sèl
1973   Poukisa Aysyin Kité Lakay-Yo: You ankèt sou ti ayisyn Nouyok. No. 9, New York.
Sowell, Thomas
1981   *Ethnic America*. New York: Basic Books.
Sudama, T.
1983   Class, race and the state in Trinidad and Tobago. *Archipelago*. Pp. 9–47.
Takaki, Ronald
1979   *Iron cages: Race and culture in 19th century America*. New York: A. Knopf.
1987   *From different shores: Perspectives on race and ethnicity in America*. New York: Oxford University Press.
Thomas, M. and M. Hughes
1986   The continuing significance of race: A study of race, class and quality of life in America 1972–1985. *American Sociological Review* 51:830–841.
Thompson, E. P.
1963   *The making of the English working class*. New York: Pantheon Books.
Trouillot, Michel-Rolph
1986   *Les racines historiques de l'état duvalièrien*. Port-au-Prince: Editions Deschamps.
Unity
1976   No. 30. New York City.
Verdieu, Ernst.
1973a   Notes sur la communaute haïtienne de New York. *Sèl* 9:27–31;
1973b   Aspects culturels de l'immigration. *Sèl* 10:46–55.
Voltaire, Frantz, Ed.
1988 [1976] *Pouvoir noir en Haïti*, 2nd edit. Montreal: CIDHICA.
Williamson, J. R.
1971   Black self-assertion before and after emancipation. In *Key issues in Afro-American experiences*, edited by N. Huggins, M. Kilson, and D. M. Fox. New York: Harcourt Brace. Vol. 1: 213–240.
Willie, C. V., Ed.
1979   *The caste and class controversy*. New York: General Hall Inc.
Wilson, W. J.
1980   *The declining significance of race*, 2nd edit. Chicago: University of Chicago Press.
1987   *The truly disadvantaged: The inner city, the underclass, and public policy*. Chicago: University of Chicago Press.
Wynter, Sylvia
1979   Sambos and minstrels. *Social Text* 1:149–156.

Limits to Cultural Accumulation: Chinese Capitalists on the American Pacific Rim

AIHWA ONG

Department of Anthropology
University of California
Berkeley, California 94720

In Northern California, the so-called "Hong Kong money elite" resides in an exclusive community on the flank of the Peninsula mountain range. All homes in Peninsula Peak (a pseudonym) cost over a million dollars. The choicest houses are set into the sides of the hills, with mountains as a backdrop, and a view of the Bay. The *feng-sui* (geomancy) is excellent. In Southern Chinese folklore, mountain ranges are inhabited by dragons, mythical creatures highly valued for their natural strength and energy, and association with royalty and ancestors. Seeking to tap these riches, wealthy Hong Kong emigrés have crossed the Pacific to make this former white enclave their new home.

Initially led by real estate agents, and later by word of mouth, the influx of wealthy Chinese has spread to suburban communities in the Bay Area. They account for fifteen percent of Peninsula Peak's population, which is around 10,000 (McLeod 1989:C6-1). Large mansions in an Asian-Mediterranean style stand on the brow of the ridges, amidst clearings where few trees remain unfelled. Many of these houses were paid for with hard cash, sometimes before the arrival of their occupants. In March, 1990, one such home was hosting a fund raiser for a prominent Chinese-American Democrat incumbent in the state government. Cars parked on the windy road included ten Mercedes Benzs, a couple of Rolls Royces, BMWs, and one Jaguar. There was also a Volvo, and two Japanese cars, one of them mine. Though all were fluent in English, practically everyone spoke Cantonese, and we could have been at an exclusive gathering in Hong Kong.

» «

From its founding in 1829, Hong Kong has been a transit point for refugees and monetary exchange. It is today the third largest financial center in the world, after New York and London. In the past decade, the emergence of a significant number of affluent Chinese communities in Southeast Asia and in the wider Asian Pacific Rim region has produced "a global network of Chinese communities" doing business with each other all over the world (Skeldon 1989:25; see also Goldberg 1985). The growth of this trans-Pacific Chinese capitalist class is a result of their localized commercial activities as well as their strategies of accumulation and investments internationally. Since the mid-1970s, Hong Kong had produced textiles, garments, electronics goods, and such for world consumer markets. Further capital accumulation entails shifting from manufacturing to real estate and the service industries, where the rate of profit returns is higher. The booming business environment is such that despite the return to mainland Chinese rule in 1997, the Hong Kong government has plans for a new container port and airport. Jan Morris notes, "But then, almost nothing has not been proposed, at one time or another, for the making of money in Hong Kong. The chief strength of this economy has always been its flexibility" (1989:197).

The risk-taking and flexibility of Hong Kong entrepreneurs must qualify the popular view that emigrants and "capital flight" are solely caused by the impending communist takeover. Indeed, the South China diaspora dating from the last century must be the historical context to view this latest wave of outmigration.[1] More specifically, the strategies of emigrating capitalists should be viewed in terms of the changing conditions of "flexible accumulation" in the world economy (see Harvey 1989:147–152). Harvey argues that since the 1970s, capitalism has become globalized through innovative financial practices. As securities were traded 24 hours, "flexible responses in labor markets, labor processes, and consumer markets" greatly increased (1989:159). These conditions favor the geographical dispersal, small-scale production, and the pursuit of special markets in a highly uncertain competitive environment. Furthermore, satellite communications facilitate swift decision-making, information access and data analysis, allowing centralized co-ordination of far flung corporate interests. For the first time, relatively small family enterprises can enter into a truly global arena once the exclusive preserve of large corporations.

» «

In keeping with Chinese tradition, the overwhelming majority of companies in Hong Kong are family-owned. Over the past decade, as many new

---

[1] The current relocation of Chinese capitalists to Western metropolitan countries should be viewed in the historical context of the South China diaspora. Since the mid-19th century, Chinese merchant families have combined profit-making and Western cultural practices in successful trade ventures. Since the 18th century, outmigration from Southern China has been a continual process. Chinese peasants from Kwantung and Fukien migrated in large numbers to areas opening up to capitalist development mainly in colonial Southeast Asia, but also across the Pacific to North America (Chan 1986; Chen Ta 1939; Freedman 1959; Purcell 1951). Throughout Southeast Asia, Chinese entrepreneurs control major businesses like rice milling and rubber production (Omohundro 1981; Skinner 1957; T'ien 1953; Wertheim 1964) and increasingly light manufacturing, lumbering, the hotel industry and finance (Lim & Gosling 1983). By the 1970s, the number of Chinese capitalists has grown, and they have begun to invest heavily in the wider Asia-Pacific region (Inglis & Wu 1990; Kwok 1987; Watson 1975; S-L. Wong 1988).

family fortunes were being made in the booming Hong Kong economy, family firms began to look outside the colony to diversify their portfolios. Entrepreneurs anywhere recognize that economies have merged ("globalized") to such an extent that investment decisions must be made in the global context. Although Hong Kong investors can make money faster locally (Millard 1989:33), they increasingly turn to American and European markets, the site of longer range plans.[2] Such financial expansion abroad provided the main point of entry for Chinese capital into the San Francisco Bay Area (Walker *et al.*, 1990:12).

This paper looks at Hong Kong emigrants in terms of their strategies of accumulation in a cultural as well as an economic sense. What is often missing in accounts of migration experiences is the necessity for the adoption of at least some cultural forms associated with the host society. I argue that the effectiveness of Hong Kong emigrants in their overseas ventures is conditional upon their acquisition of appropriate "symbolic capital" (Bourdieu 1984). Bourdieu maintains that the accumulation and display of certain credentials, luxury goods and social trappings are practices attesting to the social distinction of the owner. For the emigrant, the kinds of symbolic capital to be acquired must have recognition and value, and not only in the country of origin and the country of destination, but especially in the transnational spaces in which the paths of emigrants and local residents intersect in daily life. Whether in Hong Kong, London, Berlin, Sydney, Tokyo, New York, or San Francisco, transnational arenas are places where competing hierarchies of cultural distinction assess the symbolic worth of locals and newcomers. To operate effectively in a transnational setting, ambitious emigrants must acquire some of the signs and values of distinction as set by the local cultural elite. Although there is substantial overlap in the symbols of distinction in the "global cultural economy" (Appadurai 1990) of capitalism[3] – for example, the snob value of a Harvard M.B.A. or a Rolex watch – different societies or locales have particularized symbolic systems of good taste and prestige (Bourdieu 1980), so that, for instance, flaunting one's business degree may be considered petit bourgeois rather than haute culture in Paris.

Chinese entrepreneurs in international settings have been viewed mainly as skillful "handlers of money" (Freedman 1959; see Watson 1967, Lim and Gosling 1983), but rarely as agents actively shaping self-identity in a globalized context. This paper looks at their "symbolic work"[4] of acquiring the signs

---

[2] Even before the early 1970s, wealthy Hong Kongers had sought overseas investments, mainly in the developing economies of Southeast Asia. Some capitalists, especially those who amassed huge fortunes in the 1970s, then turned to new opportunities in North America, Australia, Japan, and Europe.

[3] For Appadurai, "the global cultural economy" is shaped by the complex flows of cultural production and interactions, characterized more by disjunctures, overlaps, difference, and uncertainty than by homogenization.

[4] I borrow this phrase from Paul Willis, who defines "symbolic work" as "the application

and symbols of cultural distinction that is necessary to their class acceptance and reproduction across national boundaries. What are the connections between the cultural values in the global economy, and the cultural performance of citizenship in the host country? In the United States, how do these Hong Kong immigrants come to represent themselves, in relation to Chinese Americans, and to the dominant "Anglo"[5] capitalists?

FROM TREATY PORT MERCHANTS TO WORLD INVESTORS

In the 19th century, Hong Kong, together with Shanghai and other Treaty Ports, were sites in which European imperialists imposed Western standards of international mercantilism. Among the prominent merchant families, Fei (1946) notes an abandonment of Confucian ethics in favor of foreign practices:

> (T)o such ports a special type of Chinese was attracted. They are known as compradors. . . . They are half-cast in culture, bilingual in speech, morally unstable. They are unscrupulous, pecuniary, individualistic, and agnostic, not only in religion but in cultural values. Treaty ports . . . are a land where the acquisition of wealth is the sole motive, devoid of tradition and culture.

> (Nevertheless,) they occupy a strategic position in China's transition. . . . As their children grow up, they give them modern education and send them abroad to attend Western universities. From this group a new class is formed . . . But being reared in a cosmopolitan community, they are fundamentally hybrids. In them are [sic] manifest the comprador characteristic of social irresponsibility (1946:646–647).

While Fei considered the dual identity of the Chinese capitalists as detrimental for society, other scholars have seen it as instrumental in modernizing China. Nurtured in colonial enclaves, the "hybrid" or "modernized" offspring of compradors were viewed as leaders who might have brought about a capitalist revolution in twentieth century China (Wang 1981; Murphey 1974). Instead, civil war and the communist victory in mainland China caused a diaspora of millions of Chinese throughout the Pacific Asia region. Subsequently European colonialism and capitalism shaped the economic and cultural character of Southeast Asian Chinese-dominated communities. Cut off from the

---

of human capacities to and through, on and with symbolic resources and raw materials (collections of signs and symbols . . .) to produce meanings. This is broader than, logically prior to and a condition of material production, but its 'necessariness' has been forgotten" (1990:10).

[5] In parts of the South, and most of Southwestern and Western United States where Hispanic populations have settled, whites or Caucasians are generally referred to as "Anglos," or the dominant (sometimes in all but numerical aspects) group vis-à-vis racial "minorities." The latter are also collectively referred to as "ethnics" (which can include dominated whites) when cultural difference is stressed, or, signalling cultural opposition, as "people(s) of color."

ancestral homeland, and the social aspects of Confucianism, the Western-educated elites pursued narrow goals of acquiring wealth and international social forms.

Over the past two generations, the emergence of a capitalist class among "Overseas Chinese" in Southeast Asia[6] has made them an increasing presence in business arenas outside Asia. These Chinese professionals and capitalists are a historical first group to undertake significant investments in Western capitalist societies, especially those on the Pacific Rim like Australia and North America. This latest wave of Chinese diaspora is dialectically linked to the capitalist tendencies of globalization (see, *e.g.*, Goldberg 1985). World integration, and specifically the technological and informational revolution, induce a profound reorientation from the local towards the "global village." The interweaving of local and global worlds has produced among wealthy Chinese a combination of transnational expertise, on the one hand, and stress on local security (family, community) on the other.[7] Individuals acquire the professional and cultural skills to maneuver in global settings, but the family firm remains the vehicle par excellence for capital accumulation in the local and international realms. This mix of cultural strategies for operating in transnational capitalism fosters both the development of rampant individualism and stress on group security, coping strategies linked to the predicaments *and* opportunities generated by postmodern capitalism. As I will argue below, emigrant entrepreneurs are active self-making agents who operate in transnational and national cultural contexts; they become as much the products as the opportunists of flexible accumulation (Harvey 1989:171). Poised to go transnational at the same historical moment of communist takeover, Chinese investors become adept at converting potential disadvantages in one arena into capital in another.

CULTURE OF EMIGRATION

Seeking to capture such postmodern realities, anthropologists have focused on the dynamic exchanges and emerging cultural landscapes of transnational flows of culture (*e.g.*, Hannerz 1989; Appadurai 1990). Less attention has been paid to agents who are part of these flows, and must manage

[6] This term is a variant of the Chinese category *huaqiao*, and conventionally refers to Chinese communities in Southeast Asia. For a historical discussion of various labels used for emigrating Chinese, see Wang (1981). There is a large literature on Overseas Chinese; for major studies, refer to footnote 2.

[7] For years, scholars have emphasized the importance of family unity and stability among the Chinese, and the entrepreneurial competitiveness of Overseas Chinese. While the tendency has always been to attribute these qualities to some essential characteristic of Chinese culture, there has been little attempt to discuss how participation in changing local and global environments may weaken or strengthen the adoption of these cultural values.

the cross-currents of cultural winds at home, in transit, and upon arrival at what will perhaps be only a temporary place of residence. Indeed, for many in the ex-colonial developing world, the poor as well as the well-off, planning to emigrate can begin in grade school, or even earlier. For instances, thousands of pregnant Hong Kong women travel to Western countries to have their babies who will obtain a foreign passport at birth. As part of their early socialization, agents in these cultures of emigration acquire diverse cross-cultural forms as they envision and map out their life trajectories in the global arena.

For the Hong Kong emigrants seeking to participate in the wider world of capitalism dominated by Western forces, the first step towards the acquisition of culturally correct capital is choosing the right schools. Bourdieu proposes that there is "a very close relationship linking cultural practices . . . to education capital (measured by qualifications) and secondarily, to social origins (measured by father's occupation)" (1984:13). Chinese emigrants lack the racial and cultural origins that would make them blend easily into Western capitalist societies, and must seek a combination of educational and class capital to facilitate their maneuvers in transnational worlds of business.

The most successful of the Hong Kong emigrant entrepreneurs had their education in British prep schools, which inculcated certain aspects of upper class British behavior. For instance, the Diocesan Boys' School (DBS), Diocesan Girls' School (DGS), and St. Paul's (coeducational) were the few Hong Kong schools to which prominent families sent their children. There, they acquired the trappings of British public schools, as revealed in British-accented speech, a smart turnout, and a muted arrogance which prepared them for dealing with Western businessmen with a degree of ease that traditional Chinese entrepreneurs found hard to muster. Since the 1960s, limited university places in Hong Kong have compelled many ambitious Chinese students to seek higher education abroad. For the offspring of the wealthiest families, overseas education at a finishing school or college is de rigueur. A Hong Kong official estimates that about 30 percent of local students have some facility with the English language. These members of the new middle class are likely to be among those said to be "educated to emigrate," and the "yompies" (young outwardly mobile professionals) lamented by the local press and government.[8]

Trained to be "quick and receptive, truly the wards of liberal (British) Empire",[9] young Hong Kongers have often been at the forefront of outmigration, blazing the trail for eventual family emigration. Even in the 1960s, boys

[8] There are about 10,000 Hong Kong students in the United States alone (Skeldon 1989: 24). In the past, many returned to work in Hong Kong, but since the late 1980s, young white collar workers and professionals have become a significant part of the Hong Kong brain drain (see the *South China Morning Post*, from 1988 onwards).

[9] In her best imperialist manner, Jan Morris bemoans the impending fate of this new middle class when Hong Kong reverts to Chinese rule in 1997: "condemned perhaps in their maturity to the straight jacket of totalitarian thought, or the deadweight of a five-thousand-year intellectual backlog!" (1985:332).

in these elite prep schools provided the peer pressure and networks for each other to pursue further studies abroad. They shared information about U.S. education, passing around thumbed-over copies of *Lovejoy's Guide to US Colleges*, and, once admitted, recruited siblings and friends to the same colleges or nearby institutions of higher learning. California is a popular destination because of its Pacific Rim location, weather, and large Asian populations.

Where there are no traceable Chinese-American relatives, young men an women on student visas often represent the first step of emigration for their families. Thousands of Overseas Chinese have graduated from Californian universities with M.B.A.'s and Ph.D. degrees in the hard sciences. I was told repeatedly that Hong Kong students graduating from U.S. universities stay on to work, and after gaining a resident permit, begin to sponsor their family members for emigration. They mediate for relatives who cannot speak English, choose schools for younger siblings, and help invest family savings in the local real estate. The offspring of wealthy families become the conduit for capital exports, and the points of family business expansion in the United States. In one case, the eldest son of a Hong Kong developer, after getting his American M.B.A., set up the North American branch of his father's company in San Francisco. In this not uncommon strategy of family business expansion abroad, sons provide the modern expertise, and in their roles as managers and heirs, the continuity for family firms and therefore unity transnationally (see Ong, n.d.).

Beyond the attainment of internationally recognized credentials, the Hong Kong entrepreneur, usually male, must be concerned with the presentation of self (Goffman 1959), maneuvering from a British- to an American-dominated transnational setting. His symbolic work of self-reconstruction includes a reworking of his Chineseness, so as to project a persona readily accepted in international business situations. Post-colonial self-formation requires as much a process of decentering from one's roots as it did under colonialism, conducted as it is under the Orientalist eye. For the Hong Kong subject seeks not to return to the cultural motherland, but to join the transnational world of capitalism that developed under European hegemony. His British education has perhaps prepared the grounds for a Western body style and interpersonal skills in the English-speaking milieux. In the Central District of Hong Kong, young professionals dress in smart European and Japanese fashions, flaunting gold watches and expensive luggage. The wealthy are driven in air-conditioned Mercedes Benzs. The construction of a bureaucratic body and spirit (Goffman 1959:56) involves intense self- and mutual-scrutiny for minute, every shifting differentiation of taste and other class markers in particular cultural and time contexts. Skiing replaces golf as the latest foreign cultural fad; taking up rich white men's sports is a way of bridging the gap between local and internationalized cultures. The expensively turned-out body is also conspicuously exercised on behalf of corporate capitalism. The ambiance is one of controlled frenzy, as well-groomed men and women seem to be in constant movement and communication across town or across the world. Mobile phones proliferate, and are widely used in taxis and restaurants, and on sidewalks. These signs, symbols, and activities of acquired cultural capital are the circulating grammar of economic competence in the global cultural economy.[10]

The mix of Western educational capital and bureaucratic values signals an active process of self-making as Chinese entrepreneurs handle the risks and opportunities of transnationalism and citizenship in Western societies. In the North American economy, they must finesse their acquired transnational personae to meet the cultural demands of citizenship. Indeed, despite their small number, the image of capital-bearing Chinese immigrants has begun to change perceptions of Asian-Americans in California.

HONG KONG INVESTMENTS IN CALIFORNIA

United States laws have been a major influence on the uneven pattern of Chinese emigration, and more recently, investments, to the country. In 1965, U.S. immigration laws allowing "family reunification" provided a major opportunity for Overseas Chinese, and their capital, to flow towards the United States (Barringer 1990). Although the majority of Chinese immigrants have come from mainland China, many also hail from Hong Kong.[11] In 1990, almost nine thousand Hong Kongers emigrated to the United States, not counting students and visitors already here on other kinds of visas. The senate recently passed a bill to grant permanent visas to 10,000 Hong Kong residents a year (Prokesch 1990). Hong Kong investors in the Bay Area are but a small fraction of the influx. Most are green card carriers, and perhaps a third have become citizens.

The San Francisco Bay Area is home to one quarter of the nation's Asians (just under 10 million).[12] The historical connections with China and other parts of Asia have made it a favorite spot for Asian visitors and immigrants.

[10] My point is not that international cultural flows lead to homogenization of the world, a view Appadurai contests (1990), but that certain signs, symbols and attitudes have become modern badges of middle and upper middle class status transnationally. This essay will argue that in particular locales, and other spheres of people's daily life, the signs and symbols take on different, local meanings.

[11] Since 1990, over 1,000 emigrants a week have left Hong Kong. Most professionals and businessmen go to Canada and Australia, but many also opt for American cities. While most of the Chinese immigrants are working and middle class immigrants, the influx includes a high proportion of students, professionals and entrepreneurs. The exodus from Hong Kong to the West coast of North America is so great that it is referred to as "the China tide" (*zhong guo chao; Asia Newsweek*, April 16, 1990:42).

[12] Currently, in historically unprecedented number Asia has become the principal source of legal migrants (40% of the total) to North America.

There are daily flights to Hong Kong. Since the mid-1970s, Hong Kongers began investing in the Bay Area, buying residential and commercial properties as a means to diversify their portfolios overseas. One Hong Kong official compares buying properties in California to health insurance (Milliard 1989:31–32), since the United States provides a safe haven for their money and a good place to raise their children.

It is impossible to keep track of the inflow of Chinese capital. There is no foreign exchange control in Hong Kong; investors can just call and transport millions of dollars overnight. Many investors do not invest overseas in their own names. They go through a banker or investment company, or buy up a U.S. company to do business. Besides, in keeping with Chinese business practices, there is a wall of silence on the subject. A San Francisco Chinese lawyer who handles Hong Kong investments exclusively told me that even lawyers did not know the full extent of the clients assets. Earlier, wealthy Hong Kong families feared "loss of face" if known to be investing overseas. Besides, those trading with China also worried about Beijing's disapproval of their international investments. Keeping an eye on the bottom line, secrecy helped to minimize estate taxes. Another popular way to circumvent taxes was to form a British company that owned the U.S. property (see also Bales 1989:19). Finally, there is fear of backlash in the United States for being seen as a new form of "yellow peril" (see below). Thus, although the increasing presence of affluent Chinese households attests to their local investments, major business transactions amounting to hundreds of millions of dollars are invisible to the public. Secrecy, diversified portfolios, and front companies conceal an increasingly dense and complex network of Chinese capital in the United States.

For analytical purposes, there are two groups of investors: middle class and upper class family enterprises. Many middle class Hong Kongers came to California to join their relatives. For others, what began as overseas speculation in the 1970s became a search for stable investments and family residences by the late 1980s. Those investors with children in American schools and/or who are waiting to fulfill residency requirements are likely to buy houses. A Bay Area realtor reports that even a Hong Kong cook can pay up front for a $200,000 property in cash (Askin 1989). Others invest in shops, and small apartment and office buildings worth from $1 to $25 million (Totty 1987; Bales 1989). For instance, the recent Kong case, in which the Kongs disappeared after failing to pay hundreds of garment workers as well as real estate loans, reveals a popular strategy, though without the criminal infractions. They were reported to "own a portfolio of 15 pieces of property [in different cities], including four commercial stores, an office complex, six apartment houses, and an industrial building," in addition to two expensive homes (Wallace 1991: A16). Although most middle class investors operate on a more modest scale, the pattern and mix of acquisition reflects a preferred immigrant Chinese portfolio diversification. The goal is to capitalize on the real estate boom in the

Bay Area; that is, to follow the Hong Kong get-rich-quick formula which is also the "tried and true American road to wealth: real estate investment and landlordism" (Walker *et al.* 1990:23–24).[13]

The second group consists of big league investors, including the top sixty Hong Kong business families (each with capital assets of over 400 million). Since 1975, these families have sought in the United States steady income-producing investments over the long-term (Totty 1987:16). With their massive capital buildup, the California investments, in contrast to their Hong Kong properties, were made without any expectation for a quick return. In the Bay Area, they seek urban renewal projects and suburban developments, many of which serve an increasingly Pacific Rim clientele. Even local restrictions on high rises are considered an opportunity that will enable them to recoup their real estate investments in hotels, office and condo buildings in the long run. It is widely estimated that by the early 1980s, Hong Kong money came to control about ten percent of the San Francisco downtown area (Millard 1989:32). Much of the investments were made through intermediaries, while the company head quarters and owners remained in Hong Kong. The more visible aspect of their investments are classy Chinese restaurants and hotels, as well as storefronts selling T-shirts and cameras, giving rise to fears of what the columnist Herb Caen calls the "Hongkongization" of San Francisco. Altogether, the local Hong Kong business association reports at least 54 major Hong Kong companies and a membership list of over 1,500. In total, Overseas Chinese are said to have invested anywhere from $2 to $10 billion throughout California.

CULTURAL CITIZENSHIP AND THE LIMITS OF CULTURAL ACCUMULATION

When was the last time . . . fabulously rich people, talented, with
their families, were looking to live and work in your city?
Hong Kong-born banker

Coming to the Bay Area, Hong Kong entrepreneurs suddenly find themselves viewed as members of an "ethnic" (not nationality) group. As extremely class conscious subjects, they are offended by the popular American view of Chinese as laundry or restaurant workers. Their high social and economic profile in the Hong Kong world is often not immediately apparent to local residents. Thus, in order to reproduce their class privilege in the Bay Area, Hong Kong investors have to meet the cultural criteria of the local Anglo

---

[13] For a description of the political economy the San Francisco Bay Area in the 1980s, with its base in high tech manufacturing, blue chip finance, property boom, and recreation industries, see Walker *et al.*, 1990.

upper class. Such requirements of "cultural citizenship," as transmitted through institutions, the media, and popular culture, of course vary across class and racial groups. The languages of race, class and culture, while overlapping and shifting, have distinctive morphological and historical lineages. Thus, the Chinese entrepreneur immigrants have to contend with the historical perception of Asians in the United States, and the current politics of minority and class representations.

The history of the Chinese in California has been shaped by hegemonic constructions, ranging from 19th-century images of morally degraded coolies (Archdeacon 1983:147–8; Chan 1986) to the current epithet of the "model minority." While the earlier stereotype was used to exclude Chinese immigrants, the current one is a cultural requirement of belonging as law-abiding and productive members of the middle class.[14] The historical perception of Chinese as a laboring class vies with the more contemporary image of horn-rimmed highly trained technicians, making their cultural acceptance by the dominant Anglo society a qualified one. Furthermore, the "model minority" image of Asians as politically subordinate is reinforced by academic representation of recent immigrants as poor and powerless groups (see *e.g.*, Foner 1987). While the Hong Kong entrepreneurs may benefit from the image of technical competence, they wish to gain social prestige and political power traditionally not associated with Asian-Americans.

However, Hong Kong immigrants seeking to break into the highest social circles encounter limits to their attempts at flexible cultural accumulation. Their class distinction, as displayed in consumer objects, university degrees, and a jet-setting life is not sufficient to attract the embrace of the local white upper classes. A Hong Kong-born developer complains "We have the qualifications to compete. But it'll take a few more generations to crack the old boy network. Meantime, we're creating our own network" (Itow 1987:D-5). The buzz word used is "glass ceiling," a term more often applied to women and middle class minority professionals whose rise in corporations are obstructed

[14] The Chinese have always had a tenuous presence in California. They were excluded as a racial group in the Chinese Exclusion Act of 1882. In 1924, an immigration law established a restrictive quota on immigrants from outside the Western Hemisphere. Only the end of racial exclusion in 1943 allowed for the formation of stable Chinese communities (Chen 1981:160–178). The decades in between saw a cowed Chinese population confined to their businesses in Chinatown, while second, and third generations moved to the suburbs, becoming acculturated in speech and behavior, to the wider society. In the 1960s, the Civil Rights Movement inspired college-educated Chinese Americans to found social service agencies to help Chinese and other Asian poor and newcomers whose numbers increased rapidly after 1965. Groups like Chinese for Affirmative Action appeared to watch for and protest all kinds of discrimination against Asians. Such political activism was not well received by the old Chinatown leadership. Merchants founded home country district associations, collectively referred to as Six Companies, confined themselves to affairs within Chinatown, trying to be good citizens keeping out of trouble with the wider authorities. After 1965, the influx of students from Taiwan and Hong Kong, many of whom stayed on as professionals, has created a new Asian-American middle class whose interests are not represented by the old Chinatown leadership.

by an invisible barrier of discrimination. Other wealthy entrepreneurs complain about "hitting a wall," for the obstruction is to movement both vertical and lateral; they feel excluded from business contracts and exclusive neighborhoods, but also from the major cultural events linked with the city's white upper crust. Another Hong Kong investor warns:

> If the established SF power doesn't invite us to their [opera] balls, we have our own balls. They don't want to do business with us, we do business among ourselves. If they don't let us into Pacific Heights, we create our own Chinatown. (Calandra and Matier 1989a:A6)

The Hong Kong entrepreneurs thus retreat into their own exclusive networks and clubs, attempting to recreate the elite circles of their homeland in the Peninsula. Their Hong Kong alma maters provide important networks for linking up with other affluent Chinese immigrants, and together with the founding of other social clubs, create a sense of security and solidarity in their upper class enclave.

In the emerging post-colonial Hong Kong, only the rise of a significant number of Chinese capitalists has occasionally breached class barriers; the imperial, racial domination remains. For generations, colonial educational policy excluded instruction on politics and Chinese history, for fear of inciting social upheaval. The focus of education was the trades and professional skills. In recent decades, a few members of the industrial and commercial elite have been invited to serve on the legislative and executive councils, as well as on advisory boards (see also Wong 1986:130–31). Isolated by their wealth and power from the ordinary people, the affluent families pursued their own interests, with the assumption that these coincided with those of the general population. A Hong Kong official reports that the scion of a powerful family in a recent speech declared that democracy "consists of the rule by the controllers of wealth." This principle of rule by the wealthiest reflects the view that capitalists have an automatic claim to community leadership, and that it is quite the thing to do to play 'money politics'–or using wealth to gain access to political influence and appointments.

In a society that concentrates on making wealth, few came to acquire a deep understanding of politics and high culture. Indeed, a British civil servant from Hong Kong notes that when Chinese entrepreneurs fail to buy whatever they want, they complain about the glass ceiling; "that is their way of saying 'I am culturally inadequate'" in the United States. His disdain reflects on the consequences of neo-colonial policies which have created the investors' cultural dilemma; it is also an instance of the transnational racial hierarchy shared by the Californian upper class that perceives the Chinese, no matter how rich or educated, as second class world citizens.[15] Thus hampered by the limits to

[15] A historical antecedent is the white upper class discrimination against wealthy cosmopolitan Jews, a topic extensively dealt with in American novels and the theatre.

cultural accumulation, Hong Kong investors seek alliances with local politicians in the hope that business contracts will be forthcoming.

Most of the immigrant investors arrived at about the time that West coast city politicians began turning to "the Pacific Rim" for trade and resources. The new mayors of San Jose and San Francisco started their tenures by courting and competing for the favors of the top Hong Kong families. In the 1987 Art Agnos campaign for mayor of San Francisco, the Hong Kong elite contributed a quarter of a million dollars. Although most of them have the freewheeling style of Republican capitalists, they have chosen to support Democrat Agnos for his liberal stance towards "Asian-Americans."[16] In return, for the first time in the city's history, a number of seats on City commissions were awarded to Chinese. Although the appointments to the various commissions were made in the name of representing ethnic diversity in the city, most of them went to rich and recent immigrants who barely represented the interests of the wider "Asian-American" community. A Hong Kong investor boasts, "I think that (the mayor) thinks, 'This is my Asian connection. It's in my pocket.' That's okay." But members of the Chinatown community feel differently. A Chinese community activist charges that the Hong Kong entrepreneurs are making "political alliances to enhance business opportunities," rather than representing the interests of grocers, butchers, shopkeepers and waiters in Chinatown (Calandra and Matier 1989a:A6). It is widely believed that the commissioners use their influence to gain information and contacts that will benefit their own Hong Kong business interests and those of their friends, while drawing "Pacific Rim" money into the city's coffers. Furthermore, the Hong Kong entrepreneurs have gained control of the Chinatown-based Chinese Chamber of Commerce, which was a vehicle for representing the interests of small groceries, restaurants, and gift shops. From a base in this constituency, the investors claim to be spokesmen for the Chinese/Asian community at large. Albert Chou,[17] the son of a real estate tycoon in Hong Kong, explains that the "money politics" maneuvers are justified on the grounds that there has not been enough "Asian-American" representation in city institutions:

> I don't know if there is really a real vision or some grand strategy [among Hong
> Kong entrepreneurs]. . . . What is happening though is a large group of Chinese feel that we have got to be a little more visible and play a larger role in local politics. We just want to be members of the local community. I don't think we will ever be the major player. We may be one of several major players.

---

[16] More recently, Chinese Americans, most of them immigrants, contributed over one million dollars to the campaign of the Republican Wilson for Governor of California, which he won in 1991. It appears that the influence of wealthy Chinese immigrants is shifting Asian-American support towards any candidate who is perceived as pro-Asian-American, regardless of party affiliation, although most wealthy Asians express Republican sentiments.

[17] A pseudonym, like other personal names in the text.

In numerous conversations with me, the investors imply that if the local elite finds them objectionable on racial or cultural grounds, they find their "Pacific Rim" money less objectionable. For instance, a banker Ian Mak sees money politics as a way to make their wealth accessible to a Northern Californian society still unaware of the depth of its future dependency on Asian economies. Because of mayoral pressure, Ian Mak is one of three Chinese (all from Hong Kong) recently appointed to the board of the San Francisco Chamber of Commerce. He lectures:

> A vibrant city like Manhattan, Los Angeles, when they are booming like crazy, they need the kind of diversity and new money coming in. . . . [It's a matter of] whether [Northern Californians] realize what they have to change in order to become international. . . . [If they] realize they are losing a lot of market shares to Los Angeles, and they want to do something bigger . . . [they will] have to be far more international. . . . it is not a question of whether they want to accept or resist Asians, it is [a question of] if one changes then the economic success of the Asian countries provides the most ready answer.

He notes further that much as the local elite may desire European investments, the reality is that the Japanese and Chinese are the major players in California. The state's future is linked more closely to the Pacific Rim economies than to Europe's.

Other Hong Kong entrepreneurs point out that their investments in rundown parts of the city have contributed to urban renewal, creating jobs where none existed before. They refer to the building of malls, housing tracts, shops and hotels. They see themselves as increasingly indispensable, and especially as leaders to the diverse Asian populations in California. A major hotelier Kenny Pao cites his own support of projects for poor Cambodians and Vietnamese in the inner-city neighborhood adjoining his hotel. He did not mention his protracted battle with his own hotel staff, one quarter of which is Asian, to prevent union formation. Again, the model of social organization is one of limited democracy, with the capitalist as leader. He expresses a view of the Chinese entrepreneur as a patriarch of his company, and by extension, of the poorer segments of society:

> If you believe in me you can believe in the next 20 or 30 years. As a foundation, (workers) don't have to worry about job security . . . jumping ship to another company to get a promotion, because if we keep the right guidelines for the company to grow then they don't have to worry about so much politics and bureaucracy within the organization.

He maintains that Asians "are all the same" in terms of having cultural values like diligence, frugality, and strong family unity. For emigrant capitalists like him, the projection of a Pan-Asian, homogenized Asian population in California strengthens their control of property values and labor transnationally. This fact is not lost on middle class workers who blame the activities of developers for the expensive real estate and crowded living conditions, making

San Francisco an American counterpart to Hong Kong. Pao's family has invested heavily in Northern Californian cities on the certainty that Anglo and African-American leaders "recognize they will have to rely on Asians to continue to give momentum to California in the next decade or two."

While most Hong Kong immigrants stress instrumental values as investors and professionals, the more ambitious find it necessary to engage in a cultural performance of citizenship. Hong Kong entrepreneurs have acquired the economic and educational trappings of the model minority, but, in order to break through the barriers of class exclusion, they must cultivate white upper class tastes and practices. A few affluent Hong Kong immigrants have boldly entered white old money domains through participation in exclusive institutions and even through marriage. For instance, Linda Yang, daughter of a Shanghai industrialist, graduate of Berkeley and the University of Colorado, and an investor in her own right, married the scion of a wealthy San Francisco family. Following Bourdieu (1980:13), "cultural competence" refers to the informed appreciation of a work of art that one has acquired through education or the appropriate social and class background. Many of the immigrant investors have been trained in Hong Kong and in the United States to be technically competent in the business world, not in the humanities or arts. Their tastes run along lines of "The Blue Danube," Hong Kong movies, and television soap operas. In the cosmopolitan world, their cultural competence is mainly expressed in the consumption of international name brands in clothing, cars, and other personal possessions. However, through large financial contributions (which are tax deductible) to elite cultural institutions, a few Hong Kong investors demonstrate a cultural competence they may or may not actually possess. Here again, the mayor's debt becomes useful in supporting the nomination of "Asian-Americans" for the boards of the city's cultural centers. Kenny Pao and another Hong Konger are the first "Asian-Americans" to attain seats on the board of the San Francisco Symphony. Only one appreciates classical music, and he earnestly feels that Chinese philanthropy should be increased outside Chinatown. By sitting on the boards of high cultural institutions, Hong Kong capitalists can "give back" to society some of the benefits they have enjoyed in the United States. Other institutions like music and ballet schools, as well as the museums, are also seeking members of the Hong Kong money elite in their rather belated attempts to seek "ethnic diversity." Kenny Pao and Linda Yang have separately expressed an interest that their patronage will promote more "Asian art" in the institutions' programs. Such acts of cultural investments are directed at gaining the social approval of the city's white fathers through an identification with upper class philanthropy directed towards "the arts," and not to build prestige from supporting ethnic-based organizations.[18] In the process of demonstrating

[18] A Hong Kong architect, who made a fortune in California real estate, is an exception. He is a strong supporter of the Asian-American film and theatre movement.

their cultural competence, the affluent emigrants hope to become more accept-
able to Northern Californian elites, and perhaps reproduce their privileged
class status locally.

The recent influx of Hong Kong capitalists has changed the meaning of
the model minority from one that is benign to an image that is aggressive and
even sinister. The conspicuous consumption, real estate investments, and
prominent cultural patronage by Hong Kong immigrants have collectively
changed the wider American view of Asian-Americans. A prominent Chinatown activist declares that there is a shift of image from "the old lady garment
worker" to "the wealthy, well-educated entrepreneur," a change of perception
that, in her view, is critical for the political ascendancy of the Chinese in
America. However, the transformation from a feminized, weak image to a mas-
culinized, entrepreneurial one has engendered envy and anger. Protests against
"rich Asians" have increased in the Bay Area. Although Japanese corporations
are the biggest investors in California, few affluent Japanese, unlike the Chinese,
choose to reside in California. In a radio call-in show on Hong Kong investors,
white and African-American callers complained of Asians driving up real estate
prices, constructing ugly buildings, and cutting down trees. They want the
immigrants to "go home." Other complaints implied that the Chinese developers were dishonest, buying political influence when most Americans earned
their wealth and power through sheer hard work (Calandra and Matier
1989c).[19] The emergent image of Chinese Americans as greedy capitalists is
also being explored by some Asian-American writers (see *e.g.*, Jen 1991). By
buying power and advancing their own interests, and claiming to represent
all Asian-Americans, they are operating in a time-honored American tradition
of pursuing group interests. Attempts by nouveau riche immigrants (although
a few of the investors are Hong Kong old money) to break into American
upper class society are not historically unprecedented, and if they stumble,
the charge of racism to some extent masks the perception of their "cultural
incompetence" as an elite group.

» «

The Westward dispersal of Hong Kong capitalists is connected to the
changing conditions of global capitalism and late modernity. Emigrants are
engaged in fabricating cultural personae that can operate effectively in the
transnational economic arena, while their strategy of cultural accumulation
seeks to reproduce their high social status overseas. In California, Chinese investors use wealth, political alliances, and the cultural patronage of "high culture" institutions to transform old racial categories into new ones of higher

---

[19] There are overtones of the "Fu Manchu" caricature in the following statements. After a
series of articles appeared in San Francisco papers on wealthy Chinese investors, the journalist
was urged by the representative of a Hong Kong business family to stop writing about the subject
in the future, for fear of enflaming American residents further.

symbolic value. They soon discover that just as there are limits to flexible accumulation in business, so there are limits to cultural accumulation. Chinese immigrants deploying cultural forms not considered as "belonging" to their ethnic group cannot easily convert such symbolic capital into high social standing in Anglo circles. Their cultural performances as a new faction of the social elite are discredited by a perceived difference in their "money politics," their accent, and the color of their skin. A frustrated investor told me, "They [the Anglos] want your Pacific Rim money, but they don't want you." Nevertheless, the continuing influx of affluent Chinese immigrants[20] has begun a process that will change the way Asian-Americans negotiate their relations with the wider society. At least on the West coast, their economic importance will bring about new alignments with Anglo elites, and will significantly condition American class, cultural, and racial formations in the coming "Pacific century."

ACKNOWLEDGMENTS

Thanks to Paul Rabinow for his valuable comments. I also benefited from remarks by Gerald Sider and other participants in the workshop on Transnational Migration, held by The New York Academy of Sciences on May 3–4, 1990.

REFERENCES CITED

Appadurai, Arjun
    1990   Disjuncture and difference in the global cultural economy. *Public Culture 2(2)*:1–24.
Archdeacon, Thomas, J.
    1983   *Becoming American: An ethnic history.* New York: The Free Press.
Askin, M.
    1989   SF real estate firms reaching asian investors. *Asian Week,* October 29:12.
Bales, K. A.
    1989   Real estate development: Hong Kong's growing stake in America. *Pacific Rim Business Digest,* April:19.
Barringer, F.
    1990   US Asian population up 70% in 80's. *The New York Times* (national ed.) March 2:A12.

[20] If American residents have misgivings about the influx of immigrant investors, politicians do not. Recently, a new immigration law was promulgated to award green cards to investors who invest $1 million or more while creating at least ten jobs. The goal is to compete with Australia and Canada for the world's capital flight, much out of Hong Kong (Valeriano 1991:B1). The new program can be expected to draw $4 billion annually in foreign investments while creating as many as 40,000 jobs a year (*ibid.*) The California state government expects to snare the lion's share of the investments (Leung 1991:A1).

Bourdieu, Pierre
  1980   *Distinctions: The cultural construction of taste.* Cambridge, MA: Harvard University Press.
Calandra, Thom and Phillip Matier
  1989a A new money elite. *San Francisco Examiner*, August 20:A1,A12–A14.
  1989b Asian influence comes of age. *San Francisco Chronicle*, August 21:A1,A6–A8.
  1989c The Griffin show (call-in radio program) News 74, KCBS Radio Station, September 3.
Chan, Sucheng
  1986   *This bitter-sweet soil: The Chinese in California agriculture, 1860–1910.* Berkeley: University of California Press.
Chen, Kathy
  1991   Hong Kong's frequent-flyer "astronauts," *San Francisco Examiner, Sunday Punch*, January 6:4.
Chen Ta
  1939   *Emigrant communities in South China.* Shanghai: Kelly & Walsh.
Fei Hsia Tung
  1953 [1946]   Peasantry and gentry: an interpretation of Chinese social structure and its changes. *American Journal of Sociology*, pp. 1–17; reprinted in *Class, status and power*, edited by E. Bendix and S. M. Lipset. Glencoe, IL: The Free Press (1953 ed.) Pp. 646–647.
Foner, Nancy, Ed.
  1987   *New immigrants in New York.* New York: Columbia University Press.
Freedman, M.
  1959   The handling of money: A note on the background to the economic sophistication of the Overseas Chinese. *Man (o.s.)19*:64–65.
Goffman, Erving
  1959   *The presentation of self in everyday life.* New York: Anchor Books.
Goldberg, Michael
  1985   *The Chinese connection: Getting plugged into Pacific Rim real estate, trade and capital markets.* Vancouver: University of British Columbia Press.
Hannerz, Ulf
  1989   Notes on the global ecumene. *Public Culture 1(2)*:66–75.
Harvey, David
  1989   *The condition of postmodernity.* New York: Basil Blackwell.
Inglis, Christine and Chung-Tong Wu
  1990   The 'new' migration of Asian skill in the Asia-Pacific region: Its implications in theory and research. In *Patterns of Migration in Southeast Asia*, edited by Robert R. Reed. Center for South and Southeast Asia Studies, Occasional Paper no. 16, University of California at Berkeley.
Itow, Karen
  1987   Hong Kong's quiet Bay Area presence. *San Francisco Examiner* June 7:D1,D5
Jen, Gish
  1990   *Typical American.* New York: Houghton-Mifflin.
Kwok, Peter
  1987   *The new Chinatown.* New York: The Noonday Press.
Leung, J.
  1991   California tries to lure rich Asian immigrants. *San Francisco Chronicle*, February 11:A1,A19.
Lim, Linda and Peter Gosling, Eds.
  1983   *The Chinese in Southeast Asia. Vol. 1: Ethnicity and economic activity.* Singapore: Maruzen Press.

McLeod, R.
  1991   Ethnic racial diversity in Bay Area. *San Francisco Chronicle*, February 27:B1.
Millard, M.
  1989   Hong Kong investors in the Bay Area. *San Francisco Business*, February:31–33.
Morris, Jan
  1989   *Hong Kong.* New York: Vintage.
Murphey, Rhoades
  1974   The treaty ports and China's modernization. In *The Chinese city between two worlds*, edited by Mark Elvin and William Skinner. Stanford, CA: Stanford University Press.
Omohundro, John T.
  1981   *Chinese merchant families in Iloilo.* Athens: The Ohio University Press.
Ong, Aihwa
  n.d.   *Chinese family and class formation in the post-colonial diaspora.* Unpublished manuscript.
Prokesch, S.
  1990   Few willing to help British help Hong Kong emigrants. *New York Times National Edition*, March 6:A9.
Skeldon, R.
  1989   South China pilgrims. *Far Eastern Economic Review*, July 27:24–25.
Skinner, G. William
  1957   *Chinese society in Thailand: An analytical history.* Ithaca, NY: Cornell University Press.
T'ien, J.K.
  1953   *The Chinese of Sarawak: A study of social structure.* London: LSE Monograph Series.
Totty, P.
  1987   The Yen for Bay Area Real Estate. *Square Footage*, Summer/Fall:12–22.
Valeriano, L.
  1991   Green-card law means business to immigrants. *Wall Street Journal*, February 21:B1–2.
Walker, Dick and the Bay Area Study Group
  1990   The playground of US capitalism? The political economy of the San Francisco Bay Area in the 1980s. In *Fire in the hearth: The radical politics of place in America*, edited by M. Davis *et al.* London: Verso. Pp. 3–79.
Wallace, Bill
  1991   Workers left holding the bag: Sudden bankrupcy means no jobs and no last paychecks. *San Francisco Chronicle*, July 23:A.16.
Wang Gungwu
  1981   Southeast Asia *Hua-Chiao* in Chinese History Writing. *Journal of Southeast Asian Studies* 22(1):1–14.
Watson, James
  1975   *Emigration and the Chinese lineage: The Mans in Hong Kong and London.* Berkeley: University of California Press.
Wertheim, W. F.
  1964   The trading minorities in Southeast Asia. In *East-West parallels: Sociological approaches to modern Asia*, edited by W. F. Wertheim. The Hague: W. Van Hoeve Ltd. Pp. 39–82.
Willis, Paul
  1990   *Common culture.* Boulder, CO: Westview.
Wong Siu-Lin
  1988   *Emigrant entrepreneurs: Shanghai industrialists in Hong Kong.* Hong Kong: Oxford University Press.

Multiple Layers of Time and Space: The Construction of Class, Ethnicity, and Nationalism among Portuguese Immigrants

BELA FELDMAN-BIANCO

Universidade Estadual de Campinas
Instituto de Filosofia e Ciências Humanas
Cidade Universitária "Zeferino Vaz"
Caixa Postal 6110
Campinas/SP CEP 13081 Brazil

INTRODUCTION

Ever since the era of seafaring exploration in the fifteenth and sixteenth centuries, the world—rather than the nation-state—has been the spatial unit for the Portuguese. Starting with the voyages of discovery and the colonizing of new lands and later (since the nineteenth century) continuing with labor migration, the movement of people across the globe has been constitutive of the Portuguese experience.

Saudade, a word that originated in the sixteenth century[1] has been associated with the Portuguese unending wanderlust. While loosely translated as "longing" and "nostalgia," *saudade* is in fact a cultural construct that defines Portuguese identity in the context of multiple layers of space and (past) time.

On the one hand, on the level of the self or the person, *saudade* has been viewed as "the soul divided throughout the world,"[2] "the uprooted experience located between the desire of the future and the memories of the past,"[3] or simply as "the memories which touch a soul."[4] This dimension of *saudade*, referring to the symbolic representations and social practices of a time and space prior to emigration, further shapes regional identity.[5]

---

[1] For an etymological study of the origin of the word *saudade* the reader is referred to C.M. Vasconcelos, *A saudade portuguesa*, 2nd edition, Porto 1922.

[2] In D. L. Pereira da Costa and P. Gomes, *Introdução à saudade*, Lello & Irmão, Porto 1976, p. 81.

[3] Pereira da Costa and Gomes,[2] p. 112.

[4] As defined by a young Portuguese immigrant who attended my courses at the University of Massachusetts—Dartmouth.

[5] Definition based on my analysis of fieldwork data.

On the other hand, *saudade* as the collective memory of Portugal has been reconstituted as the essence of Portuguese national character and as the basis of the imagined political community.[6] Within that perspective, the collective temporal memory is invariably linked to the discovery era and to the subsequent history of immigration; while the collective spatial memory encompasses the explorations and the long separations from relatives around the world.

By focusing on the multiple layers of time and space of *saudade*, my aim in this paper is to contribute to the ongoing discussions of transnationalism and transmigration (Glick Schiller, Basch, and Blanc-Szanton, 1992, this volume; Basch, Glick Schiller, and Blanc-Szanton, n.d.; Kearney 1991). Towards that end, based on fieldwork research conducted in Portugal and New Bedford, a New England industrial city, I will: first, examine how the attempts made by Portugal's post-colonial state to create a global deterritorialized nation (Basch, Glick Schiller, and Blanc-Szanton 1991) encompassing its dispersed populations have been rooted in the reinvention of the collective memory of *saudade*; and, second, discuss how immigrants have differentially conceptualized *saudade* as the basis of their personal and collective identities in the context of their specific experiences at the intersection of Portuguese and American cultures.

From that view point, I will analyze the differential constructions of class, ethnicity, and nationalism of Portuguese immigrants against the background of changes in the global economy and of evolving Portuguese and American policies of control from the 1920s to the present. Two distinct periods in this process of identity construction will be delineated.

In the first period—beginning in the 1920s and 1930s, a period of world economic depression—the Portuguese migrants were subjected to restrictive immigration laws and second-class citizenship status both in the United States and Portugal. In addition, they were faced with two conflicting and highly charged ideologies and were confronted with the state policies of two different nation states. On one side were the pressures of the U.S. "melting pot"–policies and ideologies that stressed the supremacy of American society and American ways of life. Conflicting with these were the Portuguese colonial policies and ideologies, based on the superiority and pride of the Luzitan race, which cast aspersions on those who left Portugal and emphasized the exclusive maintenance of Portuguese culture and language.

In the second period—the 1970s and 1980s—in the context of the increasing internationalization of the global economy, both the United States and Portugal changed their approach toward the Portuguese immigrant popu-

---

[6] B. Anderson, *Imagined communities: Reflections on the origin and spread of nationalism*. Verso, London/New York, 1983.

lation. In the United States cultural pluralism now prevailed, an ideology which recognized the persistence of Portuguese culture among immigrants but which continued to encourage their incorporation into the U.S. polity. Meanwhile, the Portuguese post-colonial state, broadening the constructs of "nation" and "nationality" gave immigrants dual citizenship rights and began to consider them "Portuguese spread around the world." In the end, the forms of control exercised by both the United States and Portugal over their migrant populations led to the politicization of ethnicity as well as to an intensification and redefinition of transnationalism.

By adopting the theoretical and methodological approaches outlined by Glick Schiller, Basch, and Blanc-Szanton (this volume), I seek to bring a historical dimension to the recent inquiries which have emphasized that immigrants are increasingly becoming transnationals "creating a single field of social action that merge the home and the host societies into a single construction."[7] Insofar as these findings are mostly an outcome of research conducted among the so-called "new immigrants" (like those from the Caribbean and South Asia), analysts have tended to limit the scope of their studies to a period characterized in the United States by the restructuring of "deindustrialization." While these "New Immigrants" have replaced the Europeans as the major labor pool in the United States, segments of the Portuguese migrant population have settled for several generations in New Bedford and the surrounding region. Since the 1920s, they have constituted the major ethnic group of the city, comprising today 60% of New Bedford's 110,000 inhabitants. The continuous renewal of Portuguese immigration to New Bedford allows, therefore, for a close examination of patterns of continuity and change between past and present migrations, particularly as it concerns the interrelationship between transnationalism and the construction (and reconstruction) of class, ethnicity and nationalism in the context of the creation of a "global" Portuguese nation.

When I first began my historical analysis, I found that I was confronted with a paradox: domestic structures indicated that in the past as in the present, the lived experiences of Portuguese migrants settling in New Bedford have tended to stretch between Portugal and the United States. In the context of this prevailing pattern, there has been since the late 1970s both an intensification of old and the emergence of new forms of transnationalism. Yet, my analysis of events at the grass-roots level, together with the delineation of the organization of the Portuguese settlement in New Bedford, led me to identify a simultaneous increase of their insularity as an ethnic enclave in the city. Although they may seem contradictory, the seemingly paradoxical trends can be shown to result from the same dynamic. The growing internationalization

---

[7] Glick Schiller, Basch, and Blanc-Szanton, pp. 1–24. This volume.

of the world economy is being accompanied by the re-imagining of political communities. These newly conceptualized political communities may be spatially dispersed. In any one locale the global trends may appear as a growing ethnic insularity. Thus, this paper is directed at unveiling this paradox in the context of a shifting world economy and of corollary Portuguese and American changing mechanisms of control of international migrants.

THE REINVENTION OF *SAUDADE* AND THE CREATION OF A PORTUGUESE "GLOBAL" NATION

At least since the advent of the Portuguese Republic in the nineteenth century, the concept of nation (including the construction of successive nationalisms) has been linked to Portugal's role during the seafaring era and to its (real or mythical, imperial or colonial) overseas dominions. Camões, the author of the *Lusiadas*, the epic poem of the discoveries, was turned into the mythical embodiment of the nation and of Luzitan patriotism. After the 1974 Portuguese revolution and the loss of the last overseas dominions, governmental officials began to shift away from ideologies which recurrently portrayed an image of "Portugal, the colonizer" and which glorified the "Luzitan race."[8] Yet, we will see that these experiences have been built upon by the Portuguese state. While there are plans to celebrate the Quincentennial of the Portuguese discoveries until the year 2,000, the image of Camões has become associated with an "Immigrant Portugal."[9] The Tenth of July, formerly known as "The Day of Portugal, Camões, and the Luzitan race" was reinvented as "The Day of Portugal, Camões, and the Portuguese communities" and, thereby, transformed into a celebration of the Immigrant Communities abroad.

According to a decree established in 1977,

This day, better than any other day assembles the necessary symbolism to represent the Day of Portugal. It harmoniously synthesizes the Portuguese

---

[8] For a detailed analysis of the relationship between *saudade* and the construction of the Portuguese nation, the reader is referred to E. Lourenço, *O labirinto da saudade*, Publicações D. Quixote, 1978.

Besides profiting from Lourenço's study, I further adopted Hobsbawm's formulation of "invented tradition" as ". . . a set of practices, normally governed by overtly or tacitly accepted rules and of a ritual or symbolic nature, which seek to inculcate certain values and norms of behavior by repetition, which automatically implies continuity with the past. In fact, where possible, they normally attempt to establish continuity with a suitable historic past." E. Hobsbawm, Introduction: Inventing traditions. In *The invention of tradition*, Cambridge University Press, 1983, p. 1.

[9] E. de Carvalho, *Os portugueses da Nova Inglaterra*. A Leitura Colonial, Rio de Janeiro 1931, p. 35.

nation, the Luzitan communities spread throughout the world and the emblematical figure of the genial epics.[10]

Thus, the immigrant communities spread around the world replaced the former colonial dominions in the new and expanded construction of a "global" Portuguese nation. In 1980, the then Minister Sá Carneiro defined Portugal as a populous nation scattered over the four corners of the earth, stating that

> We can only survive, we can only believe in Portugal and in Portugal's future if we think of ourselves as a nation that embraces both residents and non-residents, all treated equally.[11]

Upon Portugal's entrance into the European Community, in conformity with the emerging construction of a "global" nation, emigrants were given dual citizenship status, including voting rights. In a meeting of the Council of Europe Dr. Manuela Aguiar justified this broader construction of nationality in the following terms:

> Migration and changing countries of residence originate new connections, new bounds and new loyalties. But this does not mean that the deep roots that bind the individuals to the land and culture of their fathers do not continue to be the structural element of their identity. For the individuals, the main thing is to be doubly accepted and wanted because they accept and love two countries. It will therefore be of advantage for the states to regulate with one another the consequences of such twofold links.[12]

The creation of a Portuguese global nation reflects dramatic redefinitions of emigration policies. At least until the 1940s, emigrants—considered second class citizens—were defined as "those passengers traveling second and third class by boat." Even after that definition was abolished, Portuguese officials still continued to consider emigration a "necessary evil" and to view illegal migration as a serious crime.[13] A major shift began to occur in the early 1960s,

---

[10] Quoted from the first Report of the Day of Portugal, Camões and the Portuguese Communities, 1977, p. 3 (author's translation).

[11] M. Aguiar, *Política de emigração e comunidades portuguesas*, Secretaria do Estado das Comunidades Portuguesas, Centro de Estudios, Série Migrações, Política-Relações Internacionais, Porto, 1986, p. 7 (author's translation).

[12] M. Aguiar, Introdução á discussão sobre a dupla nacionaidade os imigrantes do ponto de vista de um pais de emigração, presented at a round table on immigrants' dual citizenship rights, Stockholm, September 6, 1985 (author's translation). In Aguiar.[11]

[13] A detailed analysis of Portuguese emigration rules and regulations are found in F. G. Cassola Ribeiro's works, as follows:
Emigração portuguesa: Regulamentação emigratória do liberalismo ao fim da Segunda Guerra Mundial. Contribuição para o seu estudo. Secretaria de Estado das Comunidades Portuguesas. Instituto de Apoio à Emigração e às Comunidades Portuguesas, Serie Migrações, Politica, Relações Internacionais, Porto, 1987.

when Portugal's colonial state, taking into account the prevailing international division of labor, recognized the need for developing emigration policies within the framework of labor policies. In 1965 the Portuguese government established a national employment service, which made the government itself in charge of the recruitment, placement, and return of migrant workers. Later, with Portugal's entrance in the European community, post-colonial governmental policies began to emphasize the human rights of laborers rather than the supply of labor. Furthermore, in preparation for the unification of Europe, the term "immigrant" was recently abolished and replaced by the expressions "Portuguese abroad" and "Portuguese spread around the world."

In the past, Portuguese immigrants were stigmatized and discriminated against. By designating immigrants as Portuguese abroad, the government recognized the transnational character of Portuguese immigration. However, in Portugal's everyday life, immigrants are still seen as individuals who have assimilated into the culture of the country to which they had immigrated. They are still pejoratively called "French," "Canadian," "Brazilians," "Americans." Yet, since the late 1970s (and particularly since the early 1980s), along with their newly acquired full dual citizenship rights, Portuguese immigrants (or better, the Portuguese abroad) have a dual responsibility: "to integrate in[to] the host society without assimilating and to establish the presence of Portugal in the world."[14]

With the inclusion of emigrants in the conceptualization of a "global" nation, emigration services were placed under the Ministry of Foreign Affairs. In addition, the Central Government created a Ministry of Portuguese Communities with the aims of a) strengthening the persistence of Portuguese culture and language in the world; and b) the economic, social and cultural cooperation among Portuguese communities abroad as well as between those communities and the different regions of Portugal. Similar divisions were formed by the autonomous regions of the archipelagos of Madeira and the Azores, and currently a World Ministry of Portuguese Communities (with the participation of representatives of different Portuguese Communities abroad) is being organized.

The recognition by Portugal's post-colonial state of the transnational character of Portuguese immigration and the incorporation of its dispersed population into the creation of a global deterritorialized nation is mirrored and reinforced by Portuguese poet Fernando Pessoa's image of Portugal as a

Emigração portuguesa: Aspectos relevantes relativos às políticas adoptadas no domínio da emigração Portuguesa, desde a última Guerra Mundial. As above, Porto, 1986.

Emigração portuguesa: Algumas características dominantes dos movimentos no período de 1950 a 1984. Secretaria de Estado das Comunidades Portuguesas, Centro de Estudos, Serie Migrações, Sociologia, Porto, 1986.

[14] Aguiar,[11] p. 18.

"nation-ship aboard which we (the Portuguese) are already born departing" and thus "a Portuguese who is only a Portuguese is not a Portuguese."[15] The imagining of a Portuguese deterritorialized "global" nation has also been expressed in immigrants' poetry. Consider this poem by João Teixeira Medeiros, an 85-year-old poet, who was born in New England, lived in the Azores from age 9 to 22 and emigrated back to New England:

> the word saudade
> who felt it who made it
> made it fit the
> Portuguese heart at large
>
> saudade has happiness and sadness
> feeling and voice
> saudade is very Portuguese
> it is an offspring of all of us
>
> saudade gives flavour to entire nations
> it is part of our daily life
> saudade will be present
> in any place where there are Portuguese flags
>
> saudade travelled with us in the sea
> as well as in the thousands of hinterlands
> it is with us in the airplanes
>
> saudade God help us
> has such a deep power
> it is like a hurricane spreading us
> in the little corners of the world[16]

[15] Carvalho,[9] p. 32.

[16] Poem entitled *Saudade*, author's translation. While Portuguese experiences and the imagery of *saudade* have encompassed the world, the movement of Portuguese migration, historically linked by regionally demarcated networks of kinship, has followed the demands of labor in a changing global economy. From the last decades of the 19th century to 1960, Portuguese migrants settled primarily in the New World, mostly in Brazil and, to a smaller extent, in the United States, Venezuela, and Argentina. Subsequently, with the economic reconstruction of Europe and the creation of the European Community, there was a major shift in the direction of Portuguese labor. Since the 1960s and throughout the 1970s, Portuguese mainlanders have tended to move away from transoceanic towards intracontinental migration, settling increasingly in France, Germany, and Switzerland, among other European countries. Though in smaller proportions, through networks of kinship, they have continued to migrate to Brazil and the United States. During the same period, the Azoreans, while continuing to emigrate in large numbers to the United States, found new work alternatives in Canada, and to a lesser degree, Bermuda. In contrast, the majority of Madeirans began to settle in Venezuela and South Africa. In the 1980s, at the same time that the Portuguese emigration rate has steadily decreased, the United States became the major recipient of migrants from the Azores and the Portuguese mainland. J. C. Arroteia (*Atlas de emigração portuguesa*, Porto, 1985) and J. Serrao (*A emigração portuguesa*, Livros Horizonte, 4th edition, 1982) provide detailed data on the movement of Portuguese emigration.

In the context of the emerging world economic order, the Portuguese post-colonial state has reinvented and reelaborated the temporal memory of the exploration era into the present. At the same time, it included the dispersed emigrant populations in the new spatial conceptualization of an overseas Portugal. *Estamos todos espalhados pelos mundo* (we are all spread throughout the world) is a common statement among the Portuguese, which suggests that their lived experiences and imagery have stretched across the world. These experiences and imagery have provided a source of legitimacy for the creation of a "global" nation. Yet, Portuguese settled abroad (such as those in New Bedford, MA) have differentially reshaped their self-identities in response to these policies.

"A PORTUGUESE WHO IS ONLY A PORTUGUESE IS NOT A PORTUGUESE" OR "THE CONSTRUCTION OF A PORTUGUESE TERRITORY ABROAD"

New Bedford is one of the many Portuguese "little corners of the world." As such, it is part of a network of Portuguese enclaves in New England, a transnational space, which Onézimo T. Almeida calls "L(U.S.A.)land,"

. . . a portion of Portugal, surrounded by America from every side, (. . .) a special nation composed of communities that are neither Portugal nor America . . . (that are) rather a mixture of two cultures, a world between Portugal and America.[17]

For at least a century, labor migration, networks of kinship relations (including intercontinental marriage patterns), the circulation of material and symbolic goods, and the constant reinvention of multiple layers of Portuguese (past) time and space in an American present, have merged this "world between Portugal and America" into a single social construction.[18] By focusing on the interrelationship between transnationalism and insularity, I will trace the historical processes and the cultural meanings through which this "world between Portugal and America" has in fact become a Portuguese "territory" abroad.

The Portuguese mark 1832 as the year they began to construct their "territory" in New Bedford. At that time, Azorean and Cape Verdean males increasingly provided the labor for the whaling expeditions. However, mass mi-

---

[17] O. T. Almeida, *L(U.S.A.)landia: A décima ilha*, Serviços de Emigração, Angra do Heroismo, 1988, p. 231.

[18] This single construction further encompasses networks of kinship spread in other parts of the world. Among the Azoreans the density of social relations also includes relatives settled in California (U.S.A.), Canada, and Brazil; Portuguese mainlanders are mostly settled in Europe and Brazil; Madeirans are particularly in Venezuela, South Africa, and Brazil (see also footnote 16).

gration of families (first from the Azores and subsequently also from Madeira and the mainland) began during the last decades of the nineteenth century, reaching its height in 1910. These immigrants were mostly composed of impoverished small landholders, landless laborers, and artisans fleeing poverty in a period of Portugal's major economic decline. There are indications that, initially, the Portuguese settling in New Bedford were predominantly involved with agriculture and craftsmanship. Some eventually managed to buy land in the outskirts of the city.

The local cotton mill industry, at that time at the vanguard of American industrialization, was initially based on a labor force mainly composed of English, Irish, and French-Canadian workers. It was only by the turn of the twentieth century that the Portuguese, along with other Southern and Eastern European unskilled workers began arriving in large numbers to the area, as cheap labor in the cotton economy. By 1910, the Portuguese already represented 40% of that labor force. Estimates further suggest that, by 1930, 80% of the Portuguese were cotton mill workers while 15% were professionals and business people.[19] Even though there was a certain degree of stratification among the Portuguese, those who remained in the region were deeply affected – like other local residents – by the decline of the textile industry and the 30-year-long depression of the New Bedford economy that was to follow.

While Portuguese immigration to New Bedford never ceased, in the late 1950s, the American government issued a special decree to facilitate the arrival of the Azoreans, in view of a drastic earthquake on one of the islands. Later, with the 1965 United States Immigration Act, successive contingents from the Azores, mainland Portugal, and Portuguese Africa have settled in New Bedford. Though to a lesser degree, Cape Verdeans, Hispanics, and (more recently) Koreans have also migrated to the area.

There are indications that the Portuguese arriving since the 1970s have tended to be more stratified economically, socially and educationally than the former contingents. In contrast to the bulk of the immigrants of the past who came to New Bedford in a bid to escape destitution, there are considerable numbers of middle class Portuguese among the new migrants. While some emigrated to avoid the drafting of their sons during the colonial wars in Africa, others came to the United States "for the future of their children." Still others either left Portugal prompted by the Portuguese Revolution, or left Portuguese Africa in response to the independence of the African colonies. Some emigrated to New Bedford from other countries of the world.

Estimates indicate that 60% of today's 110,000 inhabitants of New Bed-

---

[19] Data come from *Os portugueses de New Bedford*, Montepio Luso-Americano, New Bedford, 1932 (a book published by the immigrants themselves as part of the celebration of the fifth centenary of the discovery of the Azors).

ford are of Portuguese origin. These include the so-called Luso-Americans (descendants of the older contingents of immigrants from the Azores, mainland, and Madeira), many of whom have intermarried with members of the older immigrant groups (French-Canadian, English, Irish, Polish, Italians, *etc.*); American-born Portuguese, who moved, together with their parents, to Portugal prior to or by the 1930s and have increasingly returned to New Bedford since the 1960s; as well as newer contingents of immigrants and their descendants, most of whom are linked by kinship to the older generations of migrants and their descendants. In addition, these figures also include the Cape Verdeans, who, prior to the independence of Cape Verde, were part of the Portuguese community of New Bedford.

Today, the Portuguese of New Bedford are stratified economically, socially, and educationally. While 50% of the immigrant population is still composed of factory workers, Luso-Americans and segments of the immigrant population are represented in different sectors of activity in the region.[20] There has been, however, little political representation of these Portuguese within the American governmental echelons. Overall, in spite of their numbers, the bulk of the Portuguese immigrants still remain invisible in the mainstream of life in New Bedford. They live their daily routines within segregated (and self-segregated) neighborhoods.

Exploratory analysis of 60 oral histories and 25 genealogies suggests that the successive contingents of immigrants who have settled in New Bedford in different historical periods are linked among themselves through regionally demarcated consanguineal and affinal kinship ties. In fact, there are indications that the more recent contingents of immigrants are ultimately members of the same families that emigrated to New England in the past.

The available data further suggest that, prior to the issuing of a series of increasingly restrictive immigration laws between 1917 and 1924, Portuguese immigrants (with their American-born children) moved back and forth between Portugal and the United States. While many settled permanently in New Bedford, others left Portugal to work for a few years either on the farms surrounding the city or in the local cotton mills with the aim of amassing capital to buy a plot of land in the homeland. Even though there were at that time successful entrepreneurship stories of immigrants returning to the homeland and investing their capital in local enterprises, these were solely the result of private initiative without any backing from the Portuguese state.

Later, during the decline of the cotton mill industry and the Great Depression that was to follow, return migration from New England to Portugal seems

---

[20] The socio-economic position of Portuguese immigrants in Massachusetts was analyzed in detail by Maria da Gloria Sá Pereira, *A posição sócio-economica dos imigrantes portugueses a seus descendentes nos estados de Massachusetts e Rhode Island*, Secretaria do Estado das Comunidades Portuguesas, Porto, 1985.

to have been relatively high: some immigrants returned to Portugal with their entire families, which in many cases included American-born children; others left their married offspring in the United States, returning to Portugal with their younger (American and Portuguese-born) children. To a certain extent, even during the 1930s and 1950s, when restrictive American immigration quotas only allowed 500 Portuguese to enter the United States yearly, American-born Portuguese continued to move between Portugal and the United States, sometimes bringing along their Portuguese mates. In the same fashion, given the decline of New England's mill economy, some Portuguese offspring who had been left in the United States eventually returned to Portugal. Others, while remaining in the United States, went to Portugal to find mates. Still others moved from New England to other American regions, particularly California.

» «

"Hello . . . Goodbye . . . my time to leave has come . . ."[21] is the beginning sentence of a song that narrates how emigration has been constitutive of the everyday life in Portugal. In many regions of Portugal, and particularly in the Azores, the holding of American citizenship as well as access through kinship and marriage to "American papers" have been a valuable asset enabling individuals and families to move across, and live between, Portugal and the United States. Therefore, it is not by chance that American-born offspring of the Portuguese immigrants before and after 1930 as well as their relatives who have remained in the United States, have constituted the major connecting link between past and present contingents of Portuguese settling in the United States. Even in the 1960s, at a time when the Portuguese government was attempting to redirect the movement of labor migration from the United States to Europe, webs of kinship made way for the continuous arrival of new Portuguese contingents (mostly from the Azores and, to a lesser degree, Portuguese mainland) to the United States.

In this context, the continuous arrival of kin-related immigrants to the United States was facilitated, between the 1960s and the 1980s, by American governmental policies fostering chain migration. In fact, these policies enabled many families to reunite in New England and, at the same time, reinforced the common family strategy of choosing mates for their daughters and sons in the homeland.

In addition, the tendency of the local factories to engage in the paternalistic labor strategy of hiring family members of "docile" workers made way for the entrance of newly arrived immigrants into the labor force. Therefore, independent of their class origins, many new arrivals found their first job op-

---

[21] Song by Dionisio Costa, a Portuguese immigrant from Faial (Azores), who has settled in Taunton, MA.

portunities in the labor-intensive factories which have progressively replaced the faded textile industry of the area.

Since recruitment tended to follow ethnic lines, the labor force in the local factories came to consist mainly of Portuguese male and female workers. Yet, particularly for some younger men and women, industrial work was merely the first channel of employment. The possibility of learning English to study a skill or to pursue further studies or of accumulating some capital (even if this meant working two shifts) provided them with an opportunity to enter other occupations, such as commerce, clerical work, or the liberal professions. In addition, some men were also able to leave the factory and make a livelihood in the local fishery (whose fleet is mainly composed of Portuguese mainlanders) and in construction work. However, for most immigrants, industrial work continued to be the main avenue of employment. In fact, until the turn of this decade, when many factories began to close down their local plants, it was not unusual to find immigrants working in the same factory, together with their relatives, for over fifteen or twenty years. But even within the factory, promotion was possible for those with a knowledge of English. While many immigrant workers speak only Portuguese, supervisors as well as union representatives are bilingual.

The advent of social security in the United States in the 1930s together with medicare benefits for the elderly in the 1960s shifted the ideal from amassing capital to buy a plot of land in the homeland to the attainment of retirement in the United States and, thus, to the usufruct of the American structure of social benefits. This goal led to the postponement of return or, in many cases, to permanent settlement in the United States. Nonetheless, in view of the prevailing ideal of return, many "new" immigrants have kept their houses, land, and even cars in the homeland. At the same time, they have tended to buy, as soon as they could, a house in the United States, which symbolized in their own words, "their share of the American Dream." In view of this ever-postponed return to the homeland, their sons and daughters were able, at least since the 1970s, to increasingly pursue a U.S. education. Particularly those offspring who were able to earn a college degree have provided a brokerage role between immigrants and American institutions. In view of the prevailing ideology of cultural pluralism and of their bilingual and bicultural skills, many were able to enter occupations within the local governmental structure and the bilingual educational system as well as the Portuguese institutions which were created in the 1970s with the aid of American grants. At the same time, therefore, that this cultural brokerage has helped immigrants to cope with the American system and American institutions, it has further reinforced the insularity of the Portuguese within New Bedford.

However, particularly after the issuing of dual citizenship rights in Portugal, older immigrants have in fact returned to Portugal (and to a betterment of conditions), leaving younger relatives behind in the United States. These immigrants have lived simultaneously between Portugal and the United States, making full use of their dual citizenship rights (and of special privileges issued by the state to returning immigrants) and accumulated property in both countries. This trend seems to have intensified even more these days when, in view of the ongoing recession in the United States, larger numbers of retired immigrants are returning to the homeland.

Given Portuguese extended family patterns, this phenomenon made way for the intensification of a transnational family structure in which decisions in everyday life are dependent upon and encompass relatives living in Portugal and the United States. While younger members of these families often live more in the American milieu, taking into account that other bicultural and bilingual offspring often perform a brokering role for their Portuguese-speaking parents, this transnational family structure has tended to increase the isolation of these families within New Bedford.

In the past, Portuguese literature and oral histories have portrayed the arrival of trunks full of goods with the smell of America. Many immigrants still spend the year collecting goods and send their trunk to Portugal, thereby laying claim to social prominence in Portugal by trying to assert their social mobility in the United States through these material goods. Formerly, this circulation of material goods was essential for the domestic economy of those relatives who were left behind in the homeland; now, however, immigrants are increasingly confronted with the higher social mobility of those relatives who were able to gain access to the free educational system of post-Revolution Portugal as well as to profit from the ongoing process of capitalist penetration. More and more, these relatives in Portugal request specific American brands, marking the transnationalization of consumption and of the domestic economy. In this context, the increasing incorporation of Portugal into the world economy and the betterment of standards of living in Portuguese regions also made for an intensification of visits of relatives living in Portugal to New England as well as for an increase in the circulation of material goods.

THE MEANING OF PORTUGUESE (PAST) TIME AND SPACE IN EVERYDAY LIFE AT THE INTERSECTION OF CULTURES

These transnational networks which mark the Portuguese of New Bedford as members of a global nation encapsulate them and so insulate these immigrants within the social life of New Bedford. Symbols of the Portuguese past, in fact, of different layers of Portuguese time and space, are a constitutive part of immigrant neighborhoods in New Bedford. For instance, a layer of time, representing the Portuguese major role during the exploration era, (*i.e.*, the collective historical memory of the Portuguese) is found here and there: the fifteenth century costumes of the Prince Henry Society (a type of Portuguese Rotary Club, formed in the 1980s), the many caravelles (the sailing ship of the discoverers) displayed in storefronts and homes, and the Prince Henry Monument in nearby Fall River. Another layer of time related to the past prior to immigration is reflected in the spatial organization of homes, with an American upstairs (represented by the symbols of consumption in the U.S.), a Portuguese downstairs (the major setting of everyday interaction and of social practices associated with the homeland), and in the yard reproductions of Portuguese gardens. In the neighborhood outside the house are Portuguese stores.

Leisure-time activities include the continuance of the *serões* (storytelling and musical gatherings reminiscent of a strong oral tradition). The use of time and seasons may also place immigrants within a Portuguese world. While during the year, factory work shapes the lives of many, during the summer (as at the end of the harvest in rural Portugal), immigrants continue to ritualize their memories of the homeland in a succession of regional folk-religious festivals.[22] Discussions between family members, neighbors, and co-workers are filled with stories from the ethnic media (newspapers, radio, TV), which also brings Portugal into the everyday life of immigrants.

This sense of a certain immutability of time, given by the continuous incorporation of different layers of the past into the present, is perhaps characteristic of immigrant neighborhoods anywhere. In a way, these neighborhoods resemble still photographs of a past that was already lived and does not exist anymore in the homeland. Yet, these different layers of past time and space are dynamic representations of the ways in which immigrants cope with changing conditions of existence.

In the reconstruction of Portuguese identity on the level of the self or the person, the collective historical memory may, in some instances, permeate interactions with non-Portuguese, particularly in situations of discrimination. Self-esteem is re-asserted by comparing the United States to the Portuguese mythical past in such ways as "How old is America: and who discovered America? And who are the Americans, anyway?"

Reconstructions of identity, which are mediated by symbolic representations of different layers of the Portuguese past, vary according to social class, regional background, generation, and gender.[23] Particularly, those women

---

[22] I have analyzed these festivals in A reinvenção da memória em festas imigrantes (The reinvention of memory in immigrant feasts), a paper presented at the International Seminar, Feasts: Tradition and Innovation, organized by Dr. M. B. Rocha-Trindade, at the Universidade Aberta, Lisbon, November 11–13, 1991. The reader is further referred to S. L. Cabral, *Tradition and transformation: Portuguese feasting in New Bedford*. AMS Press, 1989.

[23] I have analyzed (with Donna Huse) gender as constitutive of the construction and reconstruction of immigrant identity in The construction of immigrant identity: The case of the Portuguese of southeastern Massachusetts (in *Spinner: People and culture in southeastern Massachusetts*, vol. 5, edited by J. Thomas, a special issue on the Portuguese of southeastern Massachusetts, in press).

and men whose immigration history encompasses the transition from pre-industrial task-oriented activities in Portugal to industrial work in the United States tend to develop a romantic nostalgia, or *saudade da terra*, for their immediate past of non-industrial labor. The reinvention of their immediate past reflects their experiences with and perceptions of different rhythms and different meanings of time, work, and life in Portugal and the United States: from more natural rhythms to the time discipline of industrial capitalism.[24]

This romantic nostalgia for a past when work was intermingled with multiple dimensions of social intercourse gives meaning to hard lives marked by abrupt change—representing a strategy to resist total immersion in industrial time. Therefore, it is not by chance that they tend only to remember the beneficial aspects of their lives prior to migration.[25] In the context of dramatic changes caused by immigration and the pressures imposed by the regularities of industrial work, the homeland (which is remembered in terms of their village or region of origin) turns into utopia. This romantic nostalgia is further translated into social practices associated with that past of non-industrial labor, such as gardening, wine making, sewing embroidery. While during their work shift they are proletarians, in their free time they continue to be peasants and artisans. Above all, these symbolic representations and social practices of their past of non-industrial labor further provide the basis for self reconstitution as Azoreans, Madeirans and mainlanders, thus demarcating their strong regional identities. In their everyday life, these regional identities tend to be stronger than (and sometimes conflict with) Portuguese national identity.

In contrast, American-born descendants of immigrants as well as younger immigrants who have advanced socially, educationally and economically and who have become cultural brokers between immigrants and the larger American society have tended either to juxtapose their Portuguese and American identities or to shift progressively to an American identity. Endemic cleavages, expressing conflicting identities (in terms of regional origin, generation, and gender) mark the actions and interactions among these cultural brokers. Major divisions cut particularly across the relationships between immigrants and the so-called Luso-Americans (descendants of immigrants who settled in New Bedford before the mid-1950s). Yet, in their attempts to represent a rather heterogeneous (and probably unviable) "Portuguese community," members of this stratum, particularly since the early 1980s, have tended to

[24] This analysis is based on E. P. Thompson's distinction between "natural time" and the "time-discipline of industrial capitalism" (Time, work-discipline and industrial capitalism. *Past and Present 38*, Dec. 1967).

[25] I am drawing a distinction between "memory" and "tradition." Like Scott, I am suggesting that the reinvention of the memories of the past is directly related to the struggles in the present (J. C. Scott, *Weapons of the weak: Everyday forms of peasant resistance*, Yale University Press, 1985). On the subject, the reader is further referred to R. Williams, *The country and the city*, Oxford University press, 1973.

reinvent the Portuguese exploration era in their mobilization as an ethnic group striving to establish itself as a majority (not a minority) in the pluralistic society of New Bedford.

The past is, therefore, not a matter of fading memories and superfluous sentiment. Incorporated are the reimagings and reinventions of Portuguese identity, which both the Portuguese state and the transnational population play a part in producing. Perceiving themselves as a people spread throughout the world, the Portuguese immigrants make full use of their dual citizenship rights. In the context of the growing internationalization of the world economy, they make way for new emerging forms of transnationalism. These immigrants have differentially reelaborated their Portugueseness in the context of their concrete experiences of migration, changing work habits, and of the interconnection of lives lived between Portugal and the United States.

REINVENTIONS OF PORTUGUESE IDENTITY: HISTORICAL PROCESSES AND THE ROLE OF THE PORTUGUESE AND AMERICAN STATES

Contrasting American and Portuguese nationalisms – including different definitions of race – together with the immigrants' structural position in New Bedford are essential to gain an understanding of the cultural and social processes underlying the construction of class, race, ethnicity, and nationalism as collective movements. In the 1920s and 1930s, the earlier years of settlement, as well as today American officials have tended to view immigration essentially as a "race question" and be concerned with which racial strains of immigrants were desirable to U. S. society. After issuing highly restrictive immigration laws, a major Americanization campaign was launched to educate (white) immigrants to become part of American society and, thus, assimilate. Although the prevailing ideology did not include blacks, the major slogan was "America Belongs to Everyone."[26]

On the other hand, Portuguese ideologies linked to Portugal's mythical role during the seafaring exploration era recurrently emphasized the patriotic pride of the "Luzitan race." This pride was also based on the existence of their overseas colonies, whose populations were primarily defined culturally as Portuguese rather than in terms of genetic definitions of race. In this context, those who emigrated were considered a "necessary evil" and second class citizens. Persons who left Portugal and settled in the United States (immigrants) were viewed pejoratively by both states and faced discrimination from both governments: discrimination was implicit in the very concept of "immigrant."

---

[26] Headline of a pamphlet distributed by the Portuguese-American Civic Association.

At the time, the Portuguese were already the largest immigrant group in New Bedford. However, the so-called Portuguese colony was in fact composed of four distinctive groups: the Azoreans, mainlanders, Madeirans, and Cape Verdeans (who, as part of Portugal's overseas colonies were considered – and considered themselves – Portuguese). There was in addition a Luso-American contingent, which included descendants of the whalers and farmers who had settled in the region before the turn of the twentieth century, some of whom had attained economic prosperity. While the Portuguese were highly stratified, the majority was part of the lower economic echelons of local society. Structurally, they were economically, socially and politically in a position inferior to other immigrant groups, particularly the English, Irish, French-Canadians and Jews. Moreover, while immigration itself was considered to be a "race issue," the presence of Cape Verdeans within the Portuguese group further earned them the stigma of "Black Portugee."

This was a population that had already established transnational family networks and projects connecting their aspirations for a better life to their connections in both worlds. Yet, in the context of the prevailing Portuguese and American nationalisms, immigrants and descendants were continuously confronted with the necessity of choosing whether to continue to be Portuguese or to assimilate and become American. On the one hand, Americanization implied the rejection (and invisibility) of Portuguese identity and avoided the issue of race. At the same time, it provided the possibility of gaining access to political, social and economic mobility within the United States. On the other hand, Portuguese nationalism stressed the maintenance of Portuguese culture and language and the superiority of Portuguese culture.

Americanization and naturalization classes were established in New Bedford with funds channelled by City Hall and with the support of the YWCA and local industries. Among the teachers recruited for the Americanization mission were descendants of immigrants of different national origins, including Portuguese. Apparently, Americanization leaders attempted to get support from inside the foreign groups. In conformity with those goals, the Portuguese-American Civic Society (a voluntary association composed mostly of leading Luso-American professionals and businessmen who were trying to gain access to American governmental institutions) began to play a major role in that campaign. However, there is evidence of some contention between their goals and those of the governmental forces promoting Americanization. The propaganda of the Civic Society advocated: "If you want to be a good Portuguese, become an American."

In contrast to the assimilative forces, the Portuguese daily paper *Diário de Noticias*, a leading representative of Portuguese patriotic ideologies, systematically advocated the maintenance of Portuguese culture and language. Its editorials recurrently attacked the ongoing inter-ethnic marriages, the tendency to anglicize Portuguese names and the fact that Luso-Americans who spoke perfect English and whose names were anglicized were easily passing as Americans. The newspaper further called attention to those richer Portuguese families who tended to disconnect themselves from the so-called *colonia*, by, among other things, attending English–rather than Portuguese–Masses.

The maintenance of Portuguese national identity and patriotism among Portuguese and descendants was a matter of concern for Portuguese governmental officials. A case in point is the report written in 1926 by a Portuguese consul regarding the inauguration of a monument in honor of a Luso-American, born in New Bedford, who died during World War I. Apparently, that monument was part of a campaign promoting a historical memory of Luso-Americans as "true Americans":

> Side by side with patriotism, and confused with it, there is what we can call COLONIALISM, (and) that is not the love for Portugal. I could verify that fact at the time of the inauguration of the monument to Walter Goulart, son of Portuguese and the first American soldier to die at war.[27]

> The initiative of the monument was made by a committee composed almost entirely by the Portuguese of New Bedford. The American public officers classified Walter as a true American. With all my energy, I vindicated him for Portugal. I reclaimed him for us and I introduced him as Portuguese. I linked him to the motherland, our nation. For the members of the committee (composed primarily of Portuguese) and for many other men of our race present to that major ceremony, he was not either an American, nor a Portuguese of Portugal. He was a Portuguese of New Bedford, a Portuguese of the Portuguese colony.

> Walter Goulart was for the Americans a true American. *The Boston Post*, publishing in 1924 the photo of Mr. Manoel Acores, emphasized in headlines that he was also a true American. Who are, among the Portuguese born in America and those naturalized Americans, who would in fact disagree with that classification? I cannot answer.[28]

During the celebration of the anniversary of the Portuguese Republic, held by a voluntary association in nearby Fall River, another governmental officer praised the ongoing resistance toward denationalization and urged Portuguese and descendants not to reject their ancestry:

> We should praise the Portuguese . . . who in the present circumstances have patriotically resisted denationalization . . . [as] Portuguese . . .

> The motherland needs every sacrifice that we can make . . . even when she refuses us an easy economic life. We must imitate the great men, like Fernando de Magalhaes, who, even when not well appreciated in their land, never forgot it . . .

---

[27] In Carvalho,[9] p. 273 (author's translation).
[28] Carvalho,[9] pp. 273–275 (author's translation).

And even those who are forced by circumstances to change their juridical condition, as well as those who were born in America . . . those also can be a reason of pride for Portugal, if they don't negate their Portuguese ancestry.[29]

The rejection of Portuguese ancestry became a major issue in New Bedford a few years later, in 1931, when the newspaper *Diário de Notícias* published a dramatic headline: "The Portuguese-American Civic Society Rejects the Portuguese Flag." From the newspaper's editorial and coverage, that event seemed to have divided the community:

> This civic association, composed of Luso-American professionals and businessmen, decided that the Portuguese flag should never appear in their club. This action represents an insult of a bunch of snobs who don't want to be Portuguese, and who in fact don't deserve to be Portuguese (and now) the majority of the Portuguese, who had become members of that organization in the hope of gaining political prestige for the Portuguese colony, is now ready to abandon it.[30]

After a sequence of editorials and pressure from the community, the Portuguese-American Civic Society called for an extraordinary meeting, in which the author of the proposal, a lawyer named Nunes, emotionally stated:

> I thought that the public exhibition of the Portuguese flag in the club whose members are citizens, could create antagonism among the native, who are always ready to censor us and to call us foreigners . . . and this would be in a certain way an obstacle for us to gain the desired political prestige. We cannot antagonize the so-called American vote because we need their cooperation to win. I sincerely believe that by acting the way I did, I was fulfilling my duty with our club and towards our people. I thought that the subject was the club's affairs and not the public's affair. But if the well-being of the club and the well-being of the colony requires the presence of the flag in our public function, we will do it.[31]

Because of the pressure of many who attended the meeting, the decision was that the Portuguese flag was to continue to be exhibited in the club's public sessions. This dramatic event brings to the fore the pressures to reject (or at least to turn invisible) any symbols related to foreign ancestry, particularly by those who were trying to gain upward mobility and political power in the United States. It also makes clear that there were among the Portuguese in New Bedford countervailing forces to the assimilative pressures, although in this case they were not publicly acknowledged. Not only did the Portu-

[29] Part of a speech made by a consular officer in Fall River (*Casa da saudade collection*, 1930, author's translation).

[30] In *Diário de Notícias*, a Portuguese newspaper of New Bedford (1917–1970s), January 15, 1931 (author's translation).

[31] *Diário de Notícias*, January 23, 1931.

guese state play a direct role in the life of the colony, but the familial trans-national networks made identification with Portugal and Portuguese culture not a fading memory, but a continuing presence and orientation for the fu-ture. Nonetheless, oral histories suggest that the pressures to Americanize had a potent effect on the descendants of immigrants. In order to avoid discrim-ination, particularly the stigma of "Black Portugee," Luso-Americans tended to "pass" within the mainstream culture, even though in many cases they re-tained the Portuguese language and traditions. Some, but not all, intermar-ried into other immigrant groups, and–to some degree–"melted in the melting pot" (as defined by Luso-Americans).

» «

In short, the "melting pot" policies, emphasizing assimilation, the stigma of "Black Portugee," together with the long depression put major constraints upon the community. For many (particularly the descendants of immigrants), assimilation became a way to avoid discrimination, and issues pertaining to naturalization were major sources of conflict. Yet, in spite of the pressure of Americanization and of prevailing regional cleavages, the exploration era was present in the collective memory of the Portuguese. A case in point was the joint celebrations in 1932 of the fifth centenary of the Discovery of the Azores, the fiftieth anniversary of the Monte Pio Mutual Aid Society, and the cente-nary of the Portuguese colony of New Bedford. These events were extensively celebrated throughout New England with parades, lecture series, and ex-hibits.[32] In addition, under the auspices of the Monte Pio Mutual Aid So-ciety, a committee composed of Madeirans, Azoreans, mainlanders, and Cape Verdeans published in Portuguese a book documenting the history of the Por-tuguese in New Bedford. On the basis of their own transnational experience, the authors resisted the prevailing polarization between the two competing national ideologies. Instead they saw the histories of New Bedford and different regions of Portugal as inter-related parts of a single construction.[33]

The Americanization process did not seem to have had a great impact on the immigrant working class population. Those who remained in New Bed-ford after the restrictive immigration laws were coping with hard times. Many continued to keep in touch with their relatives in the homeland, and, when they could, sent remittances. For many, the symbolic representation and so-cial practices associated with the past prior to immigration provided an outlet for self-expression. In the 1920s and 1930s, alongside the proliferation of re-gional voluntary associations and mutual aid societies, Portuguese schools were established. Radio programs and six Portuguese theater groups were formed. One of these groups (the more radical), the Popular Dramatic Group

[32] These events, extensively covered by the Portuguese newspaper *Diário de Noticias*, brought to the fore the existence of deep cleavages among the Portuguese concerning the par-ticipation of the Cape-Verdeans in the celebrations. These cleavages were more profound in Provi-dence, RI than in New Bedford.
[33] This book was published under the title *Os portugueses de New Bedford*.[9]

(linked to the anti-fascist Liberal Alliance in Portugal), was an offspring of both Portuguese involvement in the 1928 six-month-long strike against the 10% reduction of wages in the local textile mills and of the fight against fascism in Portugal.[34]

In the 1970s, the Portuguese were still viewed as the "invisible minority" and the "case of the disappearing ethnics."[35] And, even today, many Luso-Americans (descendants of the older generations) are caught between feelings of shame and pride for their Portuguese ancestry. Furthermore, discrimination continues to permeate the fabric of social life in New Bedford. In the past as in the present, cultural misunderstandings have provided a main source of (sometimes) disguised and concealed discrimination in everyday life. In this context, the label of "greenhorn" has further stigmatized different contingents of immigrants upon their arrival in the United States. In particular, younger immigrants and children of immigrants recall how, by virtue different customs (including food and clothing styles) and language, they were invariably faced with prejudice at the intersection of cultures (and most flagrantly in the American schools). At the same time, regional and class differences have marked social boundaries among the immigrants themselves. Moreover, while in the past the "melting pot" policies were based on explicit discrimination, on-going American multi-ethnic policies—reinforcing ethnic boundaries—have made way for increasing segregation and self-segregation. While segregation implies (and at the same time avoids) discrimination, in times of conflict and confrontation, social prejudices come dramatically into the open.

In the last decade, there has been an emerging reconstruction of class, race, ethnicity and nationalism among the Portuguese of New Bedford. These have been prompted by a complex mix of factors:

1. American pluralistic policies, emphasizing the allocation of resources through ethnic lines in the context of an ideology that at least rhetorically views "America as a nation of immigrants;"
2. The arrival of new and more diversified contingents of immigrants;
3. The betterment of New Bedford's faded economy;
4. The relative improvement of the social, political and economic position of the Portuguese in New Bedford; and
5. The recent redefinitions of the concepts of "nation," "nationality," "immigration," and "immigrant" by the Portuguese state in the context of Portugal's increasing incorporation into the world system. Government officials have assigned new responsibilities to the so-called Portuguese abroad: to integrate in the host society without assimilating and, at the same time, establish the presence of Portugal in the world.

---

[34] In the spring of 1928, 30,000 mill workers refused to accept a 10% wage cut imposed on them by New Bedford's mill owners. The strike, the longest in New Bedford, lasted 6 months. As a result of a deep split between rival unions, the workers accepted a compromise of a 5% cut.
[35] From titles of papers by Estellie Smith, 1976.

As a part of these strategies, the central government as well as those of Madeira and the Azores have strengthened their relations with leaders of the Portuguese communities abroad. Besides stimulating extensive celebrations of the Day of Portugal, Camões, and Portuguese communities, the Ministry of the Portuguese Communities has organized conferences with leading "citizens abroad" in different parts of the world, and has recently directed particular attention to the media, creating special TV and radio programs for the communities abroad. In similar fashion, the Emigration Divisions of Madeira and the Azores, whose local constituency is larger, have increasingly strengthened their ties with leading immigrants and Luso-Americans of their region. Visits of a variety of government officials (including President Mario Soares) to the region have been frequent. Mota Amaral, President of the Azores, visits New England (especially Fall River, a Massachusetts city a few miles from New Bedford) at least four times a year.

Even before the intensification of contacts between Portuguese officials and leading community leaders, Luso-American and immigrant business people have recurrently attempted to become part of the main political, economic and social streams of society in the United States. In spite of prevailing conflicts with an emerging stratum of bicultural Portuguese social workers (composed mainly of women), Portuguese leaders decided not to join the "Affirmative Action" program and, thus, established themselves as a part of the majority.[36] As such, they have distanced themselves again from the issue of race at a time when the Cape Verdeans, already independent from Portugal, had chosen the "minority" path. However, in the early 1970s, segments of this leadership took advantage of American federal and state funds to create an "Immigrant Assistance Center" and a Portuguese branch of the local public library (whose personnel of social workers and librarians are made up of bilingual immigrants who have pursued an education in the U.S.). In contrast to the 1930s, when a government report indicated a scarcity of Portuguese personnel and interpreters, New Bedford today has a bilingual structure. Portuguese-Americans and immigrants have begun progressively to occupy bureaucratic, social service and teaching positions in the city, and have acted as brokers between the community and the larger system. A few of them have also acted as brokers between Portugal, New Bedford, and the immigrants.

While in the past, the possibility of attaining upward mobility and political power demanded the rejection or invisibility of Portuguese identity and ancestry, today there is an inverse process. This may be illustrated by the formation of organizations like the Prince Henry society mentioned earlier. This club, composed mostly of English-speaking Luso-Americans and immigrant

---

[36] Francis Rogers, a Harvard professor and himself of Portuguese descent, defends the "majority" path in his *Americans of Portuguese descent: A lesson in differentiation*, Sage Research Papers, Vol. 2, 1974.

professionals and business people, was named in honor of Prince Henry the Navigator. It is one of the few associations able to reunite Azoreans, Madeirans, mainlanders, and Luso-Americans.[37] Like the former Portuguese American Civic Society, the Prince Henry Society aims at playing a political, economic and social role in the region. In contraposition to the former civic association, the Prince Henry Society emphasizes the historical memory of the discoveries, and one of its goals is to promote Portuguese Official Culture. Besides honoring leading citizens of New Bedford, as well as the "Immigrant of the Year," this association also organizes concerts of classical music, art exhibits and conferences. The emphasis on "high culture" is intended to enhance their own class position as representatives of Portugal in New Bedford, and at the same time, change the image of the Portuguese as peasants engaging in folk-religious festivals.

The following statements by the Director of the Portuguese Cultural Foundation of Rhode Island at the time of the inauguration by President Mario Soares of a monument honoring Portuguese explorers in Newport, summarizes the ongoing process:

> Like other cultures, the Portuguese are not only farmers and fishermen. They are part of a great heritage. A monument like this allows anyone who is interested to discover the world of the Portuguese, just as the Portuguese discovered the world of America 500 years ago. It is a culmination of a dream where the past becomes the present and the future.[38]

Rather than an obsession with Portugal's historical past, or a utopian characterization of Portuguese fate, the reinvention of the discovery era into an American present represents a pragmatic cultural construction to change the image of Portugal and of Portuguese immigrants in the region. The Portuguese state as well as segments of the immigrant and Luso-American upper classes have vested interests in the on-going reinvention of tradition (using Hobsbawm's definition of the term). On the one hand, the Portuguese state, by strengthening its relationships with the leading citizens of the Portuguese "communities" abroad, has tried to establish "the presence of Portugal in the world." On the other hand, those leaders, in their attempts to establish themselves as part of the mainstream of American society have made use of the reinvention of tradition to better their position within the realm of American multi-ethnic politics.

However, since the Portuguese leadership of New Bedford is highly differentiated and fragmented (in terms of region of origin, class, generation,

---

[37] Other associations reuniting Azoreans, Madeirans, mainlanders, and Luso-Americans include a Portuguese-American Business Association and a Portuguese Anti-Defamation League. Moreover, in spite of their regional cleavages, Portuguese workers mobilize together in the local unions.

[38] Quoted from the newspaper *East Bay Window*, Newport, RI, March 1, 1989.

gender, and particularly in terms of the differential experiences of immigrants as compared to the older and more established Luso-American stratum), the politics of the Portuguese state have ultimately intensified endemic cleavages insofar as different groups have competed among themselves to represent Portugal's historical past in the region.[39] At the same time, endemic cleavages further reflect and encompass regional countervailing interests in Portugal. In fact, since the Portuguese Revolution of 1974, the Azoreans (as well as the Madeirans) have tried to gain more autonomy in relation to the centralizing forces of the state. In that historical conjuncture, the Azorean government, together with Azorean intellectuals residing in the islands and abroad, have invented the tradition of *açorianidade* (or azorianity), the Azorean "distinct way" of being Portuguese. In New England, where the Azorean constituency is the largest, *açorianidade* has increased regional cleavages among leading citizens (including among Azorean immigrants). *Açorianidade* further enabled the Azorean government to seek the help of leading New England Azoreans in establishing international accords in the region as well as in gaining direct access to the higher echelons of American politics.[40] As part of their attempts to incorporate their dispersed populations, both the Portuguese state and the autonomous government of the Azores systematically award medals and honors to leading immigrants and Luso-Americans who have gained a certain celebrity in their spheres of activity in the United States.[41]

In the meantime, the bulk of Portuguese workers, who are themselves more vulnerable to the rhythms of capitalism, are presently facing once again the closing down of local plants, salary cuts, and unemployment. As we have seen, in their everyday life, these immigrants have tended to imagine Portugal in terms of their village of origin rather than in terms of that nation's remote historical past. Hence, the symbolic representations and the social practices associated with their immediate past prior to migration have shaped their identities as Azoreans, Madeirans, and mainlanders. These strong regional identities have been strengthened even more by regionally demarcated transnational networks of kinship. In spite of the endemic regional cleavages, which have been further intensified by ongoing American and Portuguese policies of control, these immigrants have mobilized themselves in the work-place as Portuguese workers facing discrimination within the American labor force. At the same time, as members of the American labor force, these workers have become increasingly aware that their present economic vulnerability is an outcome of the on-going process of "deindustrialization" since local plants have

---

[39] These cleavages came flagrantly to the fore during the 1988 celebrations of the "Day of Portugal, Camões and the Portuguese Communities" in New Bedford.

[40] In comparison to the policies of the Portuguese state, the Azorean government has played a more direct role in the region.

[41] Obviously, the Azorean government gives awards only to Azorean immigrants and Luso-Americans of Azorean descent.

tended to relocate to other areas of the world in search of cheaper labor.[42] Taking into account the betterment of living standards in Portugal, these immigrants are beginning to realize that their "American Dream" (which they translate as their search for a "better future") lies presently in Portugal rather than in the United States.[43]

CONCLUSIONS

Immigrants the world over are known for their elaboration of images of home which become sentimentalized in song, story, and poetry. While these remembered and reinvented pasts have served as bolsters against the uprooting of migration, in the United States they have also become the stock in trade of ethnic politics. Using their reconstructed past to create a multi-class ethnic constituency, upwardly mobile immigrants have entered the U.S. political process. At first glance it would be possible to read the history of these Portuguese settlers as part of the fabric of U.S. ethnic history and to see the Portuguese of New Bedford as typifying an ethnic enclave insulated from the society in which they have settled and from connections with larger political and social currents. Earlier generations of Portuguese who migrated to the United States yielded to assimilative pressures when these pressures were dominant by learning English and by inter-marrying. However, they stood prepared to assume the role of an ethnic leadership when later generations needed representing in a redefined, culturally plural America. Certainly the memories of the past, preserved and invented, pervade the life of the Portuguese of New Bedford and contribute to the self-definition of the population.

However, underlying the apparent insularity of the Portuguese settlers is a series of paradoxes in which Portuguese ethnicity is found to be the product of forces that extend far beyond that local community and encompass Portuguese and U.S. nation-building processes. It became clear that explaining the cultural identity of these Portuguese migrants requires a different reading of Portuguese immigrant history, one in which the racial constructions embedded in the nation-building processes of both the United States and Por-

---

[42] The 1988 Carol Cable strike in New Bedford is a case in point. In that strike, which was organized by the United Electric union (U.E.), workers of Carol Cable's local plant (whose labor force was majoritarily composed of Portuguese immigrants) perceived the company's attempt to impose wage cuts and cancel workers' health insurance as "discrimination against the Portuguese." In that context, they further claimed that their salaries were already lower than those of the workers of other Carol Cable plants. In their meetings they manifested their concern with the relocation of plants to other parts of the world. While the workers won that strike, Carol Cable closed its local plant in New Bedford one year later. Since then, numerous plants have closed their operations in the city.

[43] Younger immigrants in particular have said to me "A América está agora em Portugal" (America is now in Portugal) or "A América está agora nos Açores" (America is now in the Azores).

tugal take a prominent place. The constant recreation of historical memories, crystallized for Portuguese migrants in the concept of *saudade*, has its origins within the Portuguese nation-building processes and represents a continuity of the relationship between the Portuguese migrants and the Portuguese state. And these nation-building processes themselves both reflect and reinterpret the changing relationship of Portugal to world capitalist forces. Yet Portuguese migrants, at the same time, have created themselves as inheritors of *saudade* in relationship to their experience of settlement and work within the United States.

In earlier generations, U.S. nation-building processes sought to incorporate immigrants through assimilation, but in the context in which foreignness and racial difference were stigmatized and in which Portuguese immigrants tended to be seen as dark-skinned foreigners. In response, while some upwardly mobile Portuguese migrants intermarried and assimilated, much of the working class of earlier generations of migrants developed and maintained transnational family networks that melded together their lives in the United States and Portugal into a single set of relationships. Through these transnational networks migrants located themselves within Portugal, whose "imagined political community" was based on the supremacy of the Luzitan race and its overseas possessions. However, as emigrants from Portugal, the migrants were not fully welcome or secure in a Portugal which defined leaving the country as a betrayal of the state.

In the current conjuncture of capitalism, the Portuguese state has come to redefine itself as a global nation some of whose people live beyond the confines of the state. Central to this redefinition has been the legitimization of the transnational networks of its migrants as well as the very cultural construction of *saudade*. At the very same time that U.S. efforts at immigrant incorporation have now given public acceptance to celebrations of ethnic communities as building blocks of the American social fabric. The incorporative strategies of both nation-states coincide with the interest of an educated stratum of "transmigrants" (Glick Schiller, Basch, and Blanc-Szanton, this volume). Members of this stratum gain prestige and personal advantage by claiming to speak as representatives of an insulated Portuguese ethnic community of New Bedford without forswearing the benefits they obtain from remaining citizens in the Portuguese state. Whether it serves their working-class compatriots equally well to be incorporated into both settings, surrounded by the symbols of past glory but having a future of limited economic possibilities, is a different matter.

ACKNOWLEDGMENTS

The field research in New Bedford discussed in this paper was undertaken during my tenure as University Professor of Portuguese Studies at the University of Massachusetts–Dartmouth.

Different drafts of this paper were presented at: Columbia University (University Seminar on Cultural Pluralism); University of Coimbra (Center for Social Studies); Brown University (Center for Portuguese and Brazilian Studies); Lehman College of the City University of New York, and the New York Academy of Sciences. I profited from discussions with Drs. Emilia Viotti da Costa and David Montgomery. I am greatly indebted to Drs. Nina Glick Schiller, Linda Basch, and Cristina Blanc-Szanton for the framework they developed for the discussion of transnational migration. In particular, I am very grateful to Nina Glick Schiller for her input into the final version of this paper.

REFERENCES CITED

Aguiar, Manuela
    1986 *Politica de emigração e comunidades portuguesas*. Secretaria de Estudos, Série Migrações, Politica, Relações Internacionais, Porto.
Almeida, Onésimo T.
    1988 *L(U.S.A.)landia: A décima ilha*. Serviços de Emigração, Angra do Heroismo.
Anderson, Benedict
    1983 *Imagined communities: Reflections on the origin and spread of nationalism*. London/New York: Verso.
Arroteia, J. C.
    1985 *Atlas da emigração portuguesa*. Porto.
Basch, Linda, Nina Glick Schiller, and Cristina Blanc-Szanton
    1991 Transnationalism and the construction of the deterritorialized nation: An outline for a theory of post-national practices. Paper delivered at the meeting of the American Anthropological Association held in Chicago in November 1991.
    n.d. *Rethinking migration, ethnicity, race, and nationalism in transnational perspective*. New York: Gordon-Breach. Forthcoming.
Cabral, Stephen L.
    1989 *Tradition and transformation: Portuguese feasting in New Bedford*. AMS Press.
Carvalho, Eduardo de
    1931 *Os portugueses da Nova Inglaterra*. Rio de Janeiro: A Leitura Colonial.
Cassola Ribeiro, F. G.
    1986a *Emigração portuguesa: Aspectos relevantes relativos às politicas adoptadas no dominio da emigração portuguesa, desde a ultima guerra mundial*. Contribuição para o seu estudo. Secretaria de Estado das Comunidades Portuguesas. Instituto de Apoio à Emigração e às Comunidades Portuguesas, Série Migrações, Politica. Relações Internacionais, Porto.
    1986b *Emigração portuguesa: Algumas caracteristicas dominantes dos movimentos no periodo de 1950 a 1984*. Secretaria de Estado das Comunidades Portuguesas, Centro de Estudos, Série Migrações, Sociologia, Porto.
    1987 *Emigração portuguesa: Regulamentação emigratória do liberalismo ao fim da Segunda Guerra Mundial*. As above 1986a.
Feldman-Bianco, B.
    1991 A reinvenção da memória em festas migrantes. Paper presented at the Inter-

national Seminar *Festas: Tradição e inovação*, Universidade Aberta, Lisbon, November 11–13, 1991.

Feldman-Bianco, B. and D. Huse
n.d. The construction of the immigrant identity: The case of the Portuguese of Southeastern Massachusetts. In *Spinner: People and culture in Southeastern Massachusetts*, Vol. 5, edited by J. Thomas (special issue on the Portuguese of southeastern Massachusetts). In press.

Glick Schiller, Nina, Linda Basch, and Cristina Blanc-Szanton
1992 Transnationalism: A new analytic framework for understanding migration; Towards a definition of transnationalism: Introductory remarks and research questions. In *Towards a transnational perspective on migration: Race, class, ethnicity, and nationalism reconsidered*, edited by Nina Glick Schiller, Linda Basch, and Cristina Blanc-Szanton. *Annals of the New York Academy of Sciences* 645:1–24; ix–xiv. This volume.

Hobsbawm, Eric and Terence Ranger
1983 *The invention of tradition*. Cambridge University Press.

Kearney, Michael
1991 Borders and boundaries of the state and self at the end of empire. *Journal of Historical Sociology 4(1)*: 52–74.

Lourenço, Eduardo
1978 *O labrinto da saudade*. Publicações D. Quixote.

Montepio Luso-Americano (organization)
1932 *Os portugueses de New Bedford*. New Bedford, MA.

Pereira da Costa, D. L. and P. Gomes
Introdução à saudade. Porto: Lello & Irmão.

Rogers, Francis M.
1974 *Americans of Portuguese descent: A lesson in differentiation*. Sage Research Papers, Vol. 2.

Sá Pereira, Maria da Glória
1985 *A posição sócio-economica dos imigrantes portugueses e seus descendentes nos estados de Massachusetts e Rhode Island*. Porto: Secretaria de Estado das Comunidades Portuguesas.

Scott, James C.
1985 *Weapons of the weak: Everyday forms of peasant resistance*. New Haven, CT: Yale University Press.

Serrão, Joel
1982 *A emigração portuguesa*, 4th edition. Livros Horizonte.

Thompson, E. P.
1967 Time, work-discipline and industrial capitalism. *Past and Present 38*, December.

Vasconcelos, C. M.
1922 *A saudade portuguesa*, 2nd edition. Porto.

Williams, Raymond
1973 *The country and the city*. Oxford University Press.

NEWSPAPERS AND REPORTS

Diário de Noticias, New Bedford, MA (several issues).

Standard Times, New Bedford, MA (several issues).

East Bay Window, Newport, RI, March 1, 1989.

Relatório do Dia de Portugal, de Camões e das Comunidades Portuguesas, ano de 1977.

GENERAL BIBLIOGRAPHY

Adler, J.
1973   Ethnic minorities: The Portuguese, Vol. II. Cambridge.
Aguiar, M.
1987   Emigration policy and Portuguese communities. Secretaria do Estado das Comunidades Portuguesas, Centro de Estudos, Porto.
Almeida, O. T.
1983   (Sapa)téia Americana. Serviços de Emigração, Angra do Heroismo.
1988   L(U.S.A.) landia: A décima ilha. Serviços de Emigração, Angra do Heroismo.
Alpalhão, J. A. and Rosa, V.
1980   A minority in a changing society. University of Ottawa Press.
Anderson, B.
1983   Imagined communities. London: Verso.
Arroteia, J. C.
1985   Atlas da emigração portuguesa. Porto.
Bessa, A. Marques et al.
1988   Identidade portuguesa: Cumprir Portugal. Instituto Dom Joao de Castro, Lisboa.
Bourdieu, P.
1977   Outline of a theory of practice. Cambridge.
Brettell, Caroline B.
1986   Men who migrate, women who wait: Portuguese immigration and history in a Portuguese village. Princeton, NJ: Princeton University Press.
Bruneau, T. C., et al.
1984   Portugal in development: Emigration, industrialization, the European community. University of Ottawa Press.
Cabral, Stephen L.
1989   Tradition and transformation: Portuguese feasting in New Bedford. AMS Press.
Cassola Ribeiro, F. G.
1986a   Emigração portuguesa: Algumas características dominantes dos movimentos no período de 1950 a 1984. Secretaria do Estado das Comunidades Portuguesas, Centro de Estudos, Série Migrações, Sociologia, Porto.
1986b   Emigração portuguesa: Aspectos relativos às politicas adotadas no dominio de emigração portuguesa, desde a ultima guerra mundial. Contribuiçao para o seu estudo. Secretaria de Estado das Comunidades Portuguesas. Instituto de Apoio à Emigração e às Comunidades Portuguesas, Série Migrações, Politica. Relações Internacíonais, Porto.
1987   Emigração portuguesa: Regulamentação emigratoria do liberalismo ao fim da Segunda Guerra Mundial. Contribuiçao para o seu estudo. Secretaria de Estado das Comunidades Portuguesas. Instituto de Apoio à Emigração e às Comunidades Portuguesas, Série Migrações, Politica. Relações Internacíonais, Porto.
Castro, Ferreira de
1928   Emigrantes. Lisboa.
1930   A selva. Lisboa.
Cortes, C. E.
1980   Portuguese Americans and Spanish Americans. New York: Arno Press.
Evangelista, J.
1971   Um século de emigração portuguesa (1864–1960). Lisboa.
Glick Schiller, Nina, Linda Basch, and Cristina Blanc-Szanton, Eds.
1992   Towards a transnational perspective on migration: Race, class, ethnicity, and nation-

alism reconsidered. *Annals of the New York Academy of Sciences*. *Vol. 645*. This volume.

Harris, M.
1969   *Patterns of race in the Americas*. New York: Columbia University Press.

Hobsbawn, E. T. Ranger
1985   *The invention of tradition*, Cambridge.

Lamphere, L.
1987   *From working daughters to working mothers: Immigrant women in a New England industrial community*. Ithaca: Cornell University Press.

Leonardo, Micaela di
1984   *The varieties of ethnic experience*. Cornell

Mayone Dias, E. (org.)
1988   *Portugueses na América do Norte*. Peregrinação.
1990   *Falares emigreses—Uma abordagem ao seu estudo*. Biblioteca Breve, Lisboa.

Neto, Felix
1986   *A migração portuguesa vivida e representada*. Secretaria do Estado das Comunidades Portuguesas, Porto.

Pap, Leo
1982   *The Portuguese Americans*. Ywayne Publishers.

Portes, A. and R. G. Rumbaut
1990   *Immigrant America*. University of California Press.

Rocha-Trindade, M. B.
1973   *Immigrès portugais*. Lisboa.
1981   Estudos sobre a emigração portuguesa cadernos. *Revista de História Economica e Social*.

Rogers, F. M.
1974   *Americans of Portuguese descent: A lesson in differentiation*. Sage Research Papers, Vol. 2.

Rosen, E. I.
1987   *Bitter choices*. Chicago: University of Chicago Press.

Sá Pereira, M. G.
1985   *A posição sócio-economica dos imigrantes portugueses e seus descendentes nos Estados de Massachusetts e Rhode Island*. Secretaria do Estado das Comunidades Portuguesas, Porto.

Saraiva, A. J. and C. Lepes
1955   *História da cultura em Portugal*. Lisboa.

Scott, J. C.
1985   *Weapons of the poor*. Yale University Press.

Taft, Donald R.
1924   *Two Portuguese communities in New England*.

Wallerstein, I.
1976   *The modern world-system*. New York: Academic Press.

Waters, M. C.
1990   *Ethnic options: Choosing identities in America*. University of California Press.

Williams, J.
1983   *And yet they come: Portuguese immigration from the Azores to the United States*.

Implications of Transnational Migration for Nationalism: The Caribbean Example

ROSINA WILTSHIRE[a]

Caribbean Conservation Association
Bridgetown, Barbados
and
Development Alternative with Women for a New Era (DAWNE)
Bridgetown, Barbados

INTRODUCTION

The creation of Caribbean transnational networks rests on the foundation of a transnational family, in which migrants and their families have multiple home bases with ongoing commitments and loyalties that straddle territorial boundaries. It is posited that members of these networks are likely to hold multiple national loyalties. Multiple loyalties are likely to emerge, because the family and nation transcend territorial boundaries, and the early family socialization takes place at critical points in the formation of the individuals encompassed in these networks. However, there may be intervening elements such as race and ethnicity, which may serve to exclude the migrant from full integration into the host territory, thus tempering the development or sustaining of multiple loyalties among the adult migrants. The response of adult migrants is often an intense nationalism to their Caribbean home country.

Gender is another potential intervening factor tempering the negative effects of race and ethnicity in the North American context for Caribbean adult female migrants. North America may offer women migrants greater opportunities for continuing education and income earning. These combined with the larger scale of the societies may allow women more independence and potential for breaking out of gender-stereotyped roles. This has the effect of somewhat muting their intense nationalism and desire to return home.

For the offspring of these migrants in the metropolitan host cities, their sense of national identity and national loyalty may reflect confusion rather than multiple loyalties. However, multiple loyalties are most likely to be

[a] Address for correspondence: Dr. Rosina Wiltshire, 202 Atlantic Shores, Christ Church, Barbados; FAX: (809) 429-8483.

forged during formation of the second generation, the children of migrants both in the host and donor societies. Ironically, strong multiple loyalties are most likely to be reflected in the donor societies, where the children have a mythical perception of the host as representing plenty and capacity to confer well-being. All of this has significant implications for social science theory and analysis and development policy and planning.

The arguments presented here are preliminary and draw on data and impressions emerging from a study of Caribbean regional and international migration undertaken between 1982 and 1988 among Vincentian and Grenadian migrants in New York and Trinidad and their family members with whom they were in closest contact remaining in Grenada and St. Vincent. The paper thus raises preliminary questions which need to be substantiated by further research. An important question which implicitly arises as requiring research is the extent to which the issues surrounding migration, transnational networks, and nationalism are a Caribbean phenomenon or extend more generally to other regions.

CARIBBEAN TRANSNATIONAL MIGRATION: THE EMERGENCE OF NATIONS

The creation of transnational integrative linkages has been taking place as a consequence of the massive movements of migrants across national boundaries in a global context of heightened communication links. Migration is not a new phenomenon, and Caribbean migration has been a central facet of Caribbean life since emancipation in 1838. What has dramatically changed has been the communications technology which facilitates and reinforces the economic, political, and cultural transnational networks established between migrants and their families remaining in the donor societies. These transterritorial networks affect the broader societal political, economic, and sociocultural fields of both donor and host societies. They also have broader implications for analysis of regional development premised on traditional concepts of territorially bounded nations and pivotal socializing institutions such as the family.

Where do Caribbean nations begin and where do they end? More Grenadians live outside of Grenada than within its borders. This is true for many of the smaller Caribbean islands. Caribbean migration flows have historically been a significant factor in national development. In the earliest period of intra-Caribbean migration just after emancipation, as a consequence of the massive intraregional flows in which Trinidad and Tobago and then British Guyana were the major recipients, Trinidad in the 136 years after 1844, multiplied its population more than 14 times, while Guyana's population increased over the same period by almost 8 times. In contrast, the populations of Barbados and the Leeward islands, which were the major donors, did not even double (Marshall 1984:3).

Even in this early period the movements represented backward and forward flows rather than unidirectional once for all time population shifts. The magnitude of these flows made it difficult for officials and census takers to count populations. In recognition of the population fluidity, the Barbados Census Report of 1881 stated "the Christmas holiday season will soon swell the number of the population considerably beyond what it is at present, as people will be coming from Demarara, Antigua, Grenada and elsewhere to pass the time with their relatives and friends" (Marshall 1984:17). The Guyana 1883 Immigration Report corroborated this by noting that "a large proportion of them arrive in the colony after the end of June when work becomes scarce in Barbados, and return to the island to spend Christmas and crop time" (Marshall 1984:17). Trinidad planters tried to control the backward and forward flows.

The concept of nation bounded by clear territorial boundaries was grounded in the emergence of the European nation states, with nationalism perceived as a bounded zero sum concept carrying with it implications for exclusive loyalties. The Caribbean experience indicates that this has not necessarily been part of a Caribbean reality. The concepts of nation and nation-state were also formulated to explain the emergence of the European states at a point in history when communications and technology limited transnational interaction and migration was negligible. Territorial boundaries were thus one of the most significant and reliable indicators in the delineation of nation. The major social science disciplines, political science, economics, sociology, and anthropology drawing on European experience have taken as a basic point of departure a well-delimited, territorially circumscribed unit of analysis in the examination of political, economic and socio-cultural institutions.

Not only have a relatively fixed population and clearly defined national boundaries been central to the rules and theories governing international law, politics and economics, but the assumptions have also underpinned theories of domestic politics, economics and society, and current liberal theories and strategies of development. Loyalty to a nation-state or nationalism was defined as a critical element of territorial integrity and one of the bases for defining a viable national entity. Economic analyses, projecting savings and its role in development often premise their analysis on the assumption that the average individual, unlike the multinationals, operates within a relatively well-defined territorial sphere. Economists and policy makers did not conceive of a rational economic person functioning across territorial boundaries with family, commitments and loyalties straddling territorial boundaries. For the Caribbean territories, long-term emigration has resulted in pivotal socializing institutions like the family transcending national boundaries. This holds implications for national loyalties and nationalism as well as the behavior in the economic, political and social spheres likely to derive from those loyalties. It also calls for a re-examination of the traditional assumptions and premises which continue to inform Caribbean development analysis.

Multiple loyalties where the individual identifies with and has strong loyalties to more than one political and national entity is not a new phenomenon. The Texan's loyalty to Texas as well as to the United States has been well noted. However, in the latter case one sovereign entity is involved. Migration has given rise to a phenomenon where multiple loyalties are held towards different sovereign entities occupying distinct territorial boundaries. The implications of these transterritorial multiple loyalties are particularly significant because in the modern era, the loyalties are held to territorial units with vastly unequal economic and political resources such as the Caribbean territories relative to the United States and Canada. Where the migration has been to a regional host of relatively equitable size and economic potential, the implications of the transterritorial links and multiple loyalties are likely to be different for development potential.

Because modern migration has involved movements from the economically poor third world countries to the wealthy industrial countries of the north, divided or multiple loyalties have potentially severe implications for the more vulnerable donor society in times of economic uncertainty. Billions of dollars are transferred annually in remittances from migrants in northern industrial states to families in third world donor societies. However, in unstable periods, it is possible for the outflow of savings and people to outweigh the inflows. One facet of these flows is that the more privileged and business community are more likely to export savings, while those at the lower end of the social scale for whom migration may not be an easy option would continue to be the recipients of the largest segment of remittances. Socialized into multiple loyalties, those for whom migration is possible, the young and well educated of the societies would tend to see migration as a first option when national crisis or instability looms.

THE CARIBBEAN PROFILE

This study focuses on the Commonwealth Caribbean where research was conducted on the impact of regional and international migration, examining the movements of Grenadians and Vincentians to Trinidad the major regional host and the United States (New York), the major international host territory. The research involved systematic in-depth interviews and participant observation. Interviews were conducted with 131 Grenadians and Vincentians in 78 households in New York and 98 migrants in 72 households in Trinidad. Because of the difficulty in identifying undocumented migrants through standard sampling techniques, a snowball method of identifying the samples was used. Migrant networks, churches and church leaders, and community leaders were used to identify the samples. Census and immigration data were used as frames to ensure the representative nature of the sample. In St. Vincent and Grenada approximately half the sample was identified through migrant kin living in New York and Trinidad; the other half was identified using the snowball technique.

Most CARICOM countries have experienced positive growth rates over the last decade, particularly among the smaller Organisation of Eastern Caribbean States (OECS), whose economies are dependent on tourism. However, they have had average open unemployment levels of approximately 20–25%, with particularly high unemployment levels among youth 15–25 years old. Prices of major regional exports have been falling on the world market and debt servicing is increasingly becoming a significant problem affecting the region's capacity for growth and sustainable development. Tourism represents a major growth industry, but it tends to be an industry not well integrated into the rest of the economy. With the growing sophistication of the communication technology within this service industry, local hoteliers and entrepreneurs are finding it increasingly difficult to compete with the multinationals whose hotels are linked with the airlines and travel agencies. Tourism also is a very fickle industry and economic pressures in the countries of origin or political or social instability in the tourist destinations can wipe out tourist markets overnight.

Small size and limited natural resources have made the region's human resources its greatest asset, and policy makers at a rhetorical level assert the importance of human resource development. However, at the practical policy level human capital formation has been seen more as a spin off of development than a route to development and the raison d'etre of the development process. Before independence the local population was regarded as a source of labor in the service of metropolitan profit; since independence emphasis has been placed on the role of capital in the development process with human capital development perceived as a spin off from the "more efficient" capital-intensive development. Emigration has thus tended to be perceived by policy makers as a safety valve for the outflow of surplus labor. Policy makers have tended to view as problematic only the emigration of the skilled and professional class whose "educational investment" and brainpower are seen as a loss to the donor society.

With development strategies tending to emphasize the role of capital and often seeming to place less emphasis on people and human resource development, Caribbean people have continued to seek jobs and status enhancement in metropolitan host centers.

CARIBBEAN MIGRANT FLOWS AND
TRANSNATIONAL LINKAGES

Since emancipation, emigration has provided an important route to education, employment, and status mobility for both the migrant and the family. These massive flows have continued into the post-independence period as development strategies continue to marginalize the region's human resources. In the 30-year period spanning 1950–1980 it is estimated that net emigration from the Caribbean totalled approximately 4.2 million with Caribbean Community (CARICOM) countries accounting for 1.4 million. CARICOM countries have a combined population of approximately 5.5 million. The movements continue to be regional and international, with Trinidad one of the traditional regional hosts and the United States and Canada the largest international recipients.

The Networks

Transnational networks are forged and sustained through a variety of mechanisms. These include regular communications through the telephone, visits and correspondence, economic remittances, childcare, and general social support. The elements often overlap and there is reciprocity. While money and food stuffs were sent by the migrants in Trinidad to their relatives back home, those remaining in the donor societies tended to send agricultural foodcrops grown on the family plots back to the migrants. Because of the geographical distance, the reverse remittances were not a strong facet of the New York flows. Relatives in the donor societies manage property and savings for migrants in both regional and international hosts. One third of the migrants had stayed with relatives when first migrating and relatives helped with finding the first job and getting settled.

The Gender Dimension

The early flows were predominantly male, but the 1960s represented the period in which women began to migrate in significant numbers. There were several factors at work, the most important of which were the technological revolution in manufacturing and industry and the growth of the service sector. There is now relative equity in the numbers of males and females emigrating from the region.

Gender is not a significant factor differentiating the strength of migrant linkages with home. However, gender is a significant factor in defining who are the pivotal points in the transnational network in the donor societies. Both male and female migrants maintained the strongest links with a female member of the family, often a mother, sister, or grandmother in the donor society.

Women are the greatest beneficiaries of migrant remittances from abroad because they are also the poorest and carry the heaviest family responsibilities. Our data revealed that families at the lowest end of the income scale received the most remittances. Migrants at the upper end of the income scale tended to send gifts for birthdays and Christmas to the family remaining behind, while those at the lower end of the income scale tended to receive remittances regularly. Eighty-one percent of the sample earning less than US$5,000 received regular remittances, while only 27% of those families earning above US$30,000 received regular remittances.

The levels of remittances thus reflected not the income earning levels of the migrants but the needs of the family remaining behind. Because women were in the lowest income group, representing the poorest of the poor, women tended to receive more remittances than men. These women spend the money on the household for food, health, education and shelter. The remittances indicated families attempting to slightly attenuate the larger societal prejudices which lead to discrimination against women and the poorest in the allocation of resources.

Child care was an important dimension of the network and has implications particularly for the socialization of the young. Just over one-third of the sample in the donor countries were taking care of children of migrant relatives and all of the child-minders were women. The largest in this category were grandmothers, had only primary education and were at the lower end of the income scale. Less than 10% of this group was dissatisfied with the level of remittances and support which they got from the parents of the children in their care.

A large segment of the female huckster trade appeared to be part of the transnational network. Women relatives in the donors who made their living by buying and selling goods, often traveled far afield in their trade, using their migrant relatives' homes abroad as bases for accommodation. For these women many of whom had only primary school education, traveling to New York, Trinidad, Panama or Aruba held no fears or surprises because they had second homes or because they had an international perspective nurtured by the migration network.

The female in the donor society represented the hub around which the networks were forged and the transnational family emerged as the critical institution underpinning the transnational networks and socializing its members into multiple national loyalties.

NATIONALISM AND THE TRANSNATIONAL FAMILY: PIVOTAL SOCIALIZING AGENCY

The Transnational Family

Multiple loyalties to donor and host societies become inculcated early in members of the transnational family. The genesis of nationalism lies with the family where socialization takes place at the earliest formative stages of the individual's life. It is within the family that attitudes are first molded and loyalties instilled to community and nation. The direction of these loyalties and their strength have important consequences for the development potential of a state.

Traditionally it has been assumed that the family was demarcated by the household existing within defined territorial boundaries. Increasingly, however, in the third world, economic crisis and limited opportunities for work at home have meant that the work place for a large proportion of those between the ages of 15 and 40, is located outside of the national territorial boundaries. Research on Caribbean migration has indicated that for a wide range of individuals the work place is located outside the territorial boundaries.

The transnational family is a large amorphous structure made up of conjugal and nuclear units as well as consanguinal segments that spread across national boundaries. The transnational family is characterized by a network of interdependent linkages. Critical family functions such as economic support, decision-making and nurturing are divided among the central links in the network. As was noted, traditionally the tendency was for the migrant father to reside in the host societies, while children, mother, and grandmother remained at home in the donor country. Increasingly with the growth of the service sector and industries that favor the use of cheap female labor, mothers are as likely to be migrants as fathers.

While for some families migration represents cutting ties, for the majority it represents the creation or reinforcement of a mutually interdependent support network which is neither bounded by the household nor national boundaries. It provides an opportunity for its members to adapt to and partially transcend the realities of unemployment, economic crises, limited opportunity, and mobility which have characterized the majority of the third world states. Migrant parents in the host societies often perform the breadwinner role by sending back remittances on a regular basis to supplement the meager earnings of the family members remaining in the donor society. Over 65% of the migrants in both regional and metropolitan hosts indicated that they sent remittances back home, and this was corroborated by the families in the donor communities. The units share in decision-making on issues which involve major household expenditure such as home rebuilding and major investments as well as decisions relating to the children's education and health care.

TRANSNATIONAL LINKS AND MULTIPLE LOYALTIES

The Donor Context

Children growing up in the donor society receive early messages about the host society as representing the land of opportunity, money and gifts, which are reinforced by the media stereotypes. The myth of North America as the promised land is one which becomes embedded in the regional psyche. There are extremely few Caribbean families today who have no experience of migration. This is true even of the regional host territories whose populations were built on the basis of migrant labor and who lose populations just as rapidly during periods of instability. Fifteen thousand migrants from Trinidad left the island and claimed refugee status in Canada in one year when the drop in international oil prices sent the economy into a tailspin. In the tiny islands such as Grenada and St. Vincent, whose populations number approximately 100,000, we asked our interviewers if they could identify one family which did not have close migrant relatives, and not a single family was found.

Even when the migrant has to maintain more than one job to help the family, the migrant and the family behind become co-conspirators in the myth of success in the borrowed homeland. Myra, one of our respondents in New York epitomizes the pattern. Myra is making US$12,000 a year, is threatened with eviction by her landlord, but sends the barrel of foodstuff and clothing back to her family in St. Vincent four times per year and money once per month. She believes that a migrant's first obligation is to help the family back home financially (Wiltshire, Basch, and Wiltshire 1990).

On the occasions when the migrants visit their relatives back home, they often travel even when coming from the most depressed slums of New York or Toronto, laden with boxes and suitcases crammed with gifts of food and clothes for the relatives remaining behind. For the young, the images of two home bases, one offering opportunity and plenty is implanted indelibly. It is no wonder, that at the first pinch of economic crisis in the donor territories, all roads lead to the alternative home in the North American paradise with massive legal and illegal outflows. Only personal experience alters the images, but, although individual attitudes and allegiances shift, as migrants they become active players in the drama of "Paradise Found."

The Host Context

Race, Ethnicity and Gender: Intervening Factors

Race and ethnicity are powerful intervening factors in mediating the development of multiple loyalties and strong nationalist identification with the host territories. In this regard, there is a sharp dichotomy between the regional host territories and the international hosts. Once the reality of the metropolitan host context is tested, the Caribbean migrant finds the fact of belonging to a minority racial underclass a major deterrent to open opportunity and integration. In an attempt to distance themselves from the low status designation, Caribbean migrants cocoon themselves in their Caribbean national identities and become more firmly wedded to their nations of birth than they perhaps ever were previously. The proliferation of voluntary organizations among Grenadians and Vincentians in New York is one indication of this strenthened home identification. While there were officially 2,700 Vincentians and 5,000 Grenadians in New York, there were 18 Vincentian and 20 Grenadian voluntary organizations (Basch and Wiltshire 1990). Similarly the strength of nationalism is nowhere as strong as among the Caribbean migrant national association groupings in Canadian metropolitan centers.

Within New York, migrants regardless of sex were more likely to identify themselves as Grenadian or Vincentian than as American. It was normal to hear migrants who had lived for 20 years in the United States to speak of home as Grenada or St. Vincent. Most migrants expressed the wish to return home eventually, although an interesting gender difference emerged. Migration imposed on males the need for less rigidity in observing gender-differentiated roles. Female migrants were as likely to have jobs outside the home as male migrants. The New York context thus seemed to allow women greater income earning capacity and more flexibility within the household. In spite of the fact that women generally tended to earn less than their male counterparts, the relative freedom from the rigid gender roles in their small societies made women less likely to express a desire to return home than their male counterparts.

Our data collection did not involve formal interviews with the second generation raised in the host community, although participant observation did allow some informal discussions and insights into the formation of their national identity. This second generation is more likely to be confused about their national identity than to reflect the classic pattern of multiple loyalties to the host country in which they are reared and to the home country from which their parents originate. One child of migrants who had been born and reared in New York confessed to a great deal of confusion and disappointment on the first visit back to the Caribbean. She confessed that she had always thought of herself as Vincentian because that is what she had learned from her parents. However, on returning "home" for her first visit, other children called her foreigner and American and continually commented about her accent. She admitted that she became very confused about her identity and still had not worked out clearly whether she was West Indian or American, even though she is now an adult. Her parents define themselves as Vincentian and home as St. Vincent even though they have lived in the United States for over 30 years.

For the child of Caribbean migrants brought up in Canada the allegiances to a particular country are likely to be even more confused. The United States admits of a category called black Americans or Afro-Americans. In Canada, apart from the acknowledgment of native Indians, who fall at the base of the social ladder, there is still a general perception that non-whites are foreigners regardless of how long they or their ancestors have been part of the society. For the children of migrants, the confusion of national identity may have implications for their mental and social well-being and achievement potential, but there is little research on this group. Much more research is indicated to understand the intersection of migration, race, ethnicity and nationalism. The regional host offered some insights because of the different significance of race and ethnicity for the Caribbean migrant within the Trinidad setting.

The pattern of nationalist identification shifted dramatically in the interviews with migrants in the regional host, Trinidad. Grenadian and Vincentian form the largest group of migrants in Trinidad. There are 21,127 Grenadian and 13,500 Vincentian migrants according to the 1980 national Census figures. Trinidad has a population of approximately 1.5 million. Blacks and (Asian) Indians make up the two numerically dominant groups, unlike most CARICOM states in which blacks are the overwhelming majority. Important for the status and integration of the Grenadian and Vincentian migrants, however is the fact that there is not the horizontal stratification of blacks which exists in America with blacks at the bottom of the social ladder. The regional host is stratified vertically with blacks and Indians at all levels of the social scale.

While migrants in New York identified themselves as Grenadian or Vincentian, their counterparts in Trinidad tended to identify themselves as Trinidadian/Grenadians or Trinidadian/Vincentians. Their contacts with home were as strong as the metropolitan migrant group and the economic remittances as important a part of the transnational network. They tended to be involved in the local political and social institutions. Interestingly, the Trinidad-based migrants tended to cluster in Baptist or fundamentalist churches regardless of their religious affiliation when entering as migrants. The religious community remained the migrants' base of contact with the community left behind, but the tendency to cluster in voluntary nationalist organizations was not replicated in the regional setting.

The phenomenon of multiple national identifications seemed to operate most purely in a context in which strong reinforcing cleavages such as race, color, ethnicity and class did not serve to limit the chances of full assimilation into the society. It must be noted that in both regional and international contexts, migrants were as likely to put down roots by giving high priority to owning their homes no matter how humble. In New York they clustered in

West Indian neighborhoods whereas in Trinidad they did not. This difference, however, is as much a reflection of the tacit racial factors at play in limiting openness on the New York housing market, as it is the choice of the migrant wishing to nurture their West Indian identity by being close to friends and family in a relatively alien environment. Migrants were also as likely to vote and participate in politics in both home and host contexts, and attempting to influence the vote of relatives back home. The importance of the migrant political constituency in New York, for the Caribbean politicians has been amply discussed by Basch (1987).

What is indicated is that for the migrant, opportunities to indicate loyalty and willingness to be more integrated in the hosts are seized even when the migrant feels that there are systemic factors limiting their integration into the host, with the result that their expression of national identification with the host is weak. Nationalist identification seemed to have more implications for the private and social spheres. It indicated who friends and social associates were most likely to be, as in the case of the voluntary associations. It also gave indications of perceptions of the host society as being hostile, a bad influence for children, and lonely. It seems that it is at the psychological levels of sense of well-being that the differences observed in the regional and international hosts are most likely to lend greatest insight. The migrants themselves seemed to compensate for the sense of social rejection by over-identification with the home. At the same time there seemed to be an attempt to overcompensate in the economic sphere in order to justify the dislocation and maintain the myth of the success story. Implications for migrants' mental and general health, stress and depression related illnesses may be indicated. The issue clearly raises more questions than can be answered along a range of dimensions and with implications not only for the social sciences, but for psychology, community health and development specialists in general.

While the migrants themselves seem to arrive at compensatory balancing mechanisms, migration, the resulting transnational networks and multiple loyalties may have fundamental implications for the second generations both in the host and donor societies and for long-term development potential within the donors. There is little work on this second generation and substantial research is required in this area. These perspectives are preliminary, but the potential implications for the social sciences, development theory and policy indicate an urgent need for further research.

SELECTED BIBLIOGRAPHY

Anderson, Patricia
    1986   Migration off the record: A balance sheet of manpower losses from Jamaica,
            1979–84. Paper delivered at Caribbean Studies Association Meeting,
            Caracas, Venezuela.

Bakan, Abigail
  1987 The international market for female labour and individual deskilling: West
        Indian women workers in Toronto. *Canadian Journal of Latin American and
        Caribbean Studies 12, No. 24*:69–86.
Basch, Linda
  1982 *Population movements within the English-speaking Caribbean.* New York:
        United Nations.
  1987 The politics of Caribbeanization. In *Caribbean life in New York City: Sociocul-
        tural dimensions*, edited by C. R. Sutton and E. M. Chaney. New York:
        Center for Migration Studies. Pp. 160–181.
Basch, Linda and Rosina Wiltshire
  1990 Caribbean regional and international migration. Prepared for the Interna-
        tional Development Research Centre, (IDRC) Ottawa, Canada.
CARICOM Secretariat
  1988 Caribbean development to the year 2000: Challenges, perspectives and pol-
        icies. London: Commonwealth Secretariat
Girling, Robert *et al.*
  1985 Eastern Caribbean Human Resource Development. Sector Assessment Pre-
        pared for the USAID Regional Development Office, Caribbean.
Guengant, Jean Pierre
  1984 Recent Caribbean migrations. Paper Delivered at CARICOM Population
        Awareness Conference, St. Lucia.
Marshall, Dawn
  1982 *The history of Caribbean migrants: The case of the West Indies.* Vol. 11. No. 1.
  1984 Migration within the eastern Caribbean 1835–1980. Paper presented at the
        Conference on Cultural Contacts and Migration in the Caribbean, Barbados.
Massiah, Joycelin
  1983 Women as heads of households in the Caribbean. Paris: UNESCO.
Simmons, A. and J. Guengant
  n.d.   Caribbean exodus and the world system. In *Global interactions: International
        migration systems in an interdependent world*, edited by M. Kritz, L. Lim, and
        H. Zlotnik. Oxford: Oxford University Press. Forthcoming.
Simmons, A. and D. Plaza
  1991 International migration and schooling in the eastern Caribbean. Prepared
        for the Organisation of Eastern Caribbean States Commission on Education
        Reform.
Thomas-Hope, E. M.
  1985 Return migration and its implications for Caribbean development: The un-
        explored connection. In *Migration and development in the Caribbean: The
        unexplored connection*, edited by Robert Pastor. Boulder, CO: Westview.
Wiltshire, R.
  1986 The Caribbean transnational family. Paper delivered at UNESCO/ISER
        Seminar on Changing Family Patterns and Women's Role in the Caribbean.
        UWI, Cave Hill, Barbados.
Wiltshire, Rosina, Linda Basch, and W. Wiltshire
  1990 Caribbean transnational migrant networks: Implications for donor soci-
        eties. Prepared for International Development Research Centre, Ottawa,
        Canada.

"A *Lavalas* at Home/A *Lavalas* for Home"

Inflections of Transnationalism in the Discourse of Haitian President Aristide

KAREN RICHMAN

Department of Anthropology
University of Virginia
Charlottesville, Virginia 22903

Lavalas means deluge in Haitian Creole. A lavalas surges with the first torrential rains after a drought and ravages everything in its path only to fertilize the ground anew. Jean-Claude Martineau, writing and composing in exile under the pseudonym of Koralin, invoked the lavalas image in his celebrated 1975 freedom song, *Ayiti Demen* (Haiti Tomorrow), to describe an utter destruction of the Duvalierist state. A grassroots deluge propelled by "little churches" (*Ti Kominite Legliz*) indeed brought down President-for-Life Jean-Claude Duvalier in 1986. But the United States hastily intervened to install a military junta which dutifully pledged their commitment to a transition to a civilian government. Macabre incarnations of "Duvalierism without Duvalier" brutally restrained the tide for fundamental political change spilling over America's pesky dependency until October 1990, when Haitians unleashed a torrent of unprecedented solidarity known as "Lavalas." Their anthem: Martineau's *Ayiti Demen*; their slogan: "Alone we are weak, together we are strong, united together we are a lavalas!"[1]

---

[1] *Ayiti Demen* was the title song of the third album by Soley Leve. The song is commonly known as "*Lè la Libere Ayiti va Bèl*" (When it is Free Haiti will be Beautiful), taken from the words of the refrain. Jean-Claude Martineau (Koralin) composed *Ayiti Demen* during an especially fertile creative period for young Haitian exiled artists and intellectuals involved in organizing against the U.S. imperialist-Duvalierist alliance (Buchanan 1980). Their compositions enjoyed a resurgence of popularity during the mid to late 1980s, as the grassroots movement to liberate Haiti of dictatorship swelled.

So intimately was the *Ayiti Demen* song identified with the progressive, "little church" movement of the late 1980s that some assumed the song was created by one of their own, a presumption which the actual composer felt disinclined to correct. As Jean-Claude Martineau described to me, he had just delivered a performance of poems and stories at St. Jean Bosco. (Father Aristide preached from the St. Jean Bosco pulpit until September, 1988, when the militia massacred congregants attending his mass and burned down the chapel). After the performance, Jean-Claude was approached by a few young people who said they wanted to demonstrate that young militant artists back home had not been sitting idly; they, too, had been composing music of resistance.

An intrepid "little priest," the author of the Lavalas slogan, had just declared his last-minute decision to campaign for the Haitian presidency in the upcoming December elections. A masterful orator and champion of the indigent and downtrodden, Father Jean-Bertrand Aristide had been a dauntless leader in the movement to "uproot" Duvalier and, during the imperialist-junta alliance which succeeded the dictator, he thrice narrowly escaped martyrdom (Richman 1990b).

When Father Aristide announced his campaign, he minimized identification with his nominating party—a fragile alliance that splintered soon after the elections—and emphasized instead affiliation with the Lavalas "party of the people." Aristide's usage of "the people" meant Haitians "inside" the country's nine provinces and Haitians dispersed "outside" throughout "the Tenth Province" (*Dizyèm Depatman an*). Speaking at a rally before 20,000 supporters in Miami (the second largest population center of the Haitian diaspora) two weeks after his entry into the electoral race, Aristide launched "Lavalas For (the benefit of) Home" (*Lavalas Pou Lakay*). "Lavalas For Home" would descend along with "Lavalas At Home" (*Lavalas Lakay*) to clear the ground at Home:

Gen Lavalas Lakay.	There is Lavalas at Home.
Gen Lavalas pou Lakay.	There is Lavalas for Home.
Lavalas lakay se pitit kay	Lavalas at Home are our people
Ki mete ansanm pou yo desann.	Who unite together to go down.
Nou se Lavalas pou Lakay	You are Lavalas For Home
Ki bay randevou Lakay.	Who have an appointment at Home.
Si Lakay poko bèl	If Home is not yet beautiful
Lakay pral vin bèl.	Home will become beautiful.
Fòk Lakay vin bèl.	Home must become beautiful.
	(*Haïti Progrès* 7–13 November, 1990).[2]

"Lavalas For Home" financed the Aristide campaign with a flood of wages earned by Haitian migrants in Miami, New York, Montréal, Boston, Chicago, Paris and beyond. Lavalas at Home handed Aristide 67% of the vote in the 12 party contest on December 12th.

TRANSNATIONALISM AND LAVALAS DISCOURSE

The swift mobilization of "Lavalas For Home" in support of Aristide's candidacy confirms that the Haitian electoral process took place Outside as much

---

Then they sang "*their* song," *Ayiti Demen.* "Who was *I* to tell *them*," he recalled thinking to himself, "I wrote *their* song?"

   [2] The metaphor of home becoming beautiful may invoke the refrain (and informal title) of *Ayiti Demen*: "when it is free, Haiti will be beautiful" (*lè la libere Ayiti va bèl o*).

as Inside. The transnational setting of the recent Haitian political contest is one instance of a growing world phenomenon (Basch 1987; Basch, Glick Schiller and Blanc-Szanton, this volume; Lessinger, this volume). For like other workers whose movements followed and reinforced the transnational redistribution of capital over the last two decades, Haitians are constructing and reinventing social relations, religious ties, economic strategies, and political allegiances which continuously straddle international borders (Basch, Glick Schiller and Szanton-Blanc this volume; Sutton 1987; Glick Schiller and Fouron 1990; Richman 1990a and n.d.).

In the opening essay of this volume, Linda Basch, Nina Glick Schiller and Cristina Blanc-Szanton present three general patterns of transnationalism, which can guide our exploration of Aristide's discourse on the Haitian experience of migration. First, mobile laborers endure chronic, compound vulnerability in relation to both home and host societies. Second, migrants create cross-national relations, networks, and institutions as mainstays of security. Third, such strategies encompass, rather than resolve, conflicting tendencies, some overt and others latent, to resist and to accommodate incorporation into the structures of their migration.

This see-saw in the experience of international displacement figured and refigured in Aristide's forceful rhetoric with and about Haitian migrants. I would suggest that the preacher's successive transformations of this dialectic, as opposed to his resolution of it, contributed to his overwhelming endorsement by "Lavalas For Home." Aristide identified with Haitian migrants' experience of double insecurity and their contradictory proclivities both to reject and to acquiesce to it. His fervent discourse of protest, carried by an antiphonal style widely interpreted as a metaphor of popular political empowerment, exhorted migrants to reject policies of colluding home and host states contributing to their oppression. His subdued, but equally persuasive, rhetoric of accommodation, on the other hand, encouraged the birds of passage to continue following and abetting the asymmetrical migrations of transnational capital.

I wish to explore the tension between resistance and accommodation in Aristide's rhetoric covering a one year period from the spring of 1990 to the spring of 1991. Five motifs in Aristide's discourse will frame the discussion: the Cigar of Resistance, Creole Tourists, the Bank of the Diaspora, the Earring in the Goldsmith Shop, and the Tenth Province.

INSECURITY OUTSIDE: KROME AND AIDS

Two issues crystallized and exposed the chronic insecurity of Haitian immigrants in the United States during the last decade and so figured prominently in the contest of Haitian ethnic identity (Buchanan 1980; Glick

Schiller *et al.* 1987 and Glick Schiller and Fouron 1990). Both issues involved agencies of the United States government in "constructing" an alien threat to the nation and then intervening to control it. First was a menacing marine invasion of black, indigent refugees from the most reviled country in the hemisphere to which the state "responded" with a capricious–but reliably discriminatory–immigration policy (Stepick 1982). Within a few years came a second rationale for a discriminatory immigration policy and informal exclusion of Haitians from American society: the spurious branding of Haitians as carriers of the stigmatized Acquired Immune Deficiency Syndrome (AIDS) by the Center for Disease Control.

Since the late seventies, when boatloads of Haitian refugees "invaded" the south Florida coast, the Immigration and Naturalization Service has treated Haitian refugees as criminals, imprisoning them in Maimi's Krome detention center and dispersing them to federal prisons in several other states to await deportation proceedings. Most of the refugees arriving before 1982 were eventually released, thanks to reproaches by U.S. federal courts, only to be consigned to immigration limbo (actually classified as "status pending") for the better part of the decade. As Buchanan (1980) and Glick Schiller *et al.* (1987) have noted, extremely pejorative representations of destitute and desperate Haitian boat people exacerbated the class prejudices of earlier Haitian immigrants from the elite and middle class. The only Haitian groups to act as advocates for the boat people were the political left and the progressive priests, several of whom later became campaign advisors to Aristide (Buchanan 1980; Wilentz 1989 and 1990). Father Aristide consistently took up the cause of the refugees, praising migrants for their perseverance and condemning the Haitian state for its indifference to the emigrants' plight (March 1990 interview with Haitian Television Network Video Club 1990, *Haïti Progrès* 9–15 May, 1990).

Aristide demonstrated equal concern for what he termed the "tempest of humiliation of the SIDA hurricane" (*tanpit imilyasyon siklon SIDA*). The tempest raged again in early 1990 with the Food and Drug Administration's unexpected decree barring Haitians from donating blood. Haitians responded to the state's renewed attempt to brand them as transmitters of AIDS with an unprecedented display of unity. They held demonstrations in New York, Miami, Boston and Chicago and at the U.S. embassy in Port-au-Prince (*Haïti Progrès* 25 April–1 May 1990; Fouron n.d.).[3] The demonstrators expressed their perception that the "Federal Discrimination Agency" fabricated the

---

[3] Significantly, the protesters chose *Ayiti Demen*, as their anthem which voiced the exile's commitment to "beautifying" the homeland rather than the Creole song entitled SIDA (AIDS), whose biting critique of United States government policy was echoed by the marchers. SIDA was recorded by the immensely popular musician, Ti Manno, who died of the disease (Glick Schiller and Fouron 1990).

AIDS threat to license persecution of dark-skinned pariahs corrupting American society. Some apparently believed that AIDs was a means of germ warfare waged by the U.S. government (*Haïti Progrès* 2–9 May 1990).

Father Aristide visited New York shortly after the impressive April 20th, 1990 march in New York City of about 60,000 Haitian people protesting the FDA ruling. Thousands crowded into the Brooklyn church to participate in Father Aristide's electrifying antiphonal oratory. Aristide reworked the angry protesters' understandings of the broader significance of this unrelenting affront: their continued insecurity in the United States was an inevitable product of the unholy union between the Host and Home states. Aristide's speech elaborated a triadic pun based upon the rhyming Creole words of SIDA (AIDS in French or Creole) with *siga*, or cigar and the well-known idiom, *"men siga ou,"* literally, "here is your cigar," meaning, "surprise!" or "it will never happen the way you intended!"[4] Since their massive mobilization protesting the FDA policy, Haitians had become a bold cigar lit at both ends to resist the machinations of its imperialist smoker *and* the "pimps" and "house boys" campaigning in the upcoming elections back Home.

> *Depuis que "ti konkonm t ap goumen ak berejenn," l'impérialisme nord-américain a considéré le peuple haïtien comme . . . un cigare qu'il met à la bouche pour tirer dessus. Il extrait la moelle et le courage du peuple et puis il le jette. Mais il est tellement enivré par la fumée du cigare qu'il confond "siga" (cigare) et Sida (applaudissements). Et à travers la FDA, il déclare que le peuple haïtien ne peut pas donner son sang, qu'il a le SIDA. Sang pour sang, c'est nous qui avons le sang de la liberté dans nos veines; ce sont eux qui devraient prendre ce sang et le mélanger au leur pour devenir civilisés (ovation).*
>
> *Ce cigar, ils regretteront d'en avoir allumé les deux bouts. Depuis le 20 avril, il est allumé aux deux bouts, ils ne peuvent le fumer comme ils veulent. Et lorsque nous nous déclarons prêts à mourir, cela prouve bien que c'est vrai. Les Etats-Unis peuvent faire ce qu'ils veulent, ils peuvent tuer autant de gens qu'ils veulent, ils ne pourront jamais tuer entièrement le peuple haïtien (applaudissements et cris) précisément parce que le cigare est allumé aux deux bouts et ce sont cette conviction, cette fierté et ce courage nationaliste que nous font mettre debout avec tous les Haïtiens ayant ce sang dans les veines pour dire, et aux macoutes et aux impérialistes américains, "Américains, voilà votre cigare!" "FDA, voilà votre cigare!" tontons-macoutes, voilà votre cigare!" criminels, voilà votre cigare!" Haïti ou la mort! (*Haïti Progrès 9–15 May, 1990, translated from Creole)*

Since the time "the little cucumber has resisted the eggplant," North American imperialism has treated the Haitian people like a big cigar. . . . It sucks out the marrow and the strength of the people and then it discards the butt. But it is so high on the smoke that it mistakes *siga* (cigar) for *SIDA* (AIDS). (applause) And through the FDA, it has declared that the Haitian

---

[4] Jean-Claude Martineau, who contributed this translation, emphasized that this forceful expression, which is accompanied by a gesture with the third finger, is not considered swearing.

people cannot donate their blood, that they have SIDA. Blood for blood, we are the ones with the blood of freedom in our veins, they should take our blood and mix it with theirs to become civilized (ovation).

This cigar, they will regret having lit both its ends. Since (the march) on April 20, it has been lit at both ends and they cannot smoke it the way they want to. And when we declare ourselves ready to die for it, then they will understand. The United States can do what it wants, it can kill as many people as it wants, but it will never totally kill the Haitian people (applause) precisely because the cigar is lit at both ends and this conviction, this pride and this nationalist strength make us stand up with all Haitians with blood in their veins to say to the makouts and to the American imperialists, "Here is your cigar!" FDA, "Here is your cigar!" Tontons-makout, "Here is your cigar!" Criminals, "Here is your cigar! Haiti or death!" (Author's translation)

INSECURITY INSIDE: MADE IN AMERICA ELECTIONS

Aristide seized the occasion of his SIDA-SIGA sermon to analyze the effect of political events currently taking place at Home upon the lives of Haitians working Outside. The junta had just fallen and the interim civilian government was fervently preparing for elections despite the escalating violence. The emigrant masses implicitly rejected the parade of opportunistic candidates stumping across the Haitian diaspora. Aristide reworked their sentiment, exhorting them to resist the electoral exercise in legitimizing another "brown-nosed" leader who would only perpetuate the chronic insecurity of Haitians living abroad.[5] He continued:

Je respire un parfum, un parfum d'honneur, un parfum de dignité, un parfum de respect. Honneur, dignité, respect du peuple haïtien traité comme un sans-logis. Ce soir, au pays des Américains, nous qui avons du sang dans les veines, nous venons dire que nous avons une maison, même s'ils ont entre les mains l'acte de naissance du pays. Même si les candidats "tchoul," les candidats "restavèk," les candidats "ti sousou" veulent vendre cet acte de naissance, il nous faut leur arracher des mains (cris applaudissements). (Haïti Progès 9–15 May, 1990, translated from Creole)

I smell a fragrance, a fragrance of honor, a fragrance of dignity, a fragrance of respect. Honor, dignity and respect for Haitians treated as vagrants. Tonight, in the American's country, we who have blood in our veins, we have come to say that we have a home, even if they have the birth certificate of our country in their hands. Even if the "house boy" candidates, the "servant" candidates, the "little brown-nosed" candidates want to sell this deed we have to wrestle it from their hands (shouting, applause) . . . (Author's translation)

[5] It also bears mentioning that among the leading contenders for the presidency, only Aristide demonstrated a mastery of Creole, the language of most monolingual Haitian speakers. Creole was a second or even a third language for several of the transnational elite candidates. Their coarse, stultified use of Creole repelled the lower classes. (I thank Jean-Claude Martineau and Dimi Stephen for this observation.)

When, in October 1990, Aristide suddenly shifted course and entered the presidential race, he pitched his rhetoric to present an alternative message of inclusion and a promise to advocate for the rights of Haitians throughout the "four cardinal points of the diaspora." A good example was his dramatic post-victory decision to address Haitians Outside (rather than his supporters at Home). He entitled the New Year's Eve speech, "message to the diaspora." The eloquent communiqué concluded with the following words:

> *Sè m a frè m kap viv . . . nan 4 kwen dyaspora a, menm si nou pa wè fas a fas, sonje ke nou genyen yon peyi k ap gade ou nan je pou ou menm ou ka gade 1 nan je, pou fas a fas sa a fè ou vin lage kò ou nan bra 1. De bra 1 ouvè pou akeyi ou, pou bo ou, pou anbrase ou kòm pitit ki pat ale pou ale nèt, men ki te ale pou retounen bò isit (* Haïti Progrès *n.d.).*

Sisters and brothers living throughout the four cardinal points of the diaspora, even if we don't see each other, remember that you have a country that looks you in the eye so that you can look it in the eye, so that this face to face makes you want to throw yourself into its arms. Its arms are outstretched to welcome you, to kiss you, to embrace you as a child who did not leave to go away forever, but who left in order to return. (Author's translation)

THE DESCENT OF GOOD HOMEGROWN CREOLE TOURISTS

What did Aristide mean by "return"? He explained in the same Message to the diaspora. Some Haitian migrants should repatriate to invest in businesses and create jobs, but the lines of the majority should continue straddling national boundaries. The Haitian state would now make it easier for them to do so. He said

> *Nou menm ki swaf retounen . . . lè ou rive, ou pa oblije rive nèt san ou pa ka retounen kote ou sòti a . . . Sa nou vle se ke ou kapab retounen lakay ou lè ou vle e retounen kote ou ap travay kounyè a lè ou vle tou. M pa mande ou vini isit nèt pou ou bliye lòt bò nèt . . . (*Haïti Progrès *n.d.)*

You who are thirsty to return home, when you return you do not have to stay forever and give up residence elsewhere. . . . What we want is for you to be able to return home whenever you want and for you to be able to return where you are working now whenever you like. I am not asking you to return permanently and forsake the other place completely . . . (Author's translation)

Five weeks later, Aristide introduced his notion of "good homegrown Creole tourists" (*bon jan pitit kay touris Kreyol*). He pictured transnationals who would earn money abroad and return to spend it liberally on tours of patriotic "discovery of the countryside" and then, at the end of their vacations, cross two national boundaries to go back to work. Aristide reiterated his desire for

Haitians in the North American diaspora to emulate American Jews, whose donations and nationalistic pilgrimages to their "homeland" support the Is-raeli economy. He was not the first Haitian diaspora politician to promote this compelling analogy while simultaneously sidestepping the wide disparities be-tween the class and migration experiences of the two populations, let alone the very different structural relations between the respective nations and the United States (Glick Schiller and Fouron 1990:341).

THE BANK OF THE DIASPORA

The "bank of the diaspora" was the term Aristide applied to the million or so Haitians compelled to work Outside. Aristide expressed his desire for the bank of the diaspora not only to continue defraying the living expenses of relatives in Haiti but also to serve as economic emissaries of the Haitian state. During a March, 1990 interview, Aristide plainly stated his conviction that resources of the "bank of the diaspora" were the means to freeing Haiti from imperialism (Haitian Television Network Video Club 1990). Ques-tioned on the day of his announcement to run for the presidency about how he, an ardent anti-imperialist, expected to solicit support for his government, he responded that Haiti's greatest source of foreign aid was the "bank of the diaspora" (*Haïti Progrès* 31 October–6 November, 1990). Migration, the ulti-mate accommodation to the shifting asymmetries of transnational capital, should be transformed into a means of economic resistance for the Haitian state!

"FOR EVERY EAR THERE IS ONE EARRING IN A GOLDSMITH SHOP"

As Haitian migrants struggled both to survive abroad and to meet their home dependents' escalating consumption demands during the contraction and restructuring of the last two decades, they found an empathetic voice in Aristide. Aristide perceived how sustaining the transnational contract in spite of the inexorable rise of *lavi chè*–inflation–Inside and Outside inevitably breeds antagonisms between migrants and their dependents at Home. As I have described elsewhere (Richman 1990a and n.d.), some at Home feel in-dignant about their excessive dependency on emigrants' remittances. Others detect a *nouveau* arrogance among emigrants. They accuse migrants of taking a cavalier attitude when they are away and of showing off with their fancy clothes when they return. Home residents often react to these perceived in-dignities by neglecting their benefactors, by not writing to them or by ig-noring them when they visit.

Migrants meanwhile perceive that their families no longer look upon them as people but see them rather as insensate beasts of burden. Many feel that they slave away in hostile, foreign countries for the sake of people who resent them for ever having left. They worry that these relatives may not be reliable managers of their remittances. (As Portes [1978:478] has observed, working class migrants typically counter constrained opportunities for social and economic advancement abroad by repatriating savings to invest in symbols of social and economic relationship or status back home. Haitian migrants conceive of these investments as both practical short-term insurance against suddenly having to return home because of illness or injury and as long-term savings to be used when they retire there. Many speak in this way of "guaranty-ing" [*garanti*] their migration [Richman 1990a].) Frustrated with their own and their dependents' failures to get ahead, migrants frequently blame the latter for irresponsibly wasting their hard-earned wages instead of investing them for the migrants' future use.

Aristide demonstrated his sensitivity to distortions in domestic relations unleashed by international migration. During his momentous post-inaugural "meeting with the Tenth Province," he applied his eloquent oratory to diffuse some of the latent hostility between those who leave and those who remain behind. Having explained his vision of good homegrown Creole tourists circulating freely and proudly between Home and Host countries, he paused to paint a bucolic scene of a transnational returning to visit his impoverished grandparents in a remote hilltop village: "What will they see?" he asked the audience of "the Tenth."

> *Yo p ap wè youn pitit k ap vin taye banda, vin chèlbè, pou fè lòt yo santi krenn paske you pa t kapab ale pou you tounen bwodè konsa. Non. Non. Y ap santi ke "chak zòrèy (1 ap fè jès pou mounn yo pale tout ansanm avèk li) gen youn grènn zanno kay ofèv." Si chak fanmi pa t genyen youn grènn manm nan fanmi nan dizyèm depatman an— Mmm, Mmm. Ou konnen konman sa ta ye. Ou konnen konman sa ta ye. Ou fè 1, ou vle kontinye fè 1, kan menm* (Wilèk Film 1991, author's transcription).

They won't see a child who came home dressed to the hilt to show off and to make them ashamed that they couldn't go away to return all dressed up like that too. No. No. They will feel that (encouraging the audience to join in) "for every ear there is one earring in a goldsmith shop." If every family did not have one member in the Tenth Province—Hmm! Hmm! You know what would have happened. You know what would have happened. You did it; you want to continue doing it, regardless (Wilèk Film 1991, author's translation).

The earring proverb means "everybody has a skeleton in their closet"; in other words, because every family Inside depends for survival upon a gold earring in a goldsmith shop Outside, people at Home do not stand in a position to criticize migrants.[6] Despite myriad obstacles in the host society and the

---

[6] I thank Jean-Claude Martineau for providing this interpretation of the Creole proverb, "*Chak zòrèy gen youn grenn zanno kay ofèv.*"

ambivalence of the very people who will wear the gold treasure at Home, migrants continue abiding their onerous transnational contracts. Aristide's eloquent praise bolstered their self-respect and helped them persevere.

THE CONTEST OVER THE TENTH PROVINCE

Contradictions between accommodation and resistance in Aristide's discourse with and about Haitians Outside, so effortlessly subdued in his campaign rhetoric, rose to a turbulent surface when Aristide the President moved to garner the lavalas of support he had received from Outside. His fragmented approach to creating the transnational political entity of the Tenth Province, modeled selectively on the administrative structure of the nine internal provinces, was quickly exploited by political opponents and critics and surely frustrated the resolution of such fundamental problems as emigrants' rights to vote, to hold office and to enjoy binationality. Some denounced the Tenth Province as "a sham"; others called it "a constitutional aberration." Still others challenged whether wages contributed by the "bank of the diaspora" alone entitled them to political legitimacy (*Haïti en Marche* 1–7 May, 1991).

Battle lines over the organization and government of the Tenth Province were already forming when the new president called upon the resources of "the bank of the (now) Tenth Province" for a massive donation to the Home state. The ensuing controversy over the handling of funds raised by the "remitting to build up Haiti" (*voye Ayiti monte* or VOAM) marathon was predictable, as political rivals debated the relative authority of the Inside versus the Outside over dispensation of funds earned and remitted by Haitian migrants (*Haïti en Marche* 1–7 May, 1991; *Haïti Progrès* 10–16 July, 1991).

CONCLUSION

During Aristide's celebrated post-inaugural "reunion with the Tenth Province," the new president joined members of "Lavalas for Home," long reviled and feared by the previous fascist regimes, in a stirring chorus of *Ayiti Demen*, the exile's song foreseeing the massive mobilization, the lavalas utterly destroying the Duvalierist state. The "little priest" had unleashed a flood of support from "Lavalas For Home" by validating and reconstructing the complex weave of Haitian migrants' consciousness. He grasped the various threads of their profound sense of vulnerability, from the political to the interpersonal, and rewove them into a fabric of pride and dignity. He foretold the coming of an era when the Home state would look them straight in the eye, a necessary first step to stabilizing their transnational experience.

Aristide's sententious rhetoric did not, however, transcend the relationship between home and host states toward an equally powerful critique of the larger forces structuring the migrants' experience. Despite hegemonic voices accusing the "red priest" of promoting class warfare, Lavalas never aspired to clear the Haitian ground of unremitting exportation of labor and equally relentless importation of low wages, food, and other commodities. Indeed, the charismatic candidate encouraged the birds of passage to continue following and abetting cyclical migrations of transnational capital. Following the landslide victory of Lavalas, the new president offered this ultimate accommodation as a debatable symbol of resistance for the fledgling Haitian state.

ACKNOWLEDGMENTS

I wish to thank Nina Glick Schiller for encouraging me to write this paper for the panel on Rethinking Migration: A Transnational Perspective at the Women and Anthropology Conference of the International Union of Anthropological and Ethnological Sciences, Commission on Women, Lehman College, May, 1991. I thank Nina and members of the panel and audience for their comments. I also wish to acknowledge the generous contributions of Jean-Claude Martineau, Dimitri Stephen, and Joseph Metellus.

This paper is based upon ongoing bilateral research in western Haiti and in Florida and Virginia, early phases of which were sponsored by Inter-American Foundation and Organization of American States.

REFERENCES CITED

Aristide, Jean-Bertrand
  1991   *In the parish of the poor.* Translated and Edited by Amy Wilentz. Maryknoll, NY: Orbis Books.
Basch, Linda, Nina Glick Schiller, and Cristina Blanc-Szanton
  1992   Transnationalism: A new analytic framework for understanding migration. In *Towards a transnational perspective on migration: Race, class, ethnicity and nationalism reconsidered*, edited by Nina Glick Schiller, Linda Basch, and Cristina Blanc-Szanton. *Annals of the New York Academy of Sciences* 645:1–24.
Basch, Linda
  1987   *The politics of Caribbeanization: Vincentians and Grenadians in New York.* In *Caribbean life in New York City: Sociocultural dimensions*, edited by Constance Sutton and Elsa Chaney. New York: Center for Migration Studies. Pp. 160–181.
Buchanan, Susan
  1980   *Scattered seeds: The meaning of migration for Haitians in New York City.* Ph.D. dissertation. New York: New York University.
Fouron, Georges
  n.d.   AIDS and the implementation of a transnationalist identity among Haitians in New York. Paper presented to the panel on transnational identities and cultural strategies: The Afro-Caribbean and the United States. 89th Annual Meeting of the American Anthropological Association, New Orleans, November, 1990.

Glick Schiller, Nina, Josh DeWind, Marie Lucie Brutus, Carolle Charles, Georges Fouron, and Antoine Thomas
    1987   All in the same boat? Unity and diversity in Haitian organizing in New York. In *Caribbean life in New York City: Sociocultural dimensions*, edited by Constance Sutton and Elsa Chaney. New York: Center for Migration Studies. Pp. 182–201.
Glick Schiller, Nina and Georges Fouron
    1990   "Everywhere we go we are in danger": Ti Manno and the emergence of a Haitian transnational identity. *American Ethnologist 17(2)*:329–347.
Haiti Insight: A Bulletin on Refugee and Human Rights Affairs, November 1990 through January 1991.
Haïti en Marche
            October 1990 through May 1991.
Haïti Progrès
            October 1990 through July 1991.
            n.d. Transcript of Aristide's "Mesaj pou Dyaspora" Dec. 31, 1990.
Haitian Television Network Video Club
    1990   Mouvement Lavalas. Miami. VHS.
Lessinger, Johanna
    1992   Investing or going home? A transnational strategy among Indian immigrants in the United States. In *Towards a transnational perspective on migration: Race, class, ethnicity and nationalism reconsidered*, edited by Nina Glick Schiller, Linda Basch, and Cristina Blanc-Szanton. *Annals of the New York Academy of Sciences 645*:53–80.
Martineau, Jean-Claude (Koralin)
    1975   *Ayiti demen*. On *Ayiti demen*, Record 3 of Soley Leve, New York.
Portes, Alejandro
    1978   Toward a structural analysis of illegal (undocumented) migration. *International Migration Review 12(4)*:469–508.
Richman, Karen
    1990a   *Guarantying migrants in the core: Commissions of gods, descent groups and ritual leaders in a transnational Haitian community. Cimarrón 2(3)*:114–128.
    1990b   "With many hands, the burden isn't heavy": Creole proverbs and political rhetoric in Haiti's presidential elections. *Folklore Forum 23*:115–123.
    n.d.   *"They will remember me in the house": Ritual verses of contest and persuasion on cassette-letters*.
Stepick, Alex
    1982   Haitian boat people: A study in the conflicting forces shaping U.S. immigration policy. *Law and Contemporary Problems 45(2)*:163–196.
Sutton, Constance
    1987   The Caribbeanization of New York City and the emergence of a transnational socio-cultural system. In *Caribbean life in New York City: Sociocultural dimensions*, edited by Constance Sutton and Elsa Chaney. New York: Center for Migration Studies. Pp. 15–30.
Wilèk Film
    1991   *Titid ak dizyèm depatman an*. Brooklyn: VHS.
Wilentz, Amy
    1989   The rainy season: Haiti since Duvalier. New York: Simon and Schuster.
    1990   Foreword. *In the parish of the poor: Writings from Haiti*. Jean-Bertrand Aristide. Translated and edited by Amy Wilentz. Maryknoll, NY: Orbis Books. Pp. ix–xxiv.

Historical Reflections on Transnationalism, Race, and the American Immigrant Saga

BARRY GOLDBERG

Division of Social Science
Fordham University, College at Lincoln Center
New York, New York 10023

In spite of the interdisciplinary nature of critical social inquiry these days and my having been an intellectual co-conspirator with some of you here today, I must confess that when I was asked to participate in this conference I became quite self-conscious about being a historical interloper on anthropological turf. Fortunately the very theme of the conference helped alleviate my anxiety and enabled me to fashion a metaphorical identity suited to the occasion. Rather than worrying over being a "marginal" academic "immigrant," "sojourner," or "bird of passage," to cite just a few keywords of our long established professional lexicon, I have decided to make the most of my momentary status as a "transdisciplinary" scholar. Perhaps by the end of the day I will find myself part of a wider intellectual community of multiple theoretical and political origins—and increasingly uncertain theoretical and political destinations.

In order to encourage this transdisciplinary dialogue my comments today are framed as part of what I hope will be a continuing conversation between the dominant conventions of United States immigration history and the potentially disruptive insights that are emerging from studies of the new "transnational" migrants during the contemporary global re-division of capital and labor. As it will become clear, while I am by no means comfortable with many of the founding assumptions of my own discipline and believe that historians have much to gain from the concept of transnationalism, I will also argue that any reconceptualization of "the immigrant experience" must be informed by and include an ongoing re-reading of the past. Dr. Feldman-Bianco's study of New Bedford's Portuguese immigrants and Dr. Charles's analysis of Haitian migrant identity are particularly apt catalysts for this interdisciplinary endeavor since they call attention to the historically shifting, always slippery, and as we are unfortunately rediscovering, sometimes deadly, meanings of race, ethnicity, and class in the United States.

Let me begin with a brief critical interpretation of the historiography of immigration to the United States. In spite of rich empirical observations and occasionally astute analytic insights, it has only been during the last two decades that historians have begun to grasp the ignominious complexity of racial, ethnic, and class formation in the American past. Indeed, as John Bukowczyk has recently argued, immigration history developed as a "Whiggish" American narrative. Though often one step ahead of the official culture in its inclusive tolerance, in the final analysis, immigration history constructed sophisticated variants of the American celebration typified by the patriotic hoopla and fireworks of the Statue of Liberty's centennial of 1986 (Bukowczyk 1989:61). Focusing overwhelmingly on European migration to North America while evading the seamy side of class formation and the nation's role as an expansionist white settler society, immigration has been absorbed by and, in turn, has reinforced America's mission as a capitalist, if no longer Protestant, republic. Historic immigrants and contemporary native-born patriots have come to form a mutual admiration society: That immigrants chose America confirmed the nation's secularized "errand into the wilderness" and reaffirmed its continuing place as the last best hope of mankind. That America attracted these particular immigrants affirmed their own status as the most energetic acquisitive freedom lovers of the last two centuries. In a telling, if extreme, version of this faith, John Roche approved the "folk wisdom" of the American politician of German ancestry who, in the face of Nazism, explained German-American's democratic faith by commenting, "Maybe all the good ones came here" (Roche 1986:x–xi). The cultural moment of Roche's glib intervention is equally significant: the preface to a new edition of John F. Kennedy's *A Nation of Immigrants* published to coincide with "Lady Liberty's" one-hundredth birthday. With Chrysler Corporation president Lee Iacocca setting the ideological tone for the celebration, the historic immigrant, not the least of whom was his father, became the quintessential upwardly mobile American. This immigrant, as the martyred president had stressed two decades earlier, used "exceptional talent and enterprise" to break out of his (usually) "fixed place" to seek his fortune in a continental free market where "he could go anywhere and do anything his talents permitted" (Kennedy 1986:8).

Undoubtedly, immigrants were "children of capitalism," to borrow John Bodnar's apt phrase, but they were not necessarily successful uprooted individualists as the official government histories of immigration and Ellis Island argue. As Bodnar has stressed, this official story obscures the complexities of class and ethnic formation. Immigrants were overwhelmingly members of a vulnerable working class who tried to fashion security and dignity for their families. Few were entrepreneurs; few arrived committed to the "possessive individualism" of the capitalist frontier (Bodnar 1985; 1986).

Bodnar (1985) synthesizes the new direction immigration history has taken. Recent scholarship has become more sensitive to the differential global

patterns of capital and labor migration as well as class and ethnic group formation. But in certain respects, recent scholarship is not entirely free from the
weight of the past. For one thing, while no longer bound by a simplistic assimilationist paradigm, the overwhelming emphasis has remained on the process of "becoming American," as the title of one fairly recent narrative synthesis has put it (Archdeacon 1983). To coin a perhaps awkward phrase,
immigration history has been "America-centric." As even Bodnar's work reveals, the overwhelming emphasis has been on the European migration to the
United States between the 1830s and 1920s.

To pose the issue somewhat differently, immigration has its historiography
as well as its history. We need to explore the place of historical narratives in
the reconstruction of American identity. A crucial starting point is an understanding of the dialectical relationship between, on the one hand, the triumph
of immigration restriction and, on the other hand, the subsequent rise of immigration history and the incorporation of immigrants into the national saga.
In a revealing, but ignored, sentence in the preface to *Boston's Immigrants*, his
1941 harbinger of modern immigration and ethnic history, Oscar Handlin
offered an astute comment on the origins of his own field of specialization.
He wrote, "Since restrictive legislation has pushed the immigrant problem
into his sphere, the historian faces the primary obligations of analyzing it"
(Handlin:ix). Steeped in the literature of the social sciences, Handlin self-
consciously practiced and recommended an ethnography of the past. But his
acknowledged intellectual debt to his sociological predecessors masked a significant shift in the social function of the scholarly student of immigration.
The sociology of immigration, particularly that of the Chicago School, developed when immigration was a social problem; the historiography of immigration developed gradually after the nativists' triumph contained the perceived
immigrant menace. The historical profession which had been overwhelmingly
nativist during the years of mass emigration from Europe retroactively integrated the once feared newcomers into a new unifying national narrative. The
result was a more inclusive national narrative which asserted that consent to
the ideals of the nation was more important than allegedly patriotic lines of
descent. In many respects Kennedy's essay was the triumphant popular politicization of this new narrative. Kennedy's confirmation of the contribution
of the parents and grandparents of much of the population was an attack on
the national origins system of regulating documented immigration to the
United States. It was an ideological salvo in the battle that resulted in the 1965
abolition of the forty-year-old nativist definition of American "stock." But
while the revised law established the worth of the "new" immigrants who had
passed through Ellis Island at the turn of the century, it did not signal welcome to the "newer" immigrants from Asia and Latin America who have constituted the bulk of immigrants over the last decade and a half. As David
Reimers has shown, rather than trying to pry open the "golden door" to

peoples from Asia, Africa, and Latin America, advocates of immigration reform wanted to establish parity among those Europeans whose ancestors had proved their American worth. (Reimers 1985:63–90). By incorporating these historic immigrants into the national saga, Americans could symbolically redress old injustices while in no way preventing the emergence of new varieties of neo-nativism among the "ethnic" descendants of the now old "new" immigrants. In 1986, Americans once again celebrated the Statue of Liberty's historic promise to immigrants while they went about refashioning immigration law to control the influx of those whom Ronald Reagan once called the "foot people." Americans can venerate the immigrant past while fretting over the immigrant present.

I do not intend to establish a crude correlation between the legacy of academic immigration history and the popular memories that have served simultaneously as vehicles for retroactive Americanization and new varieties of American ethnic neo-nativism. A critical rereading of both assimilationist and pluralist interpretations of the immigrant past is a complex and yet to be completed chapter in the history of American identity. However, I do want to stress a troubling paradox of immigration history: As much as immigration history has been an *ex post facto* rejoinder to restrictionist fears and definitions of "The American," its desire to re-open the past coexists with tendency to foreclose the future.

Foreclosing the future does not necessarily imply restricting the entry of "new" immigrants. Indeed, though I think he overstates his case, Rudolph Vecoli may be correct in arguing that past "pluralist" historiographic victories have lessened the fundamentalist xenophobia of previous nativisms (Vecoli 1985:16). However, it does imply an unwillingness to question aspects of the mytho-historical framework of the nation's immigrant saga. Migrants from Asia, Latin America, the West Indies have been marginalized, studied by a sub- sub-discipline. Should we, for example, look at the involuntary migration of Africans to colonial North America as a somewhat deviant aspect of the flow of bound labor across the Southern hemisphere as well as a forerunner of more recent labor migrations from the post-colonial world to the Euro-American metropoles? In analytic terms the Europeans have been the "model" immigrants whose experiences have provided the raw material for framing other histories. But does the Ellis Island motif, even in its most critical rendition, help us understand the re-Hispanicization of the Southwest or Puerto Rican and Filipino arrivals from the nations' global empire? What does it mean that the most recent immigrants are descendants of once enslaved and conquered people of color? The movement of people from historically conquered and occupied nations suggests the dangers of generalizing from the Euro-American experience. To title a historical account of post-1965 immigration *Still the Golden Door* may say less about the actual continuities of the immigrant experience than it does about the historian's inclination to see the past in the present, to remain more or less Whiggish (Reimers).

Therefore, if nothing else, the concept of transnationalism is an important heuristic device for historians since it highlights recent changes in the range and depth of migrants' lived experience in multi-national social fields. In crucial respects, it argues, the present is not a replay of the past. Since the nineteenth century immigrants have been capitalism's offspring, but their parent has grown and changed. Consequently, immigrants cope with a new global reality. Whatever the validity of models of the past, historians need to be cautious about drawing lessons for future. While averse to theoretical generalizations the poetics of historical narrative tends to create a unilinear narrative. In immigration history this has been an endless repetition/revision of an archetypical American immigrant experience that rhetorically unifies diversity and domesticates past social conflict. At a minimum, today's new immigrants may signal a refiguring of the global economic and cultural landscape. In addition, since our analytic plots hinge on their unstable contemporary resolutions, it behooves us to reconsider our vision of the past. As Del Jones suggested in his comments, it is of course possible that what we are currently witnessing is a first generation phenomena and the culture and political economy of the transnational migrant experience may wither. Perhaps, what has changed may be the depth and range of such experiences. In either case, we may need to reconceptualize the significance of past "transnational" experiences: the Fenianism of nineteenth century Irish, the German-American cultural institutions, the efforts of the Italian government to shape the opinions of the Italian-American community in the 1920s, recurring Pan-African sentiments, and the growth of "captive nations'" organizations after World War II. The idea of transnationalism enables us to step outside of the teleological model of both Americanization and pluralism in order to reexamine social formations and cultural practices we have become perhaps too familiar with.

In order to help clarify the nature of past and present migration, historians (like Dr. Feldman-Bianco and Dr. Charles) need to continue the process of dismantling the historically constructed boundaries of their own subdisciplines. The decade of the restriction acts witnessed a tripartite division of the study of American class, racial, and ethnic formation (Berthoff 1962). Immigration history became the distinct specialty we have been discussing. Second, in spite of the valiant efforts of African-American scholars, the history of black involuntary immigrants was subsumed under studies of the slave south and the Civil War and Reconstruction dominated by the sons of the Confederacy. Third, labor history was established by progressive institutional labor economists who celebrated the virtues of nonideological business unionism of the AFL. In sum, the history of America's "dependent workers, slave and free," to use Herbert Gutman's phrase, immigrant and native, white, black, brown, red, and yellow, splintered into ideologically as well as topically bounded subfields (Gutman 1976:3). Thanks to Gutman and other scholars, historians have begun to remap the internal relations of class, race, and ethnicity.

The papers by Drs. Feldman-Bianco and Charles are part of this ongoing multidisciplinary project of reconsidering these interrelations. Each has much to teach historians as well as a good deal to gain from a more thorough critical encounter with the nation's past.

The clearest strength of Feldman-Bianco's study of the New Bedford Portuguese experience is its attentiveness to the construction and reconstruction of ethnic and national identity in the course of the twentieth century. By examining evolving Portuguese and American policies and ideologies regarding immigration and identity, her paper provides one of the more forceful accounts of the historically contingent and contested meaning of ethnicity. By focusing on official policies in Portugal and the United States, her evidence suggests we examine even earlier patterns of ethnic identity as a transnational experience shaped by both the juridical and symbolic power of states, on the one hand, and the immigrant actors' ability to negotiate the changing political-economies and national identities of two societies. The Portuguese experience belies both an evolutionary Americanization process and static bi-nationality. In addition, her data complement historians' recent insistence that the process of ethnic formation must be understood in the context of class formation within immigrant communities. While overwhelmingly a working class community, formal ethnic organization and festivals were dominated by the civic-minded aspiring middle classes (Bodnar 1985:85–143).

Unfortunately, however, Dr. Feldman-Bianco has fallen into a common uncritical periodization and interpretation of American ethnic ideologies. In particular we must avoid reifying and simplifying such slogans as "Americanization" and "pluralism." Undoubtedly, in the aftermath of World War I, the Bolshevik Revolution, and labor insurgency at home, the official culture waged an aggressive mobilization campaign linking lineage to cultural and political conformity. National origins quotas, capital's "American Plan," and the prosecution of Italian-American anarchists Sacco and Vanzetti were facets of this repressive Americanism. Yet the fact is Americanization may have provided basis for the ethnic working class insurgencies of the 1930s. As Michael Piore argued, the National Origins Act transformed immigrant working class communities into ethnic working class communities whose future was tied to the United States (Piore 1979:140–157). In addition, the attempt to lure "foreigners" into the emerging mass consumer society and political vocabulary of Americanism may have backfired. While such efforts did not produce a revolutionary proletariat, it did produce a working class with a common set of American material aspirations and a democratic language that could be turned against their employers and anti-labor forces in the government. For example, Gary Gerstle (1989) has argued that, paradoxically, the Americanization campaign helped break the power of the conservative French-Canadian clerical and business community in Woonsocket, Rhode Island providing secular Belgian labor radicals with an opening for militant class organization when the Depression hit. Conservative definitions of "American identity" can compel ideological conformity and silence "un-American" ideals, but so can varieties of ethnic chauvinism. The meaning of both "Americanism" and particular ethnicities have been subject to contestation and renegotiation. Ethnic ideologies must be seen in relation to other cultural practices.

This also applies to the practice and ideology of pluralism. When juxtaposed against the expectations of Anglo-conformity, pluralism signifies tolerance for, if not the celebration of, cultural diversity. But the relationship between such a cultural democracy and an egalitarian democracy is by no means clear. As both John Higham (1975:196–230) and Philip Gleason (1980) have maintained, like such terms as "the Melting Pot" and "Americanization," cultural pluralism has slippery, historically changing meanings. In particular, from its origins in the work of Horace Kallen, "pluralism's" relevance to the African-American experience has been muddy, at best. The resurgence of pluralist ideology and practice in the late 1960s was in many respects a white ethnic response to the civil rights movement and struggle for black empowerment (Jackson 1974; Steinberg 1981:201–221). Working class descendants of European immigrants had many grievances, but "the rise of the unmeltable ethnics" was not part of multi-ethnic egalitarian politics in spite of the rhetoric of some urban populists and social democrats. The "new ethnicity" was a revised language of white resentment denying the historically specific experience of African-Americans. At the risk of oversimplifying, in the late 1940s and 1950s urban white ethnics mobilized against integrated housing in the name of their "white" immigrant ancestors who built America. After the civil rights era delegitimated overt racist categorization, white ethnics now claimed justice as part of historically exploited and culturally stigmatized immigrant-derived working class. The symbolic politics of the semi-welfare state compelled groups to compete for most favored victim status when they sought governmental redress and social benefits. Ethnic spokesmen even called upon the state to inculcate overcome previous assaults on ethnic identity through passage of the Ethnic Heritage Act. In the end, the new ethnicity served a resurgent conservatism which did not extend the benefits of welfare state, but instead praised the hard work of romanticized European immigrants who never asked for a handout, unlike the lazy welfare cheat or rising minority member who sought the special privilege of affirmative action. Any assessment of the new pluralism in the Portuguese community should address its dark side.

To move beyond both the seeming clarity of the cultural repression of the 1920s and the relative pluralist openness of the late 1960s and early 1970s, it is essential to confront the ethnic, class, and racial ideologies of the crucial intervening decades, particularly between the mid-1930s and mid-1950s. This era witnessed the triumph of consensual pluralism. Along with the rise of anti-racist cultural anthropology, sociology, and immigration history, these decades saw both grass roots and state sponsored redefinitions of American identity. During the 1930s, Yugoslav-born journalist Louis Adamic led his populist campaign to elevate Ellis Island to the level of Plymouth Rock in the nation's political iconography of place (Harney 1986). And as World War II loomed on the horizon, Adamic and early advocates of "multicultural educa- tion" and intergroup tolerance joined in a state-sponsored campaign to forge unity in diversity. A radio series entitled "Americans All" typified this ethnic Americanism from above. With the outbreak of war, movies started to portray multiethnic foxholes defending the American way of life (Gleason 1981). Even Paul Robeson, controversial black communist fellow traveler, became the lead- ing voice proclaiming a new tolerant America when in the midst of the war he sang a new anthem, "The Ballad of Americans." But Robeson's tragic red- baited career after the war revealed the limits of the acceptance of diversity. The liberal tolerance of ethnic diversity and beginning of attacks of segregation in the South were accompanied by McCarthyism and Cold War liberalism. To appropriate and redeploy Herman Marcuse's phrase, Robeson became a victim of a "repressive tolerance" that valorized ethnic diversity only as long as it did not entail political dissent. The emergence of public ethnicity's cele- bration of immigrant roots remained within political parameters of the liberal capitalist semi-welfare state (Duberman 1988). In sum, we need to see plural- ism and Americanism not as discrete and opposing ethnic ideologies but as slippery terms whose meaning has remained contingent on their redefinitions and articulation within changing hegemonic and insurgent discourses. Robe- son's Popular Front pluralism was a far cry from the "end of ideology" which characterized the liberal pluralism of postwar America.

Equally important, as Robeson's tragic career suggests, is the fact that up until the end of World War II, in spite of the reconstruction amendments, African-Americans, like native Americans, were considered outside the Ameri- can community. This is not to say that race is a transhistorical given. For some native-born white Americans, the world could be divided for "whites and for- eigners," and it may be useful to speak of immigrants who long remained "not yet white" in the symbolic world of nativists of all classes (Bukowczyk 1984:69). Nonetheless, the United States had remained a *de jure* or *de facto* biracial inegalitarian society through most of its history, and people of color have not been as readily included in the narrative of "a nation of nations." In- deed, the case of the "black Portuguese" of Cape Verdean background fore- shadows the issues raised by current nonwhite migrants such as the Haitian community of New York. As Feldman-Bianco points out, during World War II, when light-skinned Portuguese joined the multiethnic foxholes in an army of ethnically diverse G.I.'s, not "Yanks," their darker Portuguese compatriots discovered that they were classified as "Negro" and placed in segregated Army units. Racial categorization took precedence over being one of the aspiring immigrant "huddled masses."

Not surprisingly, as Dr. James stresses, Haitian immigrants face particular problems negotiating the American's cultural definitions of race. Although not all African-Americans find themselves at the lower reaches of the socio-economic ladder, Charles correctly stresses it is a painful reality for many. Equally important, the culture does assign them a fixed subordinate symbolic place–"the bottom" as Baldwin put it. Haitians have to struggle to be black without becoming "black." At the same time, she correctly recognizes that the meaning of race is historical: "The creation of a subordinated place for blacks, while defined and informed primarily by race, expresses the dynamic of class conflict and other antagonisms in social relations within U.S. society." In sum, Haitians must renegotiate the meaning of blackness in the context of its de-based associations and real socio-economic liabilities in the United States.

Their very status as immigrants provides a degree of ideological leverage. As the comment of the political emigré who referred to the Harlem apartment in which activists organized and oriented newcomers as "a kind of Ellis Island for new Haitian refugees between Papa Doc country and the U.S. unknown" suggests, one strategy is to disassociate from American blacks by metaphori-cally placing themselves within the now venerable American immigrant expe-rience. However, as Charles convincingly argues, that strategy is not an at-tempt to deny blackness. Rather, Haitians have forged a popular memory of race and nationality centering on the revolution of 1791–1804. As the student put it, "The Haitian . . . has a cultural background. He is somebody. He won't deny his past. Because his past belongs to the greatest of Occidental nations. We were the first ones to vanquish Napoleon." If subordinate in the transna-tional labor market this national memory provides resources for resistance by separating economic vulnerability and thwarted desires for mobility from American definitions of blackness as the indelible inherited stain of historical subjugation.

This tradition, like all traditions, is selective. Unquestionably, as C.L.R. James (1963), Eugene Genovese (1979), and Robin Blackburn (1988) have em-phasized, Toussaint-L'Ouverture's linkage of the ideology of the French Revo-lution to the aspirations of the slaves of St. Dominique was a turning point in world history. Part of what made it a world historical event was its meaning for other blacks in the African diaspora. Haiti was a small country that had a big revolution. Particularly in the United States, it was a transnational event. Twelve thousand Haitian slaves were transported to the United States by their fleeing masters. More important was its widespread ideological ramifications among republican theorists, slaveholders, and, most importantly black Amer-icans. As David Brion Davis (1989:747–749) has observed, in spite of the ex-tent of white comment, the events in Saint Dominique "had a deeper and more lasting impact on the self-image and nascent national identity of free blacks, especially in the northern United States." Indeed, by the 1820s the Toussaint's "revolution had become a symbolic negation of everything slavery represented." David Walker's *Appeal to the Coloured Citizens of the World* asked blacks to read about the history of Haiti. Rather than seeing the revolution as a distinctive possession of Haitian nationality, African-American leaders such as James Forten, Absalom Jones, Richard Allen and Henry Highland Garnett saw it as a demonstration of the power of oppressed Africans throughout the Americas.

Paradoxically, whatever its power as cultural capital in fighting the racial codes of the dominant culture in the United States, Haitians' "usable past" ignores the tragic aftermath of the revolution as system of peasant proprietorship eventually yielded to neo-colonial domination by the United States, culminating in military occupation between 1915 and 1934. Occupying forces censored the press, jailed and killed thousands of protestors, and created a national guard. National City Bank took control of the Haitian Banque Nationale. Under these circumstances, American blacks, though also subjected to the insults of white supremacy, could see themselves as the more powerful heirs of the Haitian Revolution and the thwarted promise of the Civil War and Emancipation. At a minimum, Haitian's victimization equalled that experience by the most powerless of American blacks. James Weldon Johnson argued that Haitians who were forced to work without pay building roads "were in the same category with the convict in the Negro chain gangs" of the South (Rotberg 1971). Haitians and blacks in the United States have had interrelated and historically specific experiences of new world slavery, bourgeois democratic revolution, and the rise of America's informal regional empire. Thus, along with the power to be derived from Haitian migrant's popular memory, such nationalism seems to preclude the possible benefits of a Pan-Africanist renegotiation of blackness exemplified in the varied and sometimes conflicting traditions of W.E.B. DuBois, Marcus Garvey, James, Robeson, and Frantz Fanon.

From this perspective, the experience of Haitian immigrants reveals what may be most distinctive about the new immigration and its "transnational" character: its relation to the legacy race and colonialism. These are not the first black immigrants and the depth, extent, and duration of transnational social fields awaits further analysis. Yet one of the most salient facts of American history has been its roots as a "white settler" society that through most of its history defined Blacks, Mexicans, Asians, and Native Americans as internal and external Others: slaves, conquered "mongrels," "coolies," and "savages," respectively (Fredrickson 1981; Takaki 1979). The codification and meaning of American freedom was bound to the institutionalization and legitimization of African bondage and racial definitions of Americaness (Morgan 1975). More generally, as Richard Slotkin (1985:35–37) has convincingly argued, an evolving myth of the frontier has muted the contradictions of metropolitan capital by focusing attention on the progressing conquest and Americaniza- tion of new frontiers. On the other side of each new border lay the promise of a new Eldorado, a domain of prosperity that would resolve the social ten- sions of the Metropole. The borderlands–and the human "pioneers" who braved them–made America. "Emigration," Slotkin concludes, "was the nec- essary prelude to any truly American story, since without such a 'coming out' there could be no America." The earliest settlers defined themselves against the "New World Savage and the Old World Aristocracy." Although fearful of formal colonial Empire, by the early twentieth century frontier included po- litical, military, and economic stewardship of inferior peoples. Perhaps most important, the celebration of "pioneer" was not antithetical to urban indus- trialization "for even the growth of the Metropolis was connected with emi- gration; the cities were filled by European immigrants whose journey to America replicated that of the original colonists, while the growth of native population continued to push the borders of productive land out across the continent. Thus the association of economic development with the migration to 'new lands' was preserved." Thus, in many respects the European immi- grant could be seen as the last frontiersman, a rugged if late coming and urban individualist remaking himself by entering new, if previously settled territory. As it is well known, at first many Americans were not sure if masses of im- migrants from southern and eastern Europe had what it took to become "fron- tiersmen." Nativism resisted incorporating these newcomers into the domi- nant myth/ideological system. But while Americans debated and regulated these "new" newcomers, in future decades these Euro-Americans entered the national narrative. After all, they participated in the great trek from the Old Society to the New. They joined in the process of taming the continent and supplanting defeated people of color on the global frontier.

The current popular debate over the "browning of America" signals a more fundamental disruption of this myth/ideological system. It is hard to "place" the new migrants in terms of the nation's longstanding racial/geographic fron- tier. This is not to say the national narrative cannot be revised by, at a min- imum, emphasizing the individual initiative of all immigrants and an- nouncing the final abandonment of racial definitions of American identity. Undoubtedly, this would be far better than virulent nativist racism punctu- ated by all too familiar vicious physical assaults. But, nonetheless, the current migrants are not like the old ones; they are not only the "children of capi- talism," they are the offspring of American globalism, European colonial dom- ination, and their overlapping racial codes. For these migrants the United States is simultaneously an economic "promised land" with an openness to at least the idea of immigration, and a society whose political conscience and po- litical unconscious are steeped in traces of slavery and racial definitions of its continental and global manifest destiny. As Haitians negotiate their national and racial "place" in the United States they confront definitions of blackness that do not fit into the immigrant saga. In the language of our "mythistory," a black immigrant is an oxymoron. They embody the return of the oppressed and dispossessed, people who had their futures transformed by the Euro-American variant of "Western Civilization." The global flows of labor and capital characteristic of new migration are finally calling into question the racial imagination which marked America's first 500 years. While more difficult to gauge than other aspects of the transnational social field, the renegotiation of national racial memory may be an energizing factor in the strength and depth of "transnational" identities of post-colonial migrants. In the age of capital, all immigrants may have been "homeless," but these new migrants may remain more homeless than others—at least until we resolve the contradictions of the last 500 years.

Let me conclude with a provocation from "our" cultural past. I have been a bit disturbed by the fact that for all of the discussion about "transnationalism" no one has even alluded to Randolph Bourne's (1916) classic essay *Transnational America*. In 1916, responding to rising Anglophile and anti-immigrant "patriotic" sentiment, Bourne argued that the nation might have to accept "dual citizenship." In addition, he argued, "we shall have to accept, I think, that free and mobile passage of the immigrant between America and his native land . . . To stigmatize the alien who works in America for a few years and returns to his own land, only perhaps to seek American fortune again, is to think in narrow nationalistic terms." As a social critic he took what to American Anglo-Saxon racialists were the disturbing facts of recent immigration and re-visioned the meaning and future of the nation. As he put it, "Let us make something of this trans-national spirit instead of outlawing it." Opposed to the bloody interests of nation states and the prison house of pristine national and ethnic cultures, Bourne saw the immigrants' border crossings as a basis for creative renegotiations of cultural identities. These trans-nationals would be part of a global vanguard challenging the deadly nationalisms that had unleashed the massive carnage of war-ravaged Europe. Although often categorized as a "pluralist," Bourne was in fact a democratic cosmopolitan internationalist. Against the armed forces of political nationalism and stultifying cultural parochialism Bourne radicalized and internationalized Whitman's vision of "a nation of nations."

As we clarify the nature of the contemporary migration experience, we should think about Bourne and pause to reflect on the disrupted history of the idea of transnationalism. Why, in spite of the notoriety of Bourne's essay, did it never really enter the lexicon of politics and scholarship as we debated "pluralism," "the melting pot," and "assimilation," terms that presumed the overwhelming importance of the United States as a bounded if conflictual social field? Was it simply the result of the restriction and stabilization of unidirectional migration flows that seemed to leave only withering symbolic attachments to the old country? If so, scholars and policy experts may rapidly adopt the term as they confront the new dimensions of the global division of labor in late capitalism. Or perhaps, regardless of the observable dimensions of the transnational social fields, the idea of transnationalism – even more than pluralism – poses too much of a challenge to the mythistory of the United States. To acknowledge that the most recent offspring of capitalism are protecting their material well being and sense of self by acting within a transnational field would mean abandoning not simply the nativism Bourne confronted, but the less exclusive, but perhaps even more Whiggish and racist, American immigrant saga that will be celebrated during Ellis Island's centennial in 1992.

Of one thing we can be certain. If transnationalism *does* gain wider scholarly and popular currency as a medium of political exchange, its meaning will be contested. Already the reality of our new situation has been reduced to a series of advertising vignettes of materially, if not as yet emotionally, comfortable immigrants dialing family and friends in the old country. The complex, historically grounded flow of class, ethnic, and racial identities analyzed in these papers are thus reduced to the all too familiar world of prosperous re-rooted ethnic America. If we wish to engage this wider debate, we will have to become not only scholars remapping past and current migrants' social fields, but, like Bourne, public intellectuals re-naming a no longer "American" dream.

REFERENCES CITED

Archdeacon, Thomas
  1983 *Becoming American: An ethnic history.* New York: Free Press.
Berthoff, Rowland
  1962 The working class. In *The reconstruction of American history*, edited by John Higham. New York: Harper and Row. Pp. 119–136.
Blackburn, Robin
  1988 *The overthrow of colonial slavery, 1776–1848.* London: Verso.
Bourne, Randolph
  1916 Trans-national America. *Atlantic Monthly* 118:778–786.
Bodnar, John
  1985 *The transplanted: A history of immigrants in America.* Bloomington: Indiana University Press.
  1986 Symbols and servants: Immigrant America and the limits of public history. *Journal of American History* :137–151.
Bukowczyk, John J.
  1984 The transformation of working class ethnicity: Corporate control, Americanization, and the Polish immigrant middle class in Bayonne, New Jersey, 1915–1925. *Labor History* 25:53–82.
  1989 Migration and capitalism. *International Labor and Working Class History* 36: 61–75.

Davis, David Brion
  1989   American equality and foreign relations. *Journal of American History 76*: 729–752.
Duberman, Martin
  1988   *Paul Robeson.* New York: Alfred Knopf.
Fredrickson, George M.
  1981   *White supremacy: A comparative study in American and South African History.* New York: Oxford University Press.
Genovese, Eugene D.
  1979   *From rebellion to revolution: Afro-American slave revolts in the making of the New World.* New York: Random House.
Gerstle, Gary
  1989   *Working class Americanism: The politics of labor in a textile city, 1914–1960.* Cambridge: Cambridge University Press.
Gleason, Philip
  1980   American identity and Americanization. In *Harvard encyclopedia of American ethnic groups,* edited by Stephan Thernstrom, Ann Orlov, and Oscar Handlin. Cambridge, MA: Harvard University Press. Pp. 31–58.
  1981   Americans all: World War II and the shaping of American identity. *Review of Politics 43*:483–518.
Gutman, Herbert G.
  1976   *The black family in slavery and freedom, 1750–1925.* New York: Pantheon.
Handlin, Oscar
  1970 [1941]   *Boston's immigrants, 1790–1880: A study in acculturation.* Revised and enlarged edition. New York: Atheneum.
Harney, Robert F.
  1986   *E pluribus unum:* Louis Adamic and the meaning of ethnic history. *Journal of Ethnic Studies 14*:29–45.
Higham, John
  1975   *Send these to me: Jews and other immigrants in urban America.* New York: Atheneum.
Jackson, Agnes Moreland
  1974   To see the "me" in "thee": Challenge to ALL white Americans, or white ethnicity from a black perspective and a sometimes response to Michael Novak. In *The rediscovery of ethnicity: Its implications for culture and politics in America,* edited by Sallie TeSelle. New York: Harper and Row. Pp. 21–44.
James, C. L. R.
  1963   *The black Jacobins: Toussaint L'Ouverture and the San Domingo revolution.* 2d edition, revised. New York: Random House.
Kennedy, John F.
  1986 [1964]   *A nation of immigrants.* Revised and enlarged edition. New York: Harper and Row.
Morgan, Edmund S.
  1975   *American slavery, American history: The ordeal of colonial Virginia.* New York: W. W. Norton and Co.
Piore, Michael J.
  1979   *Birds of passage: Migrant labor and industrial societies.* Cambridge: Cambridge University Press.
Reimers, David
  1985   *Still the golden door: The Third World comes to America.* New York: Columbia University Press.

Roche, John P.
  1986   Preface: New immigrants, new problems, new hopes. In John F. Kennedy,
          A nation of immigrants. New York: Harper and Row.
Rotberg, Robert I.
  1971   *Haiti, the politics of squalor*. Boston: Houghton Mifflin.
Steinberg, Stephen
  1981   *The ethnic myth: Race, ethnicity, and class in America*. Boston: Beacon.
Slotkin, Richard
  1985   *The fatal environment: The myth of the frontier in the age of industrialization,
          1800–1870*. Middletown, CT: Wesleyan University Press.
Takaki, Ronald
  1979   *Iron cages: Race and culture in 19th-century America*. New York: Alfred A.
          Knopf.
Vecoli, Rudolph J.
  1985   Return to the melting pot: Ethnicity in the United States in the eighties.
          Journal of American Ethnic History 15:7–20.

Which Migrants?
Temporary or Permanent?

DELMOS JONES

Department of Anthropology
Graduate Center
City University of New York
New York, New York 10036

The title of this workshop is *Towards a Transnational Perspective on Migration: Race, Class, Ethnicity, and Nationalism Reconsidered* and the goal is to come up with a revised analytic framework for understanding a new form of international migration. The development of a new analytic framework is no easy task, and it is not something that is achieved by one effort alone. Thus, I am going to limit my comments, but hope that they will generate some discussion about the topics under consideration. My goal is not to critique the papers, nor to discuss each one in any considerable detail. Rather it is to try to draw out common themes they address and point out problems that need to be further clarified.

Let me first highlight a few of the factual conditions that all of these papers address. The first and most important condition is that the migrants maintain ties to their home society, and that families tend to remain functional across national boundaries. Communications are mentioned in this context: the fact that one can call, or FAX anything to almost anywhere, or receive television transmissions of programs almost anyplace is an important material fact that cannot be overlooked. The second condition is that many transnational migrants do not establish permanent residency in the host society. It is not revealed how many people remain for how long in the host society, and how many people return, at what point in time, to live in their country of birth. This point I will return to later.

Another important theme that appears in all of these papers is that the migrants are upwardly mobile. Concern with social status is an important issue that emerges over and over again: people who are migrating and working in Western cities are doing so to improve their status in their home country. "The project of the great majority of U.S. migrants is a long-term one; to accumulate sufficient resources to return and sustain themselves and their families securely in the Dominican 'middle class'" (Georges 1992, this volume). It may at some point be important to determine the proportion of these versus the proportion who would like to be successful in the United States.

Another issue concerns economic investments in the home country as
well as the host country–this is an important aspect of "making it." In this
respect I was struck by a quotation in Eugenia Georges' paper from Portes and
Walton who observed that "opportunities for wage earning are often greater
in the center, those for investment and informal economic activity are frequently greater in the periphery." Georges also talks about starting ethnic businesses in New York. It seems to me that there is a tendency, except in
Lessinger's paper, to place more emphasis on the social and cultural aspects
of the situation rather than the economic aspects. This is a situation that deserves much closer inspection.

The papers are uneven in the way they address the specific issues of ethnicity, race, and nationalism. This is not necessarily a criticism, but merely an
observation. More needs to be said about these topics. Lessinger's presentation offers a great deal of information about the investment strategies of NRIs.
But she also points to a tension between the resident Indians and the non-
resident Indians over the question of identity. She described a cultural function where the theme emerged "that there is a single Indian identity among
immigrants separated from India by thousands of miles, and in some cases several generations," and that there was a unifying Indian identity which ties the
overseas Indian community together, and links it firmly to India itself. But
the fact that there was a conference around the theme is perhaps of more significance than the conclusions arrived at. Here I refer to the effort to construct
or reconstruct a common identity. Lessinger suggests this when she writes
that there are two symbolic resolutions to the problem. One is the attempt
to create some kind of pan-Indian identity, and the other is to bring the immigrants, their talent, and their money home for reintegration into India.
However, some immigrants clearly want to remain part of two cultures.

The other common theme that emerges is the importance of these new
migrants to the home country. Lessinger's paper offers the most dramatic indication of that.

The other theme is the observation that the extended family continues to
function across national boundaries. Remember, that we have operated with
a theory that the evolution of the family in industrial society has been driven
by the demands of a certain kind of labor. That the individual, or the couple
had to be divorced from commitments to a larger unit so that they would be
mobile, able to move to where they were needed. This led to the breakdown
of the larger extended family and the emergence of the nuclear family as the
dominant form. It is interesting to see, therefore, that positive functioning of
larger family units.

So far I have attempted to summarize some of the common conditions
of the transnational migrants. Clearly they are part of a new and important
set of social, economic, and political processes taking place both in the
country of origin and the host society. (Not so much something new but

something that has increased in density and significance.) The question now is how can we look at this phenomenon in such a way as to isolate and describe what is taking place?

The paper by the workshop organizers is an attempt to provide some new conceptual clarity to the problem of the "new migrant" and the multiple social and economic situations. The idea is that our traditional manner of dealing with social issues is not sufficient to describe a situation where there are such multiple connections and relationships. Transmigrants are defined in contrast to an older version of immigrants who are permanently uprooted from their home setting and are forced to abandon old patterns and "adapt" to new circumstances. One of the typical topics that we used to deal with is the adaptation of migrants to the city. I do not think that the authors imply that the migrants no longer have to adapt to new circumstances. In fact I think Rouse's paper attempts to define a special kind of adaptation. I am intrigued by the idea in his paper that the two brothers had to struggle not just to work out how they should act and think but also to deal with the strange but insistent demand to identify themselves. The implication of this notion for the problem of identity deserves looking into. People are not just who they are. They become in part what others want them to be. They become in part what is required by the situation without anyone telling them to, and as long as it does not conflict with their social and economic roles, who cares? And they also become in part what they want to be.

Transnationalism is a situation where networks, activities and patterns of life encompass both the host and home societies. Here the migrants are conceptualized as acting in a social field embracing the home as well as the host countries. The writer goes on to state that the lives of these migrants cut across national boundaries and bring the two societies into a single social field. Nor do I think that the author is implying that it is the migrants alone who are bringing the two societies together or that the field of social action should be limited to two societies. It is noted that the world is currently bound together by a global capitalist system that has operated to create the phenomenon.

The writers outline five premises that are central to their conceptualization of transnationalism. The first is the problem of bounded social unit. The intent, I believe, is to substitute "field of social action" for this concept. This would imply that the boundaries of action are always subject to change, and difficult for the social scientist to keep up with. The second is that the experience of the transnational migrants is "inextricably linked to the changing conditions of global capitalism." Let me skip the third and go to the last because I want to make a comment relating the two. The last premise is that the existence of transnational migrants compels us to reconceptualize the categories of nationalism, ethnicity, and race. Conspicuously absent here is a reference to social class. As I see it the processes being described in most of these papers have a definite social class dimension, so much so that I suspect that transnationalism is both a product of global capitalism and contributes to the expansion of global capitalism. Rouse comes down very strong on this point. He writes that it is necessary to develop an approach that makes class central to our analysis. More specifically, we should situate migration in the context of class transformation. We should recognize that the production and reproduction of classes is not simply a socioeconomic phenomenon but also a political and cultural one. As anthropologists we run into serious conceptual problems when we juxtapose the idea of culture with the idea of social class. More on that point later.

The third premise is that transnationalism is grounded in the daily lives of people. This fact is clearly shown in the paper by Georges, and this description is very suggestive of the social class dimension of the process. It is at this level of description that we see the interaction between the fact of economic opportunism and the traditional cultural forms. The fourth premise is that the transnational migrants draw upon different identity constructs. But it is important to emphasize that different identities are being constructed.

The idea of multiple group affiliation is of course not new, and one that was described by Simmel. The notion of multiple group affiliations, which states in effect that multiple group membership is a characteristic of modern society. "In modern society . . . a person's multiple group affiliations constitute mostly crosscutting circles, and one's social position is at the intersection of numerous groups with largely different membership" (Blau, Beeker, and Fitzpatric 1984:586). One consequence of this, according to Simmel was greater freedom from group control. That is, a person could decide which group, if any, to submit to. The city, as Wirth expressed it, is the meeting place of different races, peoples, and cultures, a breeding-ground of new biological and cultural hybrids, and a setting that not only tolerated but rewarded individual differences (Wirth 1975:33).

The question is what is the context of the transnational migrants with respect to group affiliation, and choices? I get a conflicting picture of this issue, and I refer back to Lessinger's comment that while India might wish to draw the NRIs back to India some may wish to retain their dual role. This signifies the possibility that the transnational migrants may, in fact, end up having more choices than many other groups who live in cities. In this respect I am very struck with another comment by Lessinger: As the process of NRI investment continues, contributing to growing internal social stratification, both in India and in Indian immigrant communities abroad, it remains to be seen where profits are reinvested. Will they be redirected to the immigrants' adopted countries or in India? If NRIs do become a major force within overseas immigrant communities, will they remain encapsulated within their respective ethnic communities or will they merge imperceptibly with other national or international capitalist entrepreneurs? Ong's Hong Kong capitalists should also be considered in this context. The locations of their investments include Hong Kong, the United States, Europe, and probably other parts of Asia.

It seems to me that there is a tension in the conceptualization and the descriptions between two models of urban social organizations. The first is the freedom from group ties, and the second is the importance of group ties.

Freedom from Group Ties

One of the recurrent themes in urban studies is the kinds of "communities" or primary groups that exist in modern society. The issue is informed by an evolutionary and comparative perspective that views the city in contrast to previous social forms, as well as in relation to contemporary traditional and rural communities. The distinction is variously characterized: gemeinschaft–gesellschaft, folk–urban, mechanical and organic solidarity, status–contract. The idea behind these dual concepts is that substantial transformations occurred with urbanization, and this is the case whether it is the evolution of urbanism or the current migration from rural areas into cities. One notion is that the local group declines in importance as a basis of social relations to be replaced by common interest. As Park (1915:586) put it industrialization because of its increased division of labor eroded the basis of folk society. The outcome of this process is to break down or modify the older organization of society, which was based on family ties, local associations, on culture, caste, and status, and to substitute for an organization based on vocational interests (Park 1915:586, see also Simmel). Implied in this position is that primordial group attachments are incompatible with the conditions of a modern industrialized economic system.

This brings me back to the important role of the family that emerges in all of these studies. Remember, that we have operated with a theory that the evolution of the family in industrial society has been driven by the demands of a certain kind of labor.

Attachment to Group

The second perspective is related to the "New Pluralism." From this perspective primordial attachments, especially in the form of ethnic and national identity, remain important. Many definitions of ethnicity emphasize the continuation of cultural traditions. In the sociological literature this idea is something discussed in terms of cosmopolitanism and localism, where localism focuses on individualism and the liberation of the individual from primordial attachments (Hraba and Hoilberg 1983). The ethnic perspective stresses the importance of the group. Groups are not only more important than individuals, but should and must limit individual freedom and action.

From the perspective of the new ethnicity, primordial attachments provide the individual with a sense of belonging that is not satisfied in any broader associations. From the transnational perspective we see that these attachments are serving economic and social functions.

The question is which of these perspectives is the most suitable to apply to the transnational situation? My sense is that both should be applied. I think that this idea was what was being expressed when the writers said, the new conceptualization should ". . . combine an emphasis on social relations, understood as fluid and dynamic, yet culturally patterned, with an analysis of the global context." This means making an effort to talk about the significance of national states, the local community, and local cultural processes within the context of larger global events.

The Global Process

The United States has been going through something called deindustrialization. Many stable industrial jobs have been lost through the export of industries. Well-paying, unionized jobs have been replaced by service sector and clerical employment. While industries are searching for cheap labor by exporting industries, cheap labor is also imported in the form of migrants. Sweat shops, often associated with illegal migrants, and home work are proliferating. Work in the service sector is characterized by low pay with few benefits. At the same time the local economies of third world countries have been disrupted by the investments of transnational corporations, *etc*. The case study of the Dominican Republic shows how the erosion of the local economy encourages migration. Note the feedback mechanism that is also described: people are leaving to work in the United States and sending money back to support their families, an act that sounds very cultural, but at the same time many of these individuals are also investing and starting new business enterprises.

Recall, the common theme that most of these migrants are interested in achieving a higher standard of living, and they are able to achieve this better by investing at home. And while the situation is characterized by migrants sending money back home to support their families note another relationship that is emphasized by Lessinger and Georges. Georges notes that "The poorest remained behind, where they formed a pool of cheap labor available for tapping *by migrants who invested U.S. earnings in the village.*" Lessinger notes that the NRI investment contributes to a growing internal stratification, both in India and in Indian immigrants' communities abroad.

How can funds be accumulated in a situation where wages are low and benefits non-existent? The paper by Georges suggests that it is achieved by sponsoring the migration of dependents, both wives and children so they could work and save as part of the reconstituted household in New York: and commercial ventures in the village are carried out by using personal networks and extended family ties. What is interesting here is this interpretation of traditional cultural forms with a commercial venture in the context of the global economic system. This manipulation of culture by entrepreneurs is evident in Ong's Hong Kong capitalists. She noted, "these new Chinese immigrants are not Chinatown folks, and have very few connections with earlier waves of Chinese immigrants. However, by seizing the limelight and claiming to represent the 'Asian American' community, the Hong Kong investors have had a significant impact on the ways the Chinese community is locally perceived by the wider society." And at another point she notes that they have manipulated the "model minority" construct and rhetoric of discrimination to advance *their* individual political and economic ends.

I do not believe that the transmigrant situation as it is currently situated is a stable one. Look at some of the indications offered by the papers. Georges talks about the subsidization of the local middle class by remittances, and a greater demand for domestic servants, where women from the poorest households are employed as household servants. We know that the goal of many of these migrants is to return and realize their better standard of living. Will this return be something like gentrification? Ong and Lessinger seem the most impressed by the fact that many of these migrants are entrepreneurs and their analyses are guided by that fact. Lessinger suggests the possibility of a relationship with other national or international capitalist entrepreneurs. It is in this context that I do not understand the notion of resistance that crops up in several of the papers. The organizers write, "by maintaining many different racial, national, and ethnic identities, transmigrants are able to express their resistance to the global political and economic situation that engulfs them, even as they accommodate themselves to living conditions marked by vulnerability and insecurity." Is this a sort of retreat to a cultural analysis where "the group" is unified against an "other?" It could just as well be said that the different racial, national, and ethnic identities open up greater opportunities that can be manipulated to one's advantage. Rather than resisting the situation it is clear that many of these transmigrants are buying into it. This is not to say that resistance does not take place, but characterizing resistance as a characterization of *the* transmigrants is to reclose a social boundary that must remain open. Resistance and accommodation are not two things that happen in harmony with each other. Rather they reflect internal contradictions and tensions. The existence of forces of resistance and accommodation within a group produces a situation where the two are in confrontation with each other, and are manifested as internal factionalism. For example, M. Holden, Jr. noted that ". . . the single most common theme in all Afro-American culture is the hope for deliverance some day" (1973:17), but this is off-set by another theme,

cynicism-and-fear, which cautions against rocking the boat and the consequences of actions aimed at deliverance (1973:24–25).

It is here that the issue of social class and capitalist goals and motivation
must take central stage. We are talking in large part about entrepreneurs, and
their goal is to make money. What does culture have to do with it? Remember,
it was Rouse who suggested that the production and reproduction of classes
is a political and cultural process. It seems that in some situations–maybe
Ong's Hong Kong capitalists are the best example–groups are composed of
people who are both locally oriented and cosmopolitan. This is a condition
that allows the "liberated" or cosmopolitan investors to use the nationalism
or cultural identity of others for their benefit. It is Caulfield who talks about
the way in which traditional roles and statuses are distorted and made to serve
the interests of the new dominant class (1972:194–195).

Just a few more comments about the two separate settings and the related
processes that are taking place there. I am struck by Georges suggestion that
a rigidification of cultural norms may be taking place in the village. She ends
the paper by saying that migration often served to strengthen women's an-
choring in established gender roles. In the United States question can be
raised about the different kinds of ethnic alliances that are being generated
through co-residence, common treatment, intermarriage, or all of the above.

Interesting questions arise about the outcome of the events taking place
in the two settings. Are they reinforcing each other? Are they in conflict? Or
is it a combination of both? The answers to these and other questions must
not only await future research but the further evolution of the situation itself.

REFERENCES CITED

Blau, P., M. C. Beeker, and K. M. Fitzpatric
   1984   Intersecting social affiliations and intermarriage. *Social Forces 62*: 585–606.
Caulfield, M. D.
   1972   Culture and imperialism: Proposing a new dialectic. In *Reinventing anthro-
          pology*, edited by Dell Hymes. New York: Pantheon Books, a division of
          Random House.
Holden, Matthew, Jr.
   1973   *Politics of the black "nation."* New York: Chandler.
Hraba, Joseph and Eric Hoilberg
   1983   Ideational origins of modern theories of ethnicity: Individual freedom vs.
          organizational growth. *Sociological Quarterly 24*: 381–391.
Park, R. E.
   1915   The city: Suggestions for the investigation of human behavior in the city
          environment. *American Journal of Sociology 20*: 577–612.
Wirth, Louis
   1975   Urbanism as a way of life. In *City ways: A selected reader in urban anthropology*,
          edited by John Friedl and Noel J. Christman. New York: Thomas Crowell
          Company.

Comments on Rethinking Migration: A Transnational Perspective

PALMIRA N. RIOS

New School for Social Research
Graduate School of Management and Urban Policy
66 Fifth Avenue
New York, New York 10011

In several speeches delivered in New York City last year, Dr. José Francisco Peña Gómez, Vice-President of the International Socialist and presidential candidate of the Dominican Revolutionary Party, proposed, among other things, a constitutional amendment to allow the citizens of the Dominican Republic to opt for dual citizenship in order to encourage their participation in the American political process, thus giving the Dominican state a greater leverage over American policies. This proposal is one of the building blocks of Peña's blueprint for the modernization of the Dominican political structure which is needed to bring that Caribbean nation in line with globalization processes. Nationalism, Peña predicted, will be reduced to an isolationist position as multinationalism and economic integration become the dominant forms of participation in the global economy.

The Dominican Republic is not alone in formulating policy initiatives to integrate migrants into developmental and political agendas. Portugal, Jamaica, and Cuba already provide for dual citizenship. In 1989 the Commonwealth of Puerto Rico established the Department of Puerto Rican Community Affairs in the United States as a cabinet-level office entrusted with the responsibility of improving the quality of life for the more than two million Puerto Ricans who reside in the United States. Colombia and Peru already allow their citizens abroad to participate in presidential elections, and Mexico is debating the role that its nationals abroad can play in its political arena. These independent initiatives are a clear sign of the recognition within political circles that the diaspora constitutes a potential economic, political and social force, both at home and in the United States, and that state intervention on behalf of citizens who no longer reside within its territorial boundaries is a legitimate form of public policy. In very pragmatic ways, governments are institutionalizing transnational practices.

A transnational perspective can be very useful in explaining these trends and in understanding migration in the context of the global economy. The papers discussed today contribute significantly to a growing literature that attempts to break away from two competing paradigms within migration studies: assimilation and ethnic pluralism. Although descriptive in some ways, these case studies point to the need for a more dynamic and humanistic approach to the migration phenomenon, one that can capture the complexity of the experiences lived by individuals, families, and groups straddling in two worlds, and whose actions are opening new spaces for social exchanges.

Although we can agree that labor migration is a function of capital mobility, we cannot agree to reduce this experience to that of another commodity exchanged within the networks of the global economy. Migration is as much an economic process as it is a social, political and cultural movement that transforms social relations in its path. It is people—not just objects and victims—who are following capital, and who are consciously participating in the construction, deconstruction, and manipulation of their identities and roles. Immigrants are choosing when and where to play the role of the assimilated, the ethnic minority, or the foreigner. These new behaviors constitute challenges to the academic and, policy-making communities.

It is increasingly evident that today's immigrants are different from those of the past. They are most likely to come from the peripheral world, be persons of color, include a large number of professionals—although most will very likely join the ranks of the proletariat—and women are in the majority. Another distinctive feature is that they are holding on to their native cultures and traditional networks in unprecedented ways. This indicates that when immigrants cross national boundaries they also bring together two societies into a single arena for social interaction. Transnationalism has become a way of life for a growing number of people.

The cases analyzed by this panel demonstrate the usefulness of this theoretical perspective and point to its potential for public policy. Lessinger's study is closer to the Dominican phenomenon that I briefly described. The Indian government has implemented what other countries are just beginning to articulate: the use of nationalistic appeals to encourage nationals abroad to invest in their country of origin. The financial role of migrants is no longer reduced to sending remittances; the diaspora is now conceived as a partner in development. The study by Portes and Guarnizo (1990) of the Dominican economy documented that remittances constitute one of the single most important sources of income—greater than agriculture and second to tourism—and that a portion is being invested in small businesses, notwithstanding the lack of government support.

Richman and Feldman-Bianco provide additional evidence of how governments are turning to their own diaspora for assistance in their economic agendas. In Haiti, President Aristide's "tenth department" constitutes a blending of a populist agenda with a call to the diaspora for help in the development of the country. Portugal, while preparing to join the European

Common Market, took steps to incorporate its nationals abroad into its political structure.

This perspective also highlights that, in the context of the global economy,
nationalism is increasingly distancing from citizenship; the latter oftentimes
being reduced to a convenient legal formality. This notion is important for
politicians and policy makers who are called upon to identify who are the legitimate clients of the state. Furthermore, this distinction is an important element
in understanding the conflict between immigrants and African-Americans, for
whom full citizenship and participation in national affairs are still major goals.

Another significant contribution of the concept of transnationalism is that
it views ethnicity as a socially constructed phenomenon subject to deliberate
manipulation. Charles elaborates on the relationship between identity, class,
race, and ethnicity among Haitian immigrants, a phenomenon already described by Laguerre (1984) and also identified among Jamaicans (Foner 1987)
and Puerto Ricans (Rodríguez 1989). She notes that immigrants construct
their identity within multiple contexts. Also significant is the notion that immigrants manipulate their ethnicity to advance their interests and satisfy their
needs. The phenomenon of ethnic manipulation constitutes clear evidence
that ethnicity, like class, race and gender, is a socially constructed phenomenon. Hence, a transnational perspective avoids the reification bias that so
dominates ethnic studies and politics.

However, this proposed perspective is not without problems. The term
itself is problematic since it allows for different interpretations. A dictionary
will define it as a transformation or metamorphosis, a passage into another
nationality. The authors, however, use the term to mean a bridge and it is not
clear whether this bridge constitutes a blending of cultures, a transitional phenomenon, or a completely new culture.

Furthermore, one wonders whether transnationalism manifests in the
same manner in the private and public spheres of social life. Although this perspective rejects the dichotomy between home and host country, the studies
do not address how it might affect the public–private poles. An ethnographic
study of immigrant women workers in Paris found that their existence re-
volved around two poles: a cultural environment of family and countrymen
that resembled the country of origin and a culture of work and public life.
This dichotomy was expressed most explicitly in the acquisition of two autonomous language tools; an affective mother tongue used primarily within the
confines of the family and neighborhood, and a specialized language of the
workplace (Catani 1982).

The public–private dichotomy calls attention to the phenomenon of discrimination and segregation, particularly racial, and their roles in the making
of a transnational space. Laguerre noted that immigrants find "a landscape that
has been largely designed over the years by the practice of residential racial seg-

regation (1984:49). He also concluded that it was the racist structure of American society that compelled Haitian immigrants to use ethnicity in their adaptation process (1984:155). This partly explains the paradox between insularity and transnationalism pointed to by Feldman-Bianco.

There is also a problem in identifying the proper unit of analysis and its temporal framework. The studies use different standards of measurement, such as immigrants, the state, and culture. Neither do the studies clarify whether the phenomenon is temporal, that is, generational. Will later generations experience a similar process or will it fade away with the second and later generations? In pursuing this line of research one should look again at the migration experience of Puerto Ricans, probably one of the oldest transnational groups, to identify the continuities and discontinuities in the transnational praxis. Furthermore, the study of this group can provide insights into the relation between transnationalism, discrimination, and social mobility since some studies point precisely to transnational practices as factors in the high levels of poverty among Puerto Ricans.

There is a need for better clarification of the intersections of transnationality and other axes of power, primarily class and gender. Are there class differences in the experience of transnationality? Charles indicates that is the case, but there still remains the need for more studies. Likewise, we need to factor in gender differences in the understanding of transnationalism.

Another gray area is where do you fit those who did not migrate but who nevertheless participate in the transnational networks. These studies are focusing on immigrants thus neglecting those relatives and associates who participate in and benefit from the diaspora while remaining at home. Do they experience something equivalent to transnationalism? Likewise there is a need to look again at the interaction between immigrants and the host society; are native-born citizens brought into transnational networks by virtue of their geographical location within or near immigrant neighborhoods? All these questions point to the need for more studies, particularly of households and neighborhoods and of their roles in the construction of transnationalism.

A related issue is the future of the transnational. The sad truth is that, ultimately, transnationals do not fully belong to either societies in which they live. Often they are manipulated by both, and as a group remain relatively powerless at both ends. Lessinger touches upon this question in discussing the problem of defining Indianness. Puerto Ricans in the United States faced a similar dilemma when they were denied the right to participate in the proposed plebiscite to determine the final political status of the island. The derogative meaning of the terms Puerto Rican-York and Dominican-York is a painful reminder that neither group is fully accepted by their countryfolks.

It is interesting to note that most studies failed to recognize the critical role played by technological transformations in the making of transnationalism. Radical changes in communications and transportation make feasible the exchanges between immigrants and their native societies in ways that were not possible before. I always remember the strange sensation of being able to share with my sister a televised marathon that raised funds for the victims of Hurricane Hugo in Puerto Rico while I was in New York City and she was in Puerto Rico. The simple explanation is that we were watching the program while talking over the telephone. This example is just one instance of modern technology sustaining the transnational praxis.

Finally, Charles's comment on the need to redefine social context should not be ignored. The notion of separating the concept of the state from that of social formation seems insightful. Although unfortunately the idea was not elaborated, it still raises many interesting questions: are immigrants embedded in two social formations, as the paper suggests, or is the globalization of the economy obliterating the boundaries between social formations; does trans-nationalism constitute a distinct sphere of social relations? The answers to these questions can raise the level of the analysis of the transnational phenom-enon beyond its present descriptive stage to a more theoretical understanding of the immigrant experience.

REFERENCES CITED

Catani, Maurizio
  1982   Changing one's country means changing one's flag. In *Living in two cultures. The socio-cultural situation of migrant workers and their families*, edited by Ronald G. Parris. London and Paris: The UNESCO Press and Gowen Publishing Co., Ltd. Pp. 163–239.
Foner, Nancy
  1987   The Jamaicans: Race and ethnicity among migrants in NYC. In *New immigrants in New York*, edited by Nancy Foner. New York: Columbia University Press. Pp. 195–218.
Laguerre, Michael
  1984   *American odyssey. Haitians in NYC*. Ithaca: Cornell University Press.
Peña Gómez, José Francisco
  1990   The role of public policy in the modernization of the Dominican Republic. Paper presented at the Graduate School of Management and Urban Policy of the New School for Social Research.
Portes, Alejandro and Luis E. Guarnizo
  1990   *Tropical capitalists: U.S.-bound immigration and small-enterprise development in the Dominican Republic*. Washington, D.C.: Commission for the Study of International Migration and Cooperative Economic Development, Working Paper 57.
Rodríguez, Clara
  1990   *Puerto Ricans. Born in the U.S.* Boston: Unwin Hyman.

The Contradictions of Transnational Migration: A Discussion

GERALD SIDER

Department of Anthropology
The College of Staten Island and
The Graduate School and University Center
City University of New York
33 West 42nd Street
New York, New York 10036-8099

~ I ~

I would like to begin my comments with a simple but crucial point, most forcefully called to our attention by John Berger and Jean Mohr's marvelously poetic and analytically insightful book—*A Seventh Man*. This book looked at "guest workers" in northern Europe in the 1960s and early 1970s. One out of seven persons in the manual labor force in the industrial countries of northern Europe at that time was not a citizen of the country in which he/she worked, but a more or less temporary migrant from north Africa, the eastern Mediterranean or southern Europe.

What Berger emphasized[1] is that the remittances that migrant workers sent or brought back, however substantial in appearance and however important to the maintenance of the people left behind, did not come anywhere close to the actual costs, for the home country or region, of producing and reproducing these workers. I quote Stephen Castles and Godula Kosack:

> Migration involves the transfer of a valuable economic resource—human labor—from the poor to the rich countries. The workers who migrate may have been unemployed in the country of origin, but this does not alter the fact that the community has invested considerable sums in their upbringing. Economists sometimes speak of 'emigration as capital export' similar to the export of other factors of production . . .: "If the emigrants were slaves, and raised for the purpose, it would be appropriate to calculate whether it was worth-

---

[1] John Berger and Jean Mohr, *A seventh man*, (London: Penguin, 1975), esp. pp. 68–69. The source for their figures on the costs of migration is primarily Stephen Castles and Godula Kosack, *Immigrant workers and class structure in Western Europe* (London: Oxford University Press, 1974), pp. 408–429.

while for a poor country to raise slaves for export. . . . The answer would doubt-
lessly be 'no.'"

It is relevant to try to calculate the cost of a migrant for his country of
origin. . . . The costs we are concerned with are those of feeding, clothing,
and housing a person and providing health and educational and other services,
until he reaches working age. . . . Whatever the proportions [of such costs]
borne by parents and community, the total cost of raising a child is a charge
on the country's national income.

It is, of course, extremely difficult to assess the total cost of raising a child
in any country. . . . [Here the authors cite several examples, each approximately
U.S. $5,000 in the early to mid 1960s, and note that these figures are open
to doubt.] But these figures do indicate that the costs of bringing up migrants
are very high. This burden is all the more severe for poor countries. . . .[2]

And this does not count the other costs of reproducing a labor force—a
labor-force drawn from and returned to communities and kin-groups—in the
home (ironically: "donor") countries. Taking care of the elderly, the infirm,
the workers who come home sick and broken or just old—all these costs are
borne, not in the country where the workers are doing productive work and
having surplus value extracted from them both by the state and by the dominant classes, but these costs are borne by the home communities, the home
countries. These costs are often imposed upon a declining effective productive
base; a productive base where the portion of surplus value that is extracted
by multinational agribusinesses and manufacturing corporations moves out
even faster than the people, hardly ever to return.[3] To all this we must add,
as one of the further impacts of the migration of a substantial portion of the
labor force, the lost possibilities for production in the countries and communities that the migrants leave.

---

[2] Castles and Kosack, *op. cit.*, pp. 408–409. The internal quote is from C.P. Kindleberger,
Europe's postwar growth: The role of labor supply. (Cambridge, MA: Harvard University Press, 1967),
p. 98. The 1990 purchasing power of the U.S. dollar is approximately one-fourth that obtaining
in 1962.

[3] The conversion of agrarian output from local- to world-market crops, requiring multiple
commodified inputs (fertilizers, pesticides, perhaps irrigation, perhaps commercial seed), and ordinarily quickly displacing masses of people from the countryside in the context of both widespread immiseration and substantial shifts in land ownership and use (for the people who go,
however impoverished they may be individually, in the aggregate must leave behind very substantial claims on the social product and the productive forces); the advent of industry (especially
in "export processing zones" and structurally similar arrangements) paying wages just barely adequate to maintain their workers, and perhaps a dependent or two, in shanty housing lacking basic
services and on the most minimal food; agribusinesses and industries that pay taxes at, or more
likely below, the cost of providing their necessary economic and sociopolitical infrastructure and
that, moreover, repatriate most of their profits: all such "developments" cannot be counted as
part of an "effective productive base," being rather a form for accumulating disguised transfer payments from rural laborers and smallholders, as well as surplus value from the workers—in both
cases primarily from those least able to afford the cost.

» «

From this initial perspective I want to make four introductory points, to frame subsequent suggestions for discussion and further analytical engagement. These suggested points focus on transnational migration originating in impoverished rural areas of "third world" countries–the hinterlands of the hinterlands, to use (without endorsing its class-concealing simplicities) the "metropole-satellite" metaphor.[4] Such hinterland-transnational migrations are ordinarily deeply interwoven with "temporary" migrations to cities (or mines or plantations) within the migrants' country. Many of the issues raised in these four introductory points apply also to these internal migrations; indeed, the international or "transnational" migrations discussed in this conference often develop from, and intensify the effects of, the sorts of internal migrations that have been analytically addressed under the usually misleading rubric of "semi-proletarianization." It is this intensification of effects, which often enables such effects to be seen more clearly, that suggests the fruitfulness of thinking about transnational migrations from third-world agrarian hinterlands.

1. The process of working-class transnational migration is specifically and necessarily a process of sucking value out of the migrants' home countries and transferring that value to the host country. It is appropriation *above and beyond* the surplus value appropriated directly from the workers in their work– it is appropriation from the migrants' kin-groups, communities, regions, countries.

2. This particular appropriation is often a substantial part of a set of relations between the metropolitan countries and the third world, with strong implications for the internal political, economic and cultural organization of third world countries, including: the routine organization of "debt crises" so that their processing entails very substantial income transfers from poor rural people to wealthy and powerful urban elites; the manipulations and severe restrictions in access to fundamental consumer goods (such as basic food staples) that are ordinarily associated with World Bank and International Monetary Fund economy-management policies; the expanding agribusinesses in the third world which are increasingly and massively denying access to the basic resources of production and forcing a pervasive commodification of all the factors of agrarian production: both processes which lead to widespread immiseration and a very rapid, very profound, and to a far greater extent than usually realized, historically novel destabilization of agrarian social relations.

---

[4] It is important to emphasize that transnational migrations originating in urban areas in "newly industrializing countries"–*e.g.*, Korea, Taiwan–have a different consequential, if not causal, logic. Here the focus is on transnational migration from places like the rural Caribbean, Central America, West Africa, the Andes, the rural and outer-island Philippines, *etc.*

All together these constitute a set of social forces and processes that are bleeding third world countries dry, squeezing them to the point where there is almost nothing left to squeeze out.

No matter how brutal the regime, no matter how rapacious the claims to agrarian surplus, if a basic agrarian social order is not continuing at some modest level of output then this squeeze must only further wring the source dry. Characteristically, neither brutality nor rapaciousness enhances overall productive output; their appeal rests on their (only partly illusory) efficiency in defining and accumulating "surplus" value, especially in the context of declining relative world-market prices for hinterland commodities. As productive output and values decline, people themselves become the one exportable product of significant, realizable value for communities and families of small-holders. The transition from small-scale coffee production to agribusiness-produced sugar in Haiti is but one more or less typical instance of a wide-spreading situation where increasing numbers of villages and rural towns in the hinterlands of the third world have few other locally produced world-market commodities to export but an extremely costly one to produce: their own bodies.

3. The costs of the growing fiscal crisis in the major metropolitan countries—crisis of multiple causes and effects, but significantly including an increasing inability to collect third world debt, a debt that becomes more unpayable as the countrysides of the third world are bled dry—are being manipulated in the metropolitan countries so that the "middle classes" (the formerly stable working class and the petty bourgeoisie) of the metropolitan countries are bearing a very substantial portion of these unpaid and unpayable debts. One consequence of this is that the middle classes of the metropolitan countries are disaggregating—the upper portion (say the upper third, as yet another simplifying but indicative generality) rising, the lower (two-thirds or so) falling in standards of living and real income as are also, particularly after the early mid-1970s, the native-born poor. These falling classes and class sectors in the metropolitan countries are meeting, on increasingly hostile and competitive terms, an increasing wave of new migrants driven out of the third world by the progressive social collapse of the rural areas of their countries. They are meeting and struggling, with each other and with those who seek to channel and manipulate their daily and working lives, on a metropolitan terrain increasingly emptied of industrial employment opportunities, as the migrations of capital and labor turn in precisely opposite directions, labor moving into metropolitan countries, regions and specific locales while industrial capital moves out.[5]

---

[5] An excellent discussion of the changing flows of capital and labor is found in David M. Gordon, "Capitalist development and the history of American cities," in *Marxism and the metropolis: New perspectives in urban political economy*, 2nd edit., edited by William K. Tabb and Larry Sawers. (New York: Oxford University Press, 1984), pp. 21–53.

Insofar as E.P. Thompson is fundamentally right, that class emerges historically from struggle, rather than vice versa,[6] we must pay some attention to the new and complex kinds of struggles that people are driven into in this historically emerging context and newly shaped antithetical conjunction of labor and capital flows, for these struggles are, perhaps increasingly, not simply class-focused struggles, and they do not simply address conditions where people currently live and work—by choice and by necessity. The introduction to this volume invokes several instances where national governments defer to, and seek to enlist the cooperation of, their overseas residents; to this important illustration we must also add the goon squads used to hunt, brutalize and murder Central Americans in, for example, Los Angeles; together, the two sorts of illustrations call our attention to the role that politicized class-orientations in overseas migrant communities comes to play in the maintenance of class-based oppression "at home."[7]

4. To sum up, and to go beyond these introductory observations: One of the most crucial theoretical points to be derived from this increasing phenomenon of transnational migration is that we ought not to consider class as rooted in a specific mode of production, but we must reconceptualize class as a phenomenon within historically specific social formations. A brief explanation of this jargon is in order.

Traditionally, and effectively, the left has analyzed the formation and transformation of classes and class systems as phenomena occurring within specific forms, or "modes" of production: merchant capitalism, industrial capitalism, peasant-based societies, *etc.* Althusser, in one of the few useful methodological points he made, defined a "social formation" as two or more unequally linked

---

A very fine overview of the complexities of the flows, including the point that the sorts of industries most intensely moving into the hinterlands are the most likely to hire women (and often illegal) migrants in their metropolitan operations, can be found in M. Patricia Fernandez Kelly, "International development and industrial restructuring," in *Instability and change in the world economy*, edited by Arthur MacEwan and W. Tabb. (New York: Monthly Review Press, 1989).

[6] "Eighteenth-century English society: Class struggle without class?" *Social History 3, 2,* May, 1978 pp. 133–166. ". . . class struggle is the prior, as well as the more universal, concept. To put it bluntly: classes do not exist as separate entities, look around, find an enemy class, and then start to struggle. On the contrary, people find themselves in a society structured in determined ways . . ., they experience exploitation (or the need to maintain power over those whom they exploit), they identify points of antagonistic interest, they commence to struggle around these issues and in the process of struggling they discover themselves as classes . . ." (p. 149). This perspective, emphasizing the importance of the forms of struggle in the historical emergence of class, has extraordinary and as yet unexamined implications for the current developmental processes of capitalism. I will be suggesting that the increasing prominence (if not significance) of other forms of struggle than straightforward class struggles, and the increasing multiplicity of struggles that, while ultimately class-based, often carry a very large freight of other concurrent and transformative struggles, are engendering new forms of political-economic action-bases. But this is only one of several possible, actual, and quite different outcomes.

[7] This seems to be a more recent development, adding to an older use of migrants both in and by their country of destination for essentially right-wing purposes, and the use by migrants of foreign shelters to organize revolutionary assaults upon their homelands.

modes of production: for example, the slave system of cotton production in the southern United States before the Civil War and the simultaneous, and linked, industrial factory production of textiles in England: thus the cotton gin shaped the nineteenth century industrial history of the English midlands while the increasing mechanization of spinning and weaving in England and New England shaped and focused developments in the plantation South.[8] Social formations, in this sense of the term, are not at all new; they have been a feature of the landscape since the early neolithic Mesopotamian states. What is new, and illustrated in multiple forms by the papers of this conference, is the intensity of the ties between linked and diverse–often diverging–modes of production.

In the current developmental processes of capitalism, localized, regional and national "modes of production" increasingly take their shape, their dynamic and their central contradictions from their multiple processes of articulation with geographically distant productive modes in which they are implicated precisely because of, and in ways that ordinarily elaborate, the differences between them. Thus, for example, the cities and towns of West Africa (that had developed in the context both of their own forms of hinterland integration and of a history of relatively egalitarian trade relations that reached back through late medieval Europe, expanding Islam and the Roman Empire) were far more similar in fundamental social organization to their contemporary cities and towns in western Europe in the early 1600s, at the onset of the slave trade, than they were in the late 1800s when the carnage in Africa from that form of integration into a "world economy" was largely over, and the processes of class formation that it substantially subsidized in Europe were well rooted. Therefore our concepts of class and our strategies for class struggle must be rethought, resituated in a dynamic of multiple modes of production.

On this basis of such linkages between diverse and diverging (*not* integrating or homogenizing) modes of production and from the perspective of "class" as a process embedded in social formations, we can begin to see different kinds of processes of class formation and transformation, and we can do so because in this broader social context it is easier to get a handle on new kinds of class, and more than class, consciousness, and new kinds of class, and more than class, struggle. In the broadest perspective, perhaps we can also see new kinds of roles that localized cultures play as the arena both of changing forms of appropriation and of changing kinds of struggle.

---

[8] The dominance of England (or more generally, of the industrial-capitalist mode) in this social formation is not easy to see until the blockade of southern U.S. cotton shipments during the Civil War set in motion a chain of events that devastated wide areas of rural Egypt and India, which were made to function as replacement sources. "Dominance" in a social formation turns out to be expressed in, and defined by, ability to maintain essential processes of multi-modal social reproduction and to export the bulk of the costs for so doing.

~ II ~

The organizers of this conference, and the papers, repeatedly call our attention to the *cultural* consequences of transnational migrations of different classes, and it is precisely these cultural aspects and consequences that I would now like to briefly examine.

I will start with two specific points, each about what transnational migration *conceals*, and subsequently add a few more general observations and suggestions about what such migrations reveal.

1. I was struck, in the cases presented to us of the transnational migration of the bourgeoisie–the overseas wealthy Chinese and the non-resident Indians–by their ability to partially both conceal, and also to shelter themselves from, the havoc and devastation they create. They emerge in contemporary capitalism as the human version of an automobile that in the United States is called the Ford Escort.

To explain: the Ford Escort is the first real "world car"–it is so not simply because the same car, with minor trim and detail modifications, is marketed throughout the world, but more importantly because every single component for this car is manufactured in at least two different countries in the world, and in factories in which production schedules are designed to be substantially below capacity, so that they can be quickly expanded. This makes it close to impossible, or at least very much more difficult, for either the workers in the plants or even the nationals in the countries in which the plant is located, to successfully struggle against those who dominate production.

Similarly, this transnational bourgeoisie has insulated itself and a substantial part of its wealth from the suffering its wealth-creation has caused, and it has done so in ways that also help conceal the brutality of wealth-formation– *e.g.*, the overseas Asian cultural patrons in California, the non-resident Indian builders of medical centers in India. Elites almost always seek to conceal the gore on their hands; what *may* be new here are the possibilities for more effective concealment in a multi- or transnational context, and more particularly the increasing difficulty that workers will necessarily have in using the state for even partial, minuscule redress against elite depredations–minuscule forms of redress that states often provided in the context not of concern for workers but for reproducing the preconditions for social production. The worsening position of workers, suggested here, is thus to be understood as part of larger crises in the reproduction of third world relations of production; part of the same processes that fuel the so-called "debt-crisis" and the manipulations of the World Bank and International Monetary Fund and, indeed, the expansion of capitalist-organized agribusinesses. The potential for more international investments by third world bourgeoisie (the material basis for their migrations) may be one of the causal forces shifting localized class struggles into more "cultural" domains—for example, ethnic, religious-fundamentalist, even "liberation theology"—as those who exploit and dominate become less directly assailable and their depredations less containable.

2. I want to emphasize, for the second point about concealment, the very substantial difficulty people have, within the outmigrating communities of the third world, in seeing and assessing the costs of shipping emigrants out of their communities. The personal, emotional costs are obvious: absent kin, strained relations, the increased hardship and work of those left behind, but the financial costs are much more concealed—concealed by the desperation for remittances; concealed by the fact that remittances come in episodes and costs are spread over years. One major effect of these hidden and very substantial financial costs is that the material basis for local cultural protests is increasingly undermined—by the same processes that shift the center of resistance into the cultural domain—intensifying the violence of such culturally rooted movements without enhancing their effectiveness either in confronting domination or in taking care of their own. The concluding two sections of this discussion very briefly amplify and explain the causes and consequences of this process.

∼ III ∼

From and beyond these specific points, some general observations and suggestions can be provisionally formulated:

Transnational migration must generate, or markedly exacerbate, a profound contradiction within the rural communities that send out such migrants: On the one hand, migration intensifies the need for villagers to connect themselves to one another, particularly along lines of kin and neighborhood. They must do this to deal with the organization of migration (helping the people get where they are going) and to deal with the consequences of migration: the children and spouses and parents left behind, *etc*. In sum and in brief, migration generally intensifies and elaborates villagers' material and cultural connections to one another.

Simultaneously, however, migration also substantially contributes to further undermining the political-economic bases for these connections—the necessary material and social means for ordinary rural people (including those termed "peasants") providing for one-another. This political and economic basis has been, for a long time and for multiple reasons, increasingly eroded at the local level by the spread of state control and the penetration of capital, dramatically intensifying with the increasing spread of agribusiness in the third world. These processes of expanding and consolidating state control and commodified productive relations ordinarily increase and solidify substantial social and economic differentiation in hinterland communities and undermine local forms of subsistence and small-scale commodity production. Further, both the costs and the returns involved in shipping migrants out increase inequalities that are emerging among the working classes of the rural third world, most specifically between the families of those who migrate successfully on the one hand and the families of those who have failed migrations and the families who have no one who can go on the other. This is exacerbated by returning successful migrants, or the remittances from them, being used to buy land or to organize the extraction of surplus value from their less successful co-villagers (as Eugenia Georges showed). All of this is only partly offset by the sharing and spread of remittances around the village, and the social/cultural ties made or reinforced on this new material basis.

We must thus pay very close attention not just to the desperation for remittances in the hinterlands and to their centrality in maintaining ordinary social life, but also to the havoc and devastation these remittances can cause, most of all in the increasing commodification of the means of production.

~ IV ~

In sum: the most profound mistake we can make in our analysis of transnational migration is the idea that it alleviates the contradictions of capital accumulation in and from the hinterlands. It alleviates some, transforms some, deepens some, and introduces new ones. Understanding transnational migration *must* be situated within an analysis of these changing contradictions in order to understand the historical forces shaping the whole process. By way of conclusion, I would like to briefly discuss the implications of the contradiction just delineated (although it is but one of many equally important emergent contradictions of transnational migration): the contradiction between the intensifications of culturally based connections to one another in the migrants' home communities and the increasing undermining of the material and social bases of these connections, including the social disruptions intensified by the "investment" of remittances within hinterland villages.

This is, I think, an explosive situation—one whose roots and causes are far wider than transnational migration, but a situation that such migration significantly exacerbates. The current world-wide emergence and development of culturally focused revolutionary movements—not the familiar revolutions of the early- and mid-20th century, which were about land, returns to labor and justice—but the cultural intensities of, for example, Islamic fundamentalism in Iran, Egypt, Nigeria, the complex merger of culture and political economy in the Peruvian *Sendero Luminoso* movement (the leaders of which recently claimed that Garcia Marquez' novel, *One Hundred Years of Solitude*, rather than Lenin, was their manual for revolution) and also the Tupac Aymara struggles in the Andes—such movements suggest, but only suggest, and only partially, the power of the cultural contradictions set in motion by emergent forms of value extraction from the villages and hinterland regions of the third world, contradictions epitomized by but not restricted to, the extraction of surplus in the form of great multitudes of very specific individual people—fathers and mothers and husbands and wives and aunts and uncles and children and cousins and neighbors and co-workers and people who farmed the land bounding yours and in whose stubble you grazed your sheep and with whose children yours might have created theirs—people who now in their multitudes and in their individuality must ship themselves back and forth between here and there, carrying suitcases full of historically usual forms of hope and profoundly new forms of havoc.

ACKNOWLEDGMENTS

This paper took its first shape as a discussion of issues raised at the conference itself. I would like to thank, in particular, Antonio Lauria-Perricelli, Johanna Lessinger, and Philip Smukler for their insights and suggestions.

REFERENCES CITED

Berger, John and Jean Mohr
    1975   *A seventh man.* London: Penguin.
Castles, Stephen and Godula Kosack
    1974   *Immigrant workers and class structure in Western Europe.* London: Oxford University Press.
Fernandez-Kelly, M. Patricia
    1989   International development and industrial restructuring. In *Instability and change in the world economy,* edited by Arthur MacEwan and W. Tabb. New York: Monthly Review Press.
Gordon, David M.
    1984   Capitalist development and the history of American cities. In *Marxism and the metropolis: New perspectives in urban political economy,* 2nd edit., edited by William K. Tabb and Larry Sawers. New York: Oxford University Press. Pp. 21–53.
Kindleberger, Charles P.
    1967   *Europe's postwar growth: The role of labor supply.* Cambridge, MA: Harvard University Press.
Thompson, Edward P.
    1978   Eighteenth-century English society: Class struggle without class? *Social History 3(2):* 133–166.

Some Thoughts on Gendering and Internationalizing Our Thinking about Transnational Migrations

CONSTANCE R. SUTTON

Department of Anthropology
New York University
100 Rufus D. Smith Hall
25 Waverly Place
New York, New York 10003

As someone who began writing about Afro-Caribbean transnational migrations in the early 1970s, I regard the concept and conference papers, along with the two days of lively discussion they provoked, as marking a significant development in the theorizing we have deployed in the study of post-World War II cross-national migrations. I will briefly highlight what is new about the transnational perspective proposed, concretize and historicize my own experiences as an anthropologist enmeshed in Caribbean transnational circuits of migration, and then note further dimensions of transnational migrations not as yet adequately theorized: namely, the gender component of transnational migrations, its effect on the transnationalizing and reconfiguring of dual-place identities, and how this process intersects with the internationalizing of gender issues, another significant boundary-crossing phenomenon of the past twenty-five years.

The transnational perspective discussed in the concept paper (Glick Schiller, Basch, Blanc-Szanton 1992) builds on differing strands of past theory-building and extends our thinking in important directions. First, by explicitly linking current transnational migrations to the post-World War II processes of the globalization of capitalism, it provides a historical context for our present period of massive movements of people and compels us to consider the specific ways these two interconnected processes are operating at the particular localized but interconnected sites of emigration and immigration we study. As evidenced in the case studies and discussions of the conference, as well as studies which I and others have done (see Sutton and Chaney 1987), the transnational perspective situates the populations we study (both at home and abroad) in ways that permit a more finely tuned comparative analysis of the different forms and effects of transnational migration. This in turn promotes a more diverse and differentiated line of thinking about transnational migrants and the transnationalized fields of social action they construct.

Linking transnationalized fields of socio-cultural action to transnational-ized economies also highlights a new dynamic, one that juxtaposes a "foot-loose and country-free internationalization of capital" to the personal sets of localized though transnationalized social commitments and cultural practices today's migrations have generated. This in turn flags a second direction that theorizing from a transnational perspective has taken, namely, a concern with the ways in which "place" is related to meaningful "social spaces." As the lived experiences and identities of more and more people span two or more nations and boundaries between nation-states become blurred, what constitutes a meaningful social community has become respatialized across national bound-aries. Questions about the symbolic power of concepts such as "homeland" and a concern with peoples' perceptions of "other places" have become issues to be researched.

Concept paper and conference discussions all note the challenges that transnational migrations pose, both present and potential, to the political and cultural sovereignty western nation-states have exercised. Phrases such as "the empire strikes/writes back" current in discourses of subaltern cultural studies, capture the conflict expressed in a politics of cultural struggle over issues such as bilingualism and multiculturalism, to cite just two examples. Tensions be-tween nationally defined vs. transnationally assumed identities have taken the form of struggles over what constitutes "cultural citizenship" (IUP 1991). Tolo-lyan warns against a premature obituary of the nation-state as the privileged form of polity, but goes on to write of many nation-states having "to confront the extent to which their boundaries are porous and their ostensible homo-geneity a multicultural heterogeneity" (1991:5). Appadurai inflates the con-flict, stating that today "state and nation are at each other's throats, and the hyphen that links them is now less an icon of conjuncture than an index of disjuncture (1990:14)."

Finally, as emphasized in the concept paper, transnationalism, and the dis-junctures it produces in the ways place, people, and culturally distinctive tra-ditions are related, has necessitated a rethinking of the implicitly nation-bound concepts of race, class, ethnicity, as well of the territorially anchored notion of socio-cultural totalities (see Appadurai 1990; Gupta and Ferguson 1992; and Lauria-Perricelli 1989:244–272, 175–200, 359–361). Happily this work is being informed by new and exciting scholarship that is making histori-cally explicit the conditions that have produced these categories, recognizing how they intersect—including how they intersect as gendered concepts shaped by and shaping sex and gender relations (Enloe 1990; Parker *et al.* 1992; Yuval-Davis and Anthias 1989)—and examining the ways in which they are being both reproduced and contested within today's globalized hierarchies of power.

Let me turn now to showing concretely how these transnational develop-ments relate to my own experiences with the changing nature and cartography of the "social fields" in which my anthropological practice has been located over the past 35 years. The two populations among whom I have carried out extensive field work are Barbadians and the Yoruba of Nigeria. To quickly relate a history of their changing locations inscribed in my personal experiences, I have to roll back the clock to 1956 when I was sent to Barbados, along with Lambros Comitas and Sid Greenfield, on a project to train graduate students. It then took 13 hours to get there, few people I knew seemed to know where Barbados was geographically located or whether it even existed,[1] and it was only by accident that shortly before leaving I discovered the superintendent of the building in which I lived had emigrated from Barbados. "Discovered," because West Indians at that time, though possessing different accents and speech patterns, had not yet because of their "blackness" become visible as ethnic immigrants, at least to most of white America. And as I also discovered after a short time in Barbados, people in colonized regions knew a great deal more about the locales, histories, and characteristics of Euro-American populations than these populations knew about them, a knowledge asymmetry that international travel, tourism, and the media revolution has reduced but not eradicated.

We three had the distinction of being the first anthropologists to carry out field work in Barbados which has since hosted many anthropologists. During the 15-month period in which I lived in a sugar plantation studying the impact of the recent introduction of trade unionism and mass politics on the island, I also learned that most villagers received remittances from kin living in England and/or the United States; that many had themselves lived and worked abroad and others desired and expected to; and that those who lived abroad continued to be involved in village happenings, influencing both its activities and the lives of their relatives and friends. I also became aware through meeting Paule Marshall, who was then on the island writing her first novel *Brown Girl, Brownstones* (1959), that a sizable Barbadian community had existed in Brooklyn for some time. Nonetheless, I then viewed migration only as an external factor affecting the local community I studied. And I continued to retain an image of "the field" as located "over there" in the Caribbean, separated from my life in New York City, even though I visited the Brooklyn Barbadian community when I returned to New York.

However, this spatial separation and conceptual enclosing of "the field" all changed rather dramatically some five years after my return when my New York apartment became a major reception center for the villagers themselves, who, with the 1965 change in U.S. immigration laws, began to emigrate to the city in large numbers. At this point my late husband, a bit stunned by the way our private life in New York had become enveloped by Barbadians and other West Indians, dropped his famous comment about his not counting

---

[1] One friend vaguely recalled that the term "to be barbadosed" appeared in a Shakespeare play where it referred to being captured off a ship and brought to Barbados to be sold as a slave.

on my bringing the field back with me when I had gone off to do fieldwork. The comment signaled the beginning of my own recognition that "the field" was no longer "over there" but had become respatialized as "everywhere." And with this collapse of the geo-political and social distancing that field work had implied, Barbadians lost the distinction of being that alleged "exotic other." They increasingly became part of the student body who, along with other students of Caribbean origins, were taking my courses at New York University. And they were now part of the circle of friends with whom I shared my daily life.

Because I witnessed directly the impact the Black Power movement of the 1960s had on my West Indian friends who were busily repatriating its ideology, along with remittances, to the islands, I went back to my field site in Barbados in 1969 with the intent of studying how and who this movement was moving. I was accompanied by Susan Makiesky, a graduate student who remained for two years to chart the changes in village life for her doctoral thesis, and who returned with a young man from the village whom she subsequently married.

In the early 1970s, Sue and I drew on our joint experiences in an article we wrote on how migration was affecting changes in the racial identities and political consciousness of both the migrants and those who remained behind (Sutton and Makiesky-Barrow 1975). We expanded on the statement made by a character in G. Lamming's novel *In the Castle of My Skin* who upon returning to Barbados from the United States tells his friend "If there be one thing I thank America for, she teach me who my race wus. Now I'm never goin' to lose it. Never, Never" (1953:296). And it was at that time that I first formulated the notion of Caribbean migrations differing from earlier European migrations to the United States in that they created a "bidirectional" rather than unidirectional flow of goods, people, political ideologies, money, and cultural practices. We also underscored the fact that black migrants were being incorporated into a racialized not homogeneous "melting pot." It was also around this period that I began to refer to New York as a Caribbean outpost.

Some 10 years later, New York City was no longer an outpost. It had become a thoroughly Caribbeanized city in ways detailed in the articles published in *Caribbean Life in NYC* (Sutton and Chaney 1987). Peoples of Caribbean origin, including here Latinos from the Hispanic Caribbean, were no longer secluded in their ethnic neighborhoods in Brooklyn or Queens or East Harlem. They had become publicly present throughout the entire city (see Sutton 1987).

Today, the neighborhood in which I have continued to live is Caribbean, my apartment building is staffed by people from the Caribbean, and a sizable number of its residents, which include Sue Makiesky-Barrow and her family, are of Caribbean origin. Earlier, a Dominican and then a Haitian woman helped "look after" my son when he was young; a Jamaican woman helped

"care for" my parents during the last two years of their lives; and two days ago
the man rewiring my apartment was Barbadian and his plasterer partner was
a Trinidadian. More important, over the past 30 years my circle of personal
and professional friends have been largely from the islands. Nor is my experience as a Caribbean anthropologist who lives in New York unique.

If the post-modern experience means juxtaposing fragments that originated elsewhere – of living with "mixed up" vs. separated differences – then my
brief recounting of changes over a 35-year period encapsulates my own take
on the cross-over into a post-modern, post-colonial world. It has influenced
my latest remapping of where the Caribbean is located and what constitutes
a meaningful definition of a Caribbean community. With people having become the major export of the region, and Caribbeans who live outside the
region continuing to remain vitally connected to their home societies, thereby
generating what I have called a "transnational socio-cultural system" (see
Sutton 1987), it is no longer appropriate to think of the Caribbean in strictly
geopolitical terms.

In a different way, and on a smaller scale, something similar has happened
in relation to my field research with the Yoruba of Nigeria, undertaken in the
late 1970s. In this case, it was with a people who, outside of anthropology,
were viewed as even more distant in time and thought than were the Barbadians in the late 1950s. But while the Yoruba may still be thought of as an
"exotic other" living far away in Africa, I found when I returned to teaching
at New York University that an increasing number of students from the Caribbean, attracted to the Yoruba-based Afro-Caribbean religion of *Santeria*
which Cuban migrants brought with them to the city, enrolled in my courses
because they wanted to hear about the Yoruba. Then a few years ago when
the adopted Yoruba son I acquired came to live with me, I discovered the existence of a Yoruba community in Brooklyn and even began to encounter an
occasional Yoruba student in my classes at NYU. However, I admit to being
startled when the man riding next to me on the subway tapped me on the
shoulder as I was grading papers for my course on family and kinship to point
out that what the student wrote about Yoruba kinship was true here but
wrong there. Just by way of noting that this transnational phenomenon is not
confined solely to the east and west coasts of this country, the last two times
I arrived at O'Hare airport in Chicago, it just so happened I was picked up
by taxi drivers who were Yoruba, one of whom, a woman, drove me to see
a play by the much celebrated Yoruba writer Wole Soyinka. You may think
this was an accident, but my Yoruba friends and I know it was all arranged
by the ancestors.

This then is my personal testimony of how transnational migrations have
changed my relation to "the field" and changed my anthropological practice.
But what is missing from this account are my concomitant experiences and
research on West Indian and West African gender relations and on a politics

of gender produced by the international women's movement. The internationalizing of gender issues that has taken place during the same period in which
the new transnational migrations have occurred point to the need to add a
gender dimension to our transnational perspective and to our analysis of the
reconfigurations in racial, ethnic, and national identities that are occurring.
For women have not been passive ciphers in this process.

The literature on Caribbean migrations has emphasized the active participation of migrant women in the labor force and recorded the fact that not
only have female migrants outnumbered males, but that a large percentage of
the recent Caribbean migration—unlike the past migrations of Europeans and
the present migrations of Asians—has been female-initiated; that is, women
have established the first links in the chain of migration. The presence of Caribbean women in the work force as garment workers, nurses, domestics,
office clerks, small-scale entrepreneurs, as well as professionals in a number of
public institutions such as CUNY and the UN has also been well noted. And
more recently, studies have begun to document their active role in union and
community-based organizations, on school boards and in Caribbean ethnic
organizations. However, exploring and theorizing what this implies in terms
of culture transmitting and transforming processes and how this relates to identity constructions has not as yet occurred.

Recent reviews of the literature on transnational migrations note the absence of an explicit gender dimension in the theoretical models that have been
constructed. Little has been done by way of comparing how the social networks of immigrant women differ from those of men, or to "exposing"
women's work in the sphere of socio-cultural reproduction. This work has no
doubt expanded from that done by women in earlier migrations because of
the independent role women play in today's migrations, their more active involvement in the labor market, and the transnational socio-cultural fields in
which they operate. It is particularly at this nexus of transnationalized social
networks that Caribbean women bring their own distinctive stamp to the process of creating and maintaining the circuits of exchange in goods, people, and
cultural meanings, as Wiltshire underscores (1992). By adopting a more gendered view of the identities transnational migrations produce, and migrants
construct, we will all become more conscious of just how gendered a process
transnationalism is, as Lauria-Perricelli suggests (1992) in his comments on
the papers by Georges, Ong, Rouse, and Wiltshire (all 1992, this volume).
And here we need to ask more directly how, along with women elsewhere,
Caribbean women are reconfiguring their own identities. How is this in turn
affecting the multilayered meanings associated with the transnationalized concepts of nationhood or ethnicity being produced by today's migrations?

To do this adequately, we also have to assess the impact of women's grass-
roots activism which, since the mid-1970s, has produced a considerable amount
of female-centered collective activity, in the Caribbean, the United States, and

elsewhere. Fostered by the growing strength of an international women's movement, women have become increasingly engaged in collective efforts to empower themselves and their communities. In their efforts to dismantle hierarchies of power and control, they have also become involved in revamping and rewriting those "imaged/invented" traditions and histories being used to support the many actual and symbolic forms of male domination that continue to be embedded in many of today's religious, national, and ethnic projects.

It is worth noting that Caribbean women have played leading roles in both the international women's movement and at the United Nations, where they have served as representatives of their governments and on international commissions in support of women's interests. And as the recent writings by Caribbean women acknowledge, both the international women's movement and transnational migrations have together played an important role in inspiring their activity, analyses, and the visions they project.

Thus in rethinking transnational migrations from a gendered perspective, we need to raise a number of questions that go beyond considering how the experiences of transnational migrants differ for women and men. We need to ask also how women's and men's roles in the global economy differ in both the countries from which they come and to which they go, what their gender-specific roles are in sustaining and transmitting transnationalized social commitments and cultural traditions, and how as paid nurses and caretakers of others, Caribbean women nurture not only the people who hire them (Colen 1990), but also their own Caribbean traditions.

This brings us back to the ways women today are actively engaged in contesting the roles assigned them in their ethnic/national traditions, thus lending an important gendered contestatory dimension to all current identity negotiations and representations. Here it is important to consider the impact of the international women's movement in globalizing women's political consciousness and encouraging them to become the protagonists of their own racial/ethnic/national identities, identities which often challenge yesteryears' "traditions"–lived or invented. Once again we find Caribbean women, in the multi-national sites in which they are now located, are often key agents in internationalizing the meanings associated with gender, in part because of the leading roles they play as "women of color" in the international women's movement, in part because of their past and present-day relationship to Euro-American white women, but also because they draw on Afro-Caribbean traditions of female solidarity. Thus if we consider how the role of women in Caribbean transnational migrations intersects with the internationalized gender consciousness Caribbean women have acquired through their involvement with the international women's movement, we can begin to better appreciate the full weight of Caribbean women in current social movements directed at dismantling established hierarchies of power–both within and across nation-states.

I conclude, then, by urging that our next step be one that brings together two separate but related analyses and discourses: the one dealing with transnational migrations, the other with internationalized gender issues. It is time that we address the question of how these two important global movements intersect and affect each other. And we might also ask how they differ in the processes by which they sustain/create social connections and negotiate constructions of their collective identities.

REFERENCES CITED

Appadurai, Arjun
  1990   Disjuncture and difference in the global cultural economy. *Public Culture (2)2*:1–24.
Colen, Shellee
  1990   'Housekeeping' for the green card: West Indian household workers, the state, and stratified reproduction in New York. In *At work in homes: Household workers in world perspective*, edited by Roger Sanjek and Shellee Colen, pp. 89–118. American Ethnological Society Monograph Series #3.
Enloe, Cynthia
  1990   *Bananas, beaches and bases: Making feminist sense of international politics.* Berkeley: University of California Press.
Georges, Eugenia
  1992   Gender, class and migration in the Dominican Republic: Women's experiences in a transnational community. In *Towards a transnational perspective on migration*, edited by Nina Glick Schiller, Linda Basch and Cristina Blanc-Szanton. *Annals of The New York Academy of Sciences 654*:81–99. This volume.
Glick Schiller, Nina, Linda Basch and Cristina Blanc-Szanton
  1992   Transnationalism: A new analytic framework for understanding migration. In *Towards a transnational perspective on migration*, edited by Nina Glick Schiller, Linda Basch and Cristina Blanc-Szanton. *Annals of The New York Academy of Sciences 654*:1–24. This volume.
Gupta, Akhil and James Ferguson
  1992   Beyond 'culture': Space, identity, and the politics of difference, *Cultural Anthropology 7(1)*:6–23.
IUP
  1991   Inter-University Program for Latino Research Cultural Studies Working Group, Concept Paper #4. Ms.
Lamming, George
  1953   *In the castle of my skin.* London: Michael Joseph, Ltd. (Reprinted in 1970 and 1983 by Schocken Books, New York.)
Lauria-Perricelli, Antonio
  1989   *A study in historical and critical anthropology: The making of the people of Puerto Rico.* Ann Arbor: University Microfilms.
  1992   Towards a transnational perspective on migration: Closing remarks. In *Towards a transnational perspective on migration*, edited by Nina Glick Schiller, Linda Basch and Cristina Blanc-Szanton. *Annals of the New York Academy of Sciences 654*:251–258. This volume.
Marshall, Paule
  1959   *Brown girl, brownstones.* New York: Random House.

Ong, Aiwha
1992   Limits to cultural accumulation: Chinese capitalists on the American Pacific Rim. In *Towards a transnational perspective on migration*, edited by Nina Glick Schiller, Linda Basch and Cristina Blanc-Szanton. *Annals of the New York Academy of Sciences 654*:125–143.
Parker, Andrew, Mary Russo, Doris Sommer, and Patricia Yaeger (eds).
1992   *Nationalisms and sexualities*. New York: Routledge.
Rouse, Roger
1992   Making sense of settlement: Class transformation, cultural struggle, and transnationalism among Mexican migrants in the United States. In *Towards a transnational perspective of migration*, edited by Nina Glick Schiller, Linda Basch, and Cristina Blanc-Szanton. *Annals of the New York Academy of Sciences 654*:25–52. This volume.
Sutton, Constance R.
1987   The Caribbeanization of New York City and the emergence of a transnational sociocultural system. In *Caribbean life in New York City: Sociocultural dimensions*, edited by C. R. Sutton and E. M. Chaney, pp. 15–29. Staten Island, NY: Center for Migration Studies.
Sutton, Constance R. and Susan R. Makiesky-Barrow.
1975   Migration and West Indian racial and ethnic consciousness. In *Migration and development: Implications for ethnic identity and political conflict*, edited by H. I. Safa and B. M. DuToit, pp. 175–185. The Hague: Mouton Publishers. Reprinted in *Caribbean life in New York City: Sociocultural dimensions (op. cit.)* pp. 92–116.
Sutton, Constance R. and Elsa M. Chaney, eds.
1987   *Caribbean life in New York City: Sociocultural dimensions*. Staten Island, NY: Center for Migration Studies.
Tololyan, Khachig
1991   The nation-state and its others: In lieu of a preface. *Diaspora 1(1)*:3–7.
Wiltshire, Rosina
1992   Implications of transnational migration for nationalism: The Caribbean example. In *Towards a transnational perspective of migration*, edited by Nina Glick Schiller, Linda Basch, and Cristina Blanc-Szanton. *Annals of the New York Academy of Sciences 654*:175–187. This volume.
Yuval-Davis, Nira and Floya Anthias
1989   *Woman-nation-state*. London: Macmillan.

Towards a Transnational Perspective on Migration: Closing Remarks

ANTONIO LAURIA-PERRICELLI

Centro de Estudios Puertorriqueños
Hunter College, City University of New York
695 Park Avenue
New York, New York 10021

As genuinely exciting intellectual developments, the concept paper by Glick Schiller, Basch, and Blanc-Szanton, the case studies, and these discussions open up as many questions as they answer. I hope to focus on some of those questions, beginning with some general remarks on the very interesting concept paper, and then commenting on our discussions.

It would be helpful if the analysis presented in the concept paper were further contextualized. The paper itself treats of an international system which was created under U.S. domination after World War II. Many of the trends identified as "global capitalist" are in fact specific to the trajectory of U.S. capital pools, United States–based transnational corporations, and their effects on the "sending" countries in the circuit of labor power. In great measure, the international or "global" system posited in the paper is really the zone of U.S. imperial control, and should be identified as such.

The paper itself is strongly marked by the experience of the three authors with three instances of U.S. neocolonialism.[a] Indeed, all the case studies selected for discussion at this conference fall within the same orbit, where the United States is the host pole of the transnational migrant field. Furthermore the vision of that pole is very much focused on, and conditioned by, the reality of New York City. So the object we have been discussing is one piece of a global capitalist system, not the whole thing.

The concept paper seems to assume that national boundaries within the international system are stable. Decolonization apart, this is only relatively true for the period in question, and even in that period boundaries have changed, sometimes violently. In fact the violence and warfare which have also characterized that period, and have been an important part of the dynamic of migration and transnational experience, are underplayed.

The concept paper also raises the issue of how "new" the kind of cultural phenomena associated with the transnational experience may actually be. While we have to work together to grasp the qualitative specificity of the

---

[a] This is not to deny the possible pertinence to other neocolonial systems.

present moment, the concept paper in its present form may overstate that nov-
elty, glossing over the historical similarities which appear in European and
Euroamerican history and elsewhere between 1800, let's say, and 1950. Many
of the processes, attendant upon back-and-forth movement, or upon the
close "transnational" linkages between different migrating/exiled contingents
of the same people, are not novel, not exclusive to the present moment, but
can be found, for example, in the earlier moment of preponderantly European
migration to the United States.

The notion of transnationalism, and "the transnational" as laid out in the
concept paper makes it look like an evolutionary emergence, a new level or
stage recently tacked on top of older "national" ones. I do not think that this
was the authors' intention. It might help to visualize two processes, of "nationalization" and "transnationalization," which are dialectically related; to
conceive transnationalization and nationalization as aspects of a single dialectical process. This dialectic begins much earlier in the history of world capitalism, perhaps at the moment when national states are created not on pre-
capitalist but on capitalist bases, well back into the 19th century. This would
also allow us to fit the cultural processes attendant upon "internal migration"
into the schema, and understand how contingents of the same populations
can be subjected to nationalizing and transnationalizing trends simultaneously. It might also help to understand how nationalities can be created even
where there is no effective national state—which was one of the results of the
Haitian Revolution.

In our papers and our discussions, we have been dealing with hyphenated
cultural, social, ethnic categories, and with circuits of meaning; and that
"meaning" should be read as including value, value in the sense of that which
is produced and turned into capital. We have, in a sense, been examining U.S.
cultural history writ large. The starting point for such an analysis is actually
diversity itself, cultural multiplicity as *the* fact that has characterized the
national/transnational dynamic of the United States for well over a century.
We have been addressing a sample of that dynamic, comprising an enormously
complicated and particularistic set of situations in which projects of hegemony, dominance—or at the least, self-reproduction—are constructed through
the process of either appropriating or manipulating or using or repressing or
even attempting to eradicate this kind of diversity. This social dynamism takes
diversity itself as its point of departure, and is characterized by the continual
generation of diversity. This is nothing new, and I attempted to invoke it
earlier in mentioning a kind of dialectic between global world-shattering
world-transforming processes of nationalization and transnationalization that
occur together in some kind of very intricate relationship over the past 200
years. And this movement is tied to the fortunes and the development and
the transformation of capitalism as such.

Furthermore, these papers indicate that in order to grasp and analyze these processes, what we must keep in mind is not "Capitalism," not "Capital," but *capitals* and the various strategies which are employed to assure the expanded reproduction and the accumulation and survival of those capitals, just as we have to keep in mind the many strategies which are involved in the self-reproduction of those who work and labor for these capitals. Many of the papers also address the culturally fascinating history of the class-projects embedded in the efforts of families or kin groups to reproduce themselves. We have examined a range of such projects which are sometimes proletarian, sometimes peasant, sometimes petit-bourgeois, sometimes grand-bourgeois, and in some cases a very bizarre and interesting amalgam of several at once.

This is also an intensely and fundamentally gendered process; Eugenia George's and Rosina Wiltshire's papers very meticulously demonstrate just how gendered these processes are among people who are—in the U.S. context—mostly salaried workers and proletarians. We also see how the patriarchal definition of masculinity gives capital its particular aura, which is a real hyper-macho aura. It is interesting to see, as Ong shows, how the image of the Chinese in San Francisco is feminized. We see that this transformation of capital-bearing Chinese becomes a threat to a white society which despises Chinese for being passive—the same white society that socially and politically relegated the forebearers of this national category to their passivity. In the working class, Rouse's Aguililleños in Silicon Valley see themselves as feminized because *la Migra* dominates their life. They go back and forth between *la casa y el trabajo* ("the home and the workplace"). They never go into the bars, and they see this as a reflection on their masculinity—which is a very patriarchal definition of masculinity.

Aiwha Ong's paper also affords an interesting example of the *use* of cultural diversity which both classical assimilation/acculturation and utilitarian theory would misinterpret. Ong uses the term "cultural citizenship" to denote the process by which these overseas Chinese entrepreneurs are acquiring not only cultural capital of a new kind, but asserting a kind of cultural entering into certain elite social circles and terrain. This assertion of a kind of cultural citizenship is based on appropriating the patronization of certain kinds of use-values, in this case art museums and ballet companies and so on. But it does not make these entrepreneurs any less Chinese, either in their own concept, or that of the various white sectors they confront.

There is another use of the term "cultural citizenship" which is being employed by the Cultural Analysis Group of the Inter-University Project for Latino Research. This sees "cultural citizenship" as one means of the creative utilization of a cultural heritage, or of culture as having been imbedded in some kind of prior received condition, by people in forms of everyday struggle to address and otherwise redress their particular conditions of exploitation, spoilation, or illegitimation. It is a concept that is being utilized in a group of interlinked projects which include an adult literacy and oral history program in the Barrio here in New York City and a series of studies on identity-formation, consciousness, mobilization or empowerment in Chicano and pan-Latino communities in California and Texas. This underscores two things. We have different and genealogically unrelated uses of the term "cultural citizenship" to point to very different uses of cultural resources on both sides of the class divide that runs through the papers. It also exemplifies the volatility of concepts themselves—such as "transnationalism."

On another tack: struggles on transnational terrain among different class or national projects have been going on for a long time. Bela Feldman-Bianco's paper on the Portuguese points this up very neatly, as does Barry Goldberg's comment. I believe we have to consider this very carefully, because a major trend in the history of U.S. society has always been towards greater diversity. There never has been a uniform model of anything. Nobody has ever had it. Yet we certainly have a history of appropriative or repressive *projects*. And that history of appropriative or repressive projects is not a history of the American elites alone, but a history of the interrelations between their homogenizing or at least hegemonic projects, and the homogenizing or hegemonic projects in other nation-states or other political jurisdictions that are caught up in the same web of the movement of peoples. And this goes back a long time. For example, it involves the relations of conspiratorial groups in the United States trying to set up national liberation projects in their homeland, which is the point of departure for the Puerto Rican colony in New York City, in the 1850s if not earlier. It also involves such considerations as the relations obtaining among sectors of the American bourgeoisie, the U.S. state, the dominant coalition of classes in Italy, and the Fascist state during the 1920s. These groups evolved policy with respect to those who had migrated or those who were migrating or those who were no longer being allowed to migrate, and that involves people residing in Italy and people residing in the United States. Something similar was shown in Feldman-Bianco's paper about the Portuguese, in this case the relationship between the state in the United States, the migrants, and the fascist Portuguese corporate state in the 1920s and 1930s.

To further explore the transnational/migration relation, we will have to confront certain challenges in grasping the totality. The concept paper and the case studies focus almost exclusively on the two poles of the migration circuit: a locus in the United States, New York City, for example, and a locus elsewhere, in Mexico or Santo Domingo, and the cultural relations obtaining between them. This is perhaps an artifact of the conference theme and the methods employed. In doing so, we unintentionally reproduce a model of unilinear bi-polar relationships very similar to the unilinear gradients of the Chicago School's—or the modernization theorist's—geospatial images of social transformation.

Similarly, at some point, we must situate the migration-centered processes we address in the context of the other things that are going down in the communities described in some of our case-studies. It is necessary to fully analyze the "national" class relations in which the "sending" bases or the extra-United States poles of the transnational fields are embedded. For example, we have to understand what else is happening to the Dominican proletariat in the Dominican Republic in order to fully understand what Eugenia Georges's paper means.

There is another point, on which Del Jones and I were commenting privately during one of the breaks. In the 1920s the project of repressing diversity in the United States reached an apogee through the final capping of immigration from outside the hemisphere, which was the final stage of a process that began earlier with the Exclusion acts aimed at the Chinese and Japanese. This coincided with a wave of "Americanism," nativism, racist intolerance, and persecution. It also coincided with the maturation of Fordism as a form of accumulation, to which Rouse referred this morning as the development of "consumerism" in the 1920s. I think that the relationship between these things was more than accidental. The history of the 1920s shows the development of a project of accumulation in the United States which was strongly centered on the domestic economy. This is not to deny the burgeoning links of American capital to international finance, extradomestic direct investment, and export trade which, at that time, were not as important as they would later become. This strategy was centered on the expansion of the domestic market through a certain way of selling products to the labor force which we now know as consumerism. Fresh contingents of labor-power were incorporated from within the same domestic sphere (a sphere which, given the specific forms of overland U.S. imperial expansion in the 19th century, involved Mexicans in a somewhat different rhythm of inclusion/exclusion). Significantly, it is in this period with the restriction of in-migration that the process of incorporation of African-Americans from the southeastern United States really begins to take effect and take presence in the major industrial cities. This is also the period when the first significant nucleations of the Puerto Rican community in New York City begin to develop.

We should take another look at this period, with its emphasis on "Americanism" and uniformity, and the contradictory fact that the hyphens never disappeared, and the fact that the multiplicity of hyphenated categories even continued to develop throughout this period. And I not only mean the kinds of cultural syncretisms that Nancie González has been defining as the true process of transnationalization. I also mean that many kinds of definitions, self-definitions, and forms of national ("ethnic") identity are generated in these processes in the United States and elsewhere, as we have seen today in many of the discussions. This cultural process is staggeringly profound; I'm trying to point to what it is, to which we could add many particular examples.

The fact is that the hyphens in the United States did not disappear—the point of Barry Goldberg's summary of immigrant historiography is extremely important. The hyphens explicitly reappear in State policy during World War II—and what we see there is a combination of New Deal populist images of what the American people is, or what the American people are, which is very similar I think to Randolph Bourne's image of "Transnational America" in 1916. There is another confluence of the Popular Front image of what the American people are—the working people from many origins marching together—which was what Paul Robeson was singing about. And we have the statist war-related image of what the United States is, directed at keeping the hyphens committed to the war-effort. At the same time, some of the hyphens were put in concentration camps, while yet other hyphens (Italians and Germans) almost ended up there. Concurrently, all of the hyphens were subjected to a massive and articulated wave of appeals to their national-ethnic or nationality symbols, while simultaneously they were presented as being integrated into the grand American consensus. I think that is a good phrase because that was a consensual war. Then we have other things which occurred in the 1950s and the 1960s, the anti-racist and civil/human rights social movement, the so-called "new" white ethnicity, and the recomposition of labor power projected through the immigration reform. And now we have a period where there is supposed to be a new pluralism which—as Del Jones commented earlier in our discussions—fits into a new hegemonic project, so that we should not be too self-congratulatory about contemporary official multiculturalism.

The question of "generations" was raised several times in our discussions. As a notion of social time, the concept is related to how we conceive and imagine the morphology and dynamics of social totality as well as the experiences that go into the processes so identified. Assimilation/acculturation theory made explicit the notion of a linear gradient of the first generation of arrivers, the second generation of identity-confused children, and the third generation of assimilated "Americans." The perspective we are adopting refutes this.

On the one hand, we can identify complex processes extending over tens of years, and generations, generations in the biblical sense of twenty-five or thirty years, and even longer cycles perhaps even of a century or more of different kinds of presences in the United States, or in Honduras, for instance. Nancie Gonzalez spoke about one of them this morning: the reflorescence of Palestinian identity among later (at least third) generations of former immigrants in Honduras because of the Palestinian national struggle and the Intifada. Again, the paper on the Portuguese points up another case. The experience of Puerto Ricans, whose name has been called several times in our conversations, is another example. As Georges Fouron said earlier about Haitians, Puerto Ricans in New York City are at times nationalist, at times racial, at times ethnic, they are always Puerto Ricans—they often claim one or another of these identities to survive—and at all times their identity is class-based. Furthermore, Puerto Rican identity is inserted in what could be called the New York–Puerto Rico dialogue, spanning a period which is much longer than the one we were talking about with respect to Haiti. This manifold process of identity and identity-presentations and self-definitions extends over several generations, and generations which include people moving back and forth, and where some children are socialized both in Puerto Rico and New York. The process, as a kind of persistent ethnogenesis, has qualities very similar to those that Georges summarized.

This process brings up something else that Carolle Charles's and Feldman-Bianco's papers evoke. Currently, in New York and in the Northeast, the various neo-colonized migrant groups are entering a situation where they must confront the two rock-bottom instances of the way in which the concatenation of American social processes work around racism: North American blacks, native American blacks if you want to put it that way, and *puertorriqueños*. These are the two groups that are consistently at the bottom of the various hierarchies which can be defined. The incoming groups very often use various mechanisms to distance themselves from these two groups, while struggling in their own way with that same concatenation of racializing social processes. And, as Connie Sutton has noted several times, this works within and perpetuates the pre-set American categories, where preference was given to the incoming "immigrant" groups over those peoples over whom the United States acquired direct control by force.

On the other hand, the notion of "identity-confusion" in the second generation, or of the internal conflicts among "marginal men" caught between ethnic, racial or generational categories, forces us to confront two additional theoretical problems. One concerns an issue that Gerald Sider also addresses at some length: the prices people pay and are forced to pay by all of this, the blood on the floor and immense suffering and anguish. We need a vocabulary for that, and I think this is echoed in the call made earlier today for attention to the psychological dimension of generational changes among blacks and Puerto Ricans. We need to formulate and incorporate a psychology adequate to the task, because our discussion here today of the "second generation" (for example, Rosina Wiltshire's observations on the second-generation children growing up in New York) say much the same thing that the Chicago School sociologists and the related social psychology said. Roger Rouse uses the category of "schizoid" to talk about consciousness in his first generation, his pair of brothers. We need to examine these categories with care, because such terminology carries with it an implication of pathology. I submit that we need a psychological vocabulary more adequate to interpreting the meaning of the multiplicities we study, one which is not tied to essentialist and monadic assumptions about the relationship between group anchorage and personality strength.

There is no doubt, however, that there is a terrible human cost being paid. But my position is not that this is the consummate nadir of the Frankfort School's nightmare. On the contrary, at the same time there is a potential for human realization and freedom that is percolating through these processes; and I think *that's* the historical emergent, if anybody wants to have an historical emergent. So I am not looking for some traditional Ur-culture where everything was perfect and then it all got destroyed. On the contrary.

My final comment involves the empty category in our discussion today, and it is a surprisingly empty one. We have been talking about discursivity, and we have not talked about language. While concentrating on the diversity of cultural codes we've left out one of the major ones: multilingualism and everything that goes with it. Since multilingualism is central to questions of identity, let alone other phenomena, we certainly must address it.

Index of Contributors